# THE INTERNATIONAL ARMS TRADE

*Exeter Strategic & Security Studies* offers in-depth analysis of the most important issues in contemporary international security. Titles in the series address traditional topics of war and statecraft, as well as more recent dimensions of international security, including non-state violence, the impact of emerging technologies and resurgent major power competition.

The series' underlying themes emphasize grand strategy, the causes and prevention of conflict, military operations and technology, and defence policy. Employing key theoretical perspectives and using original empirical research, *Exeter Strategic & Security Studies* shapes the conversation in the academy, the policy community and among the population at large.

*Series Editors:* **Ash Rossiter**, Rabdan Academy & **David Blagden,** University of Exeter

Titles forthcoming in series:

*Tactical and Strategic Insights from the Russo-Ukrainian War: Western Security and Defence in the 21st Century*, edited by Thomas-Durell Young and Jarosław Gryz (2025)

*Defence Diplomacy and Security Cooperation in Southeast Asia: Managing Smaller Powers' Strategic Space*, Olli Pekka Suorsa (2025)

# THE INTERNATIONAL ARMS TRADE

## RECONFIGURATION OF THE DEFENCE-INDUSTRIAL LANDSCAPE

**KENNETH BOUTIN**

UNIVERSITY
*of*
EXETER
PRESS

First published in 2025 by
University of Exeter Press
Reed Hall, Streatham Drive
Exeter EX4 4QR, UK

*www.exeterpress.co.uk*



*Exeter Strategic & Security Studies*
ISSN 3033-411X Print
ISSN 3033-4128 Online

A CIP record for this book is available from the British Library

ISBN 978-1-80413-126-8 Hardback
ISBN 978-1-80413-127-5 ePub
ISBN 978-1-80413-128-2 PDF

https://doi.org/10.47788/LHAK4642

Cover image: M142 HIMARS in service with Ukrainian soldiers in the Bakhmut region. Photo by Serhii Mykhalchuk/Global Images Ukraine via Getty Images.

Typeset in Adobe Caslon Pro by S4Carlisle Publishing Services, Chennai, India

This volume is dedicated to the memory of Philippe Garigue (1917–2008),
an inspiring scholar and teacher.

# Contents

# Tables

# Abbreviations

additive manufacturing (AM)
Arms Trade Treaty (ATT)
Australia, United Kingdom, United States (AUKUS)
Aviation Industry Corporation of China (AVIC)
commercial off-the-shelf (COTS)
Committee on Foreign Investment in the United States (CFIUS)
completely-knocked-down (CKD)
conventional arms transfers (CAT)
Conventional Forces in Europe (CFE) Treaty
Coordinating Committee for Multilateral Export Controls (COCOM)
Countering America's Adversaries Through Sanctions Act (CAATSA)
Defense Security Cooperation Agency (DSCA)
Defense Technology and Trade Initiative (DTTI)
Defense Trade Security Initiative (DTSI)
End-Use Monitoring Agreement (EUMA)
End-Use Verification Agreement (EUVA)
European Union (EU)
Front de libération nationale (FLN)
global innovation network (GIN)
global production network (GPN)
High Mobility Artillery Rocket System (HIMARS)
high-performing economy (HPE)
information and communications technology (ICT)

integrated project team (IPT)
intelligence, surveillance and reconnaissance (ISR)
Liberation Tigers of Tamil Eelam (LTTE)
Logistics Support Agreement (LSA)
maintenance, repair, and overhaul (MRO)
Military Assistance Program (MAP)
Missile Technology Control Regime (MTCR)
multinational enterprise (MNE)
non-governmental organization (NGO)
non-state armed group (NSAG)
North Atlantic Treaty Organization (NATO)
Organization for Security and Co-operation in Europe (OSCE)
original equipment manufacturer (OEM)
People's Liberation Army (PLA)
private finance initiative (PFI)
Proliferation Security Initiative (PSI)
research and development (R&D)
Revolution in Military Affairs (RMA)
semi-knocked-down (SKD)
small arms and light weapons (SALW)
surface-to-air missile (SAM)
Technology Safeguard Agreement (TSA)
Ukraine Defense Contact Group (UDCG)
United Nations (UN)
United Nations Register of Conventional Arms (UNROCA)
uninhabited aerial vehicle (UAV)
urgent operational requirement (UOR)
Warsaw Treaty Organization (WTO)
Wassenaar Arrangement on Export Controls for Conventional Arms and Dual-Use Goods (WA)
weapon of mass destruction (WMD)

# Preface

This study is the product of my long-standing interest in arms transfer issues but represents a return to the subject following a long absence as I focused on other projects. My renewed attention to this important and complex aspect of the international political economy of security builds on several studies examining various facets of national and economic security that demonstrate the complex exercise involved in pursuing national and economic security in tandem following the Cold War.

While there is an understandable tendency to focus on arms transfers in national security terms, it is no less important to consider them in the context of economic security. Economic security considerations can have a significant impact on arms import and export decision making. Even where this is not the case, arms transfers often have significant economic security implications, particularly where they involve contributions by local industry. Tension between national and economic security imperatives can greatly complicate arms export and -import decision making, and tension in many states is increasing as transnational industrial integration deepens and it becomes progressively more difficult to compartmentalize the pursuit of national and economic security.

This study situates conventional arms transfers in broader industrial processes. This involves considering the impact of the ongoing structural transformation of the industrial landscapes of many states and the international defence-industrial landscape. These transformations are reconfiguring arms development and production throughout the developed and the developing world. Indeed, the international arms production and transfer systems are co-evolving. The changing basis for the development and production of arms is transforming arms transfer processes, both by promoting interstate collaboration that facilitates the emergence of new arms suppliers and by generating increasing flows of production inputs in the form of components, sub-components, and technologies. In the process, the international arms transfer system is becoming far less hierarchical, with increasing lateral transfers and transfers by states that traditionally have not featured as prominent arms exporters. This structural transformation is also providing the scope for firms and enterprises to play a far more proactive role in the international arms transfer system. These trends are expanding the opportunities for states and non-state armed groups (NSAGs) seeking defence materiel, while complicating efforts to manage and control the international arms trade.

As well as demonstrating the crucial role of arms transfers in supporting national defence, the Russo-Ukrainian war has thrown into high relief key features of the international arms transfer system which have been developing for some time. Ukraine is obtaining arms from a broad range of established and emerging arms suppliers through a variety of arrangements, including transnational arms production, collaborative supplier arrangements, and transfers that have been facilitated by third parties. Nothing demonstrates the importance of arms transfers to Ukraine so much as President Volodymyr Zelensky's efforts to secure and sustain access to arms supplies, including by touring foreign capitals, and Russia's efforts to dissuade states from supplying arms to Ukraine.[1] The impact of the war in Ukraine extends well beyond the belligerents, with the return of protracted high-intensity warfare driving increasing arms transfers elsewhere as concerned political authorities seek to address shortcomings in defence capabilities highlighted by this conflict.

# Acknowledgements

I owe a great debt to many who have supported me at various stages of this project. I would like to express my appreciation to Amitav Acharya, Rohan Bastin, Baogang He, Tanya King, David Lowe, Sorpong Peou, Ash Rossiter, Craig Snyder, and Tom Young for their support, advice, and assistance. I also would like to acknowledge Richard Bitzinger, who sadly recently passed away. While we often disagreed, as befits a realist and liberal-institutionalist, Richard and I collaborated successfully on several research projects on defence industries and arms transfers. The field is poorer for Richard's passing. I am forever indebted to my Doctoral and Master's supervisor Keith Krause, not least for helping to shape my thinking on arms transfer and defence-industrial issues. It is to Keith that I owe my more nuanced understanding of security issues in general and recognition of the importance of situating contemporary trends and developments in their historical context. Both features are reflected in the present study and in my approach to the study of security more broadly. I also would like to express my appreciation to my other colleagues past and present for their encouragement and for the opportunity to work with and learn from them. Particular thanks are due to Nigel Massen and the staff of the University of Exeter Press, and to the anonymous reviewers of the manuscript. I also would like to thank the staff at the American Political Science Association's Centennial Center for Political Science and Public Affairs in Washington, where I was based while conducting research for this book. Finally, I am grateful for the assistance of the staffs of the Library of Congress and the National Library of Australia for their help in obtaining various materials used in this study.

October 2024

# 1 Arms Transfers Between State and Industry

Transfers of armaments ('arms') are an important and complex feature of international security and economic relations. Arms transfers are understood here as direct and indirect transfers of defence-related weapons and equipment across international borders. Arms transfers may have significant strategic implications for suppliers and recipients, potentially altering the international military balance and enabling states to extend their influence while providing states which are unable to independently meet the materiel requirements of their defence establishments with the means for national defence.

Many observers perceive a close relationship between arms transfers and conflict. The international arms trade has been the subject of considerable notoriety since the interwar period, when arms producing firms widely were held to drive interstate conflict in the interest of profit.[2] The United States Senate's Special Committee on Investigation of the Munitions Industry (commonly known as the Nye Committee) argued that it was 'against the peace of the world for selfishly interested organizations to be left free to goad and frighten nations into military activity', for example.[3] The belief that arms transfers cause interstate conflict drove campaigns for the nationalization or abolition of privately owned defence firms in a number of states.[4]

The perspective that arms transfers contribute to conflict persists[5] and the 'merchants of death' label continues to resonate in some quarters.[6] Contemporary concern reflects an assumed linkage between the accumulation of extensive arsenals of arms and the pursuit of military aggression, particularly by developing states.[7] Recent international conflicts, such as the Gulf War of 1990–1991 and civil wars such as that which raged in Sudan until 2005, increased popular pressure on political authorities in many states to address the international arms trade. The importance of arms imports to Ukraine as it defends itself against Russian aggression, by contrast, is helping to present arms transfers in a far more favourable light.

Arms transfers can be controversial even where they are not illicit or 'destabilizing' and do not involve arming states with reprehensible human rights records or which generally are regarded by the international community as 'pariah' or 'rogue' states. The supply of arms to states or NSAGs engaged in conflicts which are causing substantial civilian casualties often generates significant public concern, which can give rise to restrictions on arms exports. Transfers to NSAGs are particularly sensitive. The supply of what sometimes are referred to as 'lethal' or 'offensive' arms tends to be much more problematic than 'non-lethal' arms for this reason. Though this generally does not attract the same level of concern, arms transfers also have significant economic implications. The production and trade of arms represents an important economic activity in many states but is regarded by some as diverting scarce resources from economic development. The discourse surrounding arms transfers often is framed in terms of their perceived human security impact.[8]

States represent the central pillars of the international arms transfer system. Arms often are transferred on the basis of interstate agreements, though these may represent transactions of a commercial nature. States fulfil a crucial structural role even where arms transfers are initiated and effected by industry. The development, production, and trade in arms generally are subject to close official scrutiny. The regulatory role of the state ensures that other than where many 'dual-use' items and illicit exports are concerned, official acquiescence if not support generally is required. The privileged position of states where the use of armed force is concerned reinforces their position as the principal actors in the international arms transfer system.

This study examines the international arms transfer system in the context of its co-evolution with the global defence-industrial landscape. The structural transformation of the defence-industrial landscape is caused by changing industrial dynamics. The production and even development of arms increasingly is structured transnationally, with a growing number of arms programmes drawing on offshore capability partners. Transnational arms production processes require sustained transfers of arms related production inputs. This trend is producing much more complex patterns of arms transfers and facilitating the emergence of new arms exporters. Transnational arms production can be expected to continue despite growing interest in 'inshoring' and 'friend-shoring' in the United States and other Western states.

Existing analytical frameworks need to be reconsidered in light of this structural transformation. This transformation compels consideration of the role of sub-state actors, general industrial trends, and state/industry relationships as well as the states that traditionally have constituted the analytical focus in examining the international arms transfer system. Critical industrial trends and their impact are discussed in depth in Chapter 4, but it is important here to note the key features of the arms industry. This comprises those private firms and state-associated enterprises that are responsible for the development and production of arms and the provision of arms related services. For the most part these sub-state actors are privately owned commercial entities, but the development and production of arms may be the exclusive preserve of the state and even where the defence-industrial landscape is not dominated by the state, governments still may operate arms development and production facilities. The degree of central control over state-associated enterprises varies; these may demonstrate considerable independence in what and to whom they export, even in authoritarian states.

## The Approach of this Study

This study considers the key features of the international arms transfer system, including the imperatives driving arms exports and imports, the impact of deepening transnational defence-industrial integration on arms transfers, the emergence and development of new arms suppliers, patterns of arms transfers, and the requirements of managing the international arms trade in the complex contemporary environment. In doing so it discusses the role of state, sub- and non-state actors and the relationship between them as they pursue their respective interests.

This study focuses on the trade in conventional arms. This includes what are sometimes referred to as 'non-lethal' as well as 'lethal' arms. The former includes systems such as transport vehicles and training aircraft which do not directly inflict casualties, while the latter are developed with this in mind. Arms transfers encompass the supply of dual-use articles which have civil as well as military applications, as well as articles which are developed with military requirements in mind. Dual-use systems may represent commercially equivalent versions of equipment such as helicopters which were developed to meet military requirements, or militarized versions of systems developed for the civil market. This study considers arms transfers in terms of production inputs and, to a limited extent, arms related services as well as complete systems. This broad compass is necessary given the increasing scale and importance of international flows of production inputs as transnational arms development and production have become more the norm. There is some overlap between the conventional arms transfers that are the focus of this study and transfers of weapons of mass destruction (WMDs). This involves delivery systems such as ballistic and cruise missiles, many of which are suitable for delivering conventional as well as nuclear, chemical, or biological payloads.

## Arms Transfers in the Interstate System

The international arms transfer system is shaped by the imperatives of both demand and supply. Supply and demand do not stand in isolation from each other. They often influence each other in important respects, with demand for arms reflecting what is available from arms producers and the development and production of arms influenced by market demands. The growing significance of international collaboration at the state and industry levels to the development and production of arms is strengthening the linkages between arms supply and demand.

Transfers of arms or 'war material' as these once commonly were referred to are an established feature of interstate relations and the global economy. There is evidence of the international diffusion of arms—and efforts to manage this—throughout recorded history. The scale of arms transfers grew in concert with the emergence of mass armies and the development of mass production techniques prior to and particularly during the Second Industrial Revolution which emerged in Europe in the latter part of the nineteenth century.[9] These trends generated increasing and sustained demand for arms while enabling states to produce arms in quantities far beyond their requirements, with the surplus being available for export.

Arms transfers will remain an important feature of the international system for the foreseeable future. Self-sufficiency in arms has proven increasingly elusive as technological frontiers have advanced and the costs of developing and producing advanced arms have soared, and now represents the exception rather than the rule. Few states can satisfy national requirements without recourse to imports of complete arms or arms related components, subcomponents, technologies, or services. Even those that are in such a position may elect to draw on offshore sources of arms for reasons of economy or convenience, or as a means of acquiring arms that are more advanced than those available from local firms and enterprises. States with strong production capabilities also might resort to arms imports where domestic industry cannot satisfy arms demands generated by pressing security requirements. States may be hard pressed to independently meet their arms requirements in a timely manner during periods of conflict or heightened international tension.

The landscape of international arms transfers is highly uneven. Arms transfers traditionally involved a general pattern of unidirectional diffusion outward or downward, as this conventionally was conceptualized, from a relatively small group of supplier states. There were considerable differences in the capabilities and market niches of the supplier states and while contours of the arms transfer system varied over time as established suppliers declined and new suppliers emerged, change in the ranks of the arms exporters was gradual and this general pattern remained quite stable. This was the case even following the end of the Second World War. While the Cold War had significant consequences through its effect of generating unprecedented demand for arms and saw the emergence of the United States and the Soviet Union as dominant arms exporters on a global level, this did not represent a transformation of the international arms transfer system.

A fundamental shift in the arms transfer system began to emerge toward the end of the Cold War and has progressively deepened, driven by the transformation of the basis of arms development and production. The international arms transfer environment is growing more complex as the number of supplier states increases and transnational production arrangements become more widespread. This transformation can be seen in the supply of arms to export customers through offshore subsidiaries and cases where governments have promoted the export of arms that were produced by a firm headquartered in another state, in the interest of supporting local industry.[10] The ranks of the arms exporting states are expanding as more firms and enterprises contribute to defence R&D and production and as security and economic imperatives encourage increasing political support for arms production. The form of state support for arms production reflects local industrial capabilities, strengths, and policy objectives, and often testifies to the imperatives driving arms exports and imports. The general forms that arms production can take and their implications for arms transfers are outlined in Table 1.1.

Arms production, and thus exports, in many arms producers is dependent to some extent on sustained inputs in the form of components, sub-components, and technologies from offshore suppliers. The arms production processes of many states, including the emerging arms suppliers, are likely to be structured transnationally as much out of necessity as choice due to limited national defence-industrial capabilities. Production in emerging arms suppliers, particularly where this involves more advanced systems, often is limited to co-production or assembly, rather than (relatively) complete production.

The requirements generated by transnational production processes contribute to changing arms transfer patterns. Familiar arms transfer patterns have been transformed by the spatial redistribution of arms production and the consequent requirement to transfer components, sub-components, and technologies to offshore capability partners. The far less unidirectional flow of arms that this involves includes growing lateral transfers of arms by states that previously were not prominent arms exporters. The contemporary international arms transfer landscape more resembles a complex mosaic than a stratified arrangement of suppliers with clearly defined production capabilities.

Arms transfers are inherently political. While they do not necessarily reflect the state of supplier/recipient security relations, security considerations often

**Table 1.1: Forms of Arms Production and their Implications for Arms Exports and Imports**

| Form of Arms Production | Implications for Arms Exports | Implications for Arms Imports |
|---|---|---|
| **Independent Production** | Capacity to independently supply arms; strong incentive to export to offset developmental costs | No reliance on foreign suppliers for arms imports or post-delivery services |
| **Co-production** | Limited capacity to supply arms; some incentive to export to offset developmental costs | Some reliance on imported components/sub-components and post-delivery services |
| **Assembly** | No capacity to supply arms without the acquiescence and support of the licensing firm | Dependence on imports of components/sub-components and post-delivery services |

figure prominently in arms export and import decision making, and arms transfers can represent important political statements on the part of suppliers or recipients. The supply of arms as a form of military assistance is a well-established practice and where commercial arms sales are concerned, political authorities in many states consider the security implications of proposed exports and more readily approve transfers of arms to states which are allies or with which they otherwise enjoy close political relations. Arms import decisions often reflect political considerations such as interest in strengthening security ties or in avoiding dependence on suppliers that are regarded as problematic or as likely to seek to exploit arms transfers as a vehicle for influence.

Its more politicized nature is not the sole respect in which the international arms market differs from the civil market. The arms market is characterized by far more extensive state oversight and regulation. This reflects the politico-military sensitivity of arms transfers. As well as their implications for interstate military balances, arms transfers have considerable potential to threaten bilateral relations with third parties. American arms transfers to Taiwan are a case in point. This is an issue of great concern for China, where such transfers are regarded as interference in its internal affairs and as a facet of an American strategy of 'containment'. The supply of arms to Taiwan places considerable strain on the Sino-American relationship as a result, undermining American efforts to engage China on security issues, as well as negatively impacting on economic relations.[11] The sensitivity of arms transfers ensures that arms flow far less freely internationally than any other licit product.

The international arms market also differs from the domestic arms market in important respects. The international market for arms is far less oligopolistic than the domestic market. The market for defence goods and services is relatively closed in most states. The greater uncertainty that characterizes the international arms market encourages defence firms and enterprises to engage in practices that contribute to the development of a transnational arms industry and encourages state intervention on their behalf. Political authorities in many states support arms exports. This can take a variety of forms, from marketing support through the demonstration of arms for prospective export customers, the provision of credit facilities, and guaranteeing the performance of firms or enterprises that are supplying arms. In some cases, state financial assistance has enabled exporters to offer arms at a price below the cost of production.[12]

The international arms market is comprised of what commonly are referred to as the 'grey' and 'black' markets as well as the legitimate or 'white' market of officially sanctioned transfers. The grey market occupies an intermediate position between the legitimate arms market and the black market and involves the state-sponsored illicit or surreptitious supply of arms. As discussed in Chapter 2, arms may be transferred in this manner as a means of supporting states or NSAGs where doing so openly would incur unacceptable domestic or international costs. The international political cost can be particularly high when this involves the supply of arms that are the subject of formal international sanctions.

The black market is distinguished by the illegality of arms exports from the perspective of the state which is the source of the arms or by states in general. This involves sub-state or non-state actors supplying arms to states or NSAGs without state sanction. Areas of unrest or conflict traditionally have constituted the sources of supply for arms trafficking by NSAGs. The black market for arms often features transfer processes that are far more complex than those of licit arms transfers and the costs of arms often are higher as a result. Iran reportedly was paying up to three times the normal price for aircraft spares obtained through intermediaries during its war with Iraq in the 1980s, for example.[13] In practice, however, it can be difficult to distinguish between the activities of black-market traffickers and the states through which they smuggle arms.[14]

The black and grey markets for arms expanded during the Cold War and remain important. This reflects both demand for arms by states and NSAGs which cannot be satisfied through mainstream channels and the interest of some suppliers in obscuring their role in supplying arms. Strong demand for black- and grey-market arms often is occasioned by conflict situations. It has been estimated that up to US$2 billion worth of arms were supplied to the warring parties in Bosnia in 1993 despite the United Nations (UN) arms embargo, for instance.[15] The difficulties inherent in suppressing the illicit arms trade are such that this will remain an issue for concerned authorities.

## *Sub-State Actors and the Arms Trade*

Sub-state actors play a crucial role in the international arms transfer system. The significance of industry has increased as the development and production of arms has become more globalized and as political authorities in a growing number of arms producing states have pursued defence-industrial liberalization. In most states, primary responsibility for the development, production, and marketing of arms rests with profit-driven privately owned firms. State-associated enterprises, in which the profit motive may be less prominent, remain an important feature of the defence-industrial landscape, but the general inefficiency of state-run defence industries compared to their private-sector counterparts encourages political authorities to draw on the services of the latter even when they are strongly prejudiced against private-sector involvement in defence research and development (R&D) and production. This has been the case in China, where recognition of the potential contribution of private firms is encouraging limited defence-industrial liberalization despite the dictates of its official socialist ideology.[16]

It is important to note the different types of sub-state actor. These can perform distinct functions, with important implications both for the supply of arms and for arms control. The relationship of sub-state actors to the states in which they are based and in which they operate is crucial. Some firms effectively constitute quasi-state actors due to the closeness of their ties to the state and the extent to which they serve as state instruments. The different types of sub-state actor and their roles and impact on the arms transfer system are summarized in Table 1.2.

The relative independence of firms can be cause for considerable official concern. The economic rationality of the private sector corresponds to state interests only in part. While many firms involved in the development and production of arms adhere to relevant national regulations, others are prepared to supply arms and support foreign arms R&D and production with little or no regard for national security considerations. Some firms with a high tolerance for risk are prepared to supply arms and support offshore arms programmes illicitly. Such firms have a disproportionate impact on national security due to their potential to contribute to the diffusion of advanced arms and the development of defence-industrial capabilities in states that are the subject of official concern, if not formal sanctions.

The part played by independent experts has been the subject of particular concern following the Cold War. What are referred to by some as 'technological mercenaries' are by no means a new feature of the international arms transfer system, but the demand for scientists and engineers with arms related expertise

Table 1.2: Types and Roles of Sub-State Actors

| | Function | Impact |
|---|---|---|
| **Defence firm/ enterprise** | Develop and produce arms | Primary supplier of arms on the international market |
| **Design house** | Provide specialist design services to defence firms and enterprises | Support defence R&D, including in emerging arms producers |
| **Independent expert** | Provide specialist expertise to defence firm and enterprises | Facilitate R&D and production in emerging arms producers, including in states which are subject to sanctions |
| **Arms dealer** | Supply surplus arms, including spares for obsolete/obsolescent arms | Important supplier of arms to states with limited means to produce or procure modern arms |
| **Logistical firm** | Transport arms for black- and grey-market suppliers | Facilitate illicit arms transfers |

has expanded as an increasing number of states initiate ambitious defence-industrial development programmes. The attraction of the opportunities provided by such programmes was reinforced by the defence-industrial shock produced by the end of the Cold War. Political authorities in several developed industrial states responded to the changed international security environment by scaling back or terminating arms development and production programmes. This resulted in considerable industrial over-capacity which led to widespread plant closures and redundancies as firms and enterprises downsized and restructured. Substantial numbers of scientists and engineers made redundant in the former Soviet Union found employment abroad, for example. At one point an estimated 30–40,000 Russian scientists were working abroad.[17]

Experts from several states have contributed to the diffusion of advanced arms through their support for offshore defence-industrial programmes. States such as China, Iran, and the Democratic People's Republic of Korea (North Korea) actively recruited former Soviet personnel as a means of accelerating their defence-industrial development.[18] The most infamous postwar technological mercenary was Canadian artillery expert Dr Gerald Bull. He consulted for several established and emerging arms producers, supporting artillery development programmes in states as varied as China, Spain, and South Africa. Bull is best known for leading Project Babylon, the Iraqi programme which sought to develop long-range artillery capable of striking targets as far away as Israel.[19] It is noteworthy that private firms were central to Bull's efforts to manufacture the components for the artillery he was designing for Iraq.[20]

## The Nature of Arms Transfers

Arms transfers involve far more than the supply of complete operationally ready hardware. Arms transfers encompass spares for arms, components and sub-components required for arms production, arms related technologies, and arms related services as well. Arms transfer agreements generally provide for associated training and the post-delivery support necessary to sustain arms over the course of their service life. This typically includes spares, engineering and technical support, test equipment, and relevant documentation. Transfer agreements also may provide for industrial packages supporting local participation in production and technology transfer. States may contract for the support of arms and for their modernization to prolong their useful service life independently of the original supplier.

The importance of transfers of components, sub-components, technologies, and services has grown in concert with the development of transnational arms production and the emergence of new arms suppliers. Transfers of arms related products and services independently of orders for complete systems are increasing as arms production in non-traditional centres expands and as the contribution of emerging arms suppliers to production processes led by established arms producers increases. Recent years have seen considerable growth in the provision of technical assistance for defence R&D and production programmes on a commercial basis.

The fact that arms transfers can involve products that have civil as well as military applications has important implications. The applicability of dual-use items to defence requirements is such that they feature prominently in the arms trade to states where resources for defence modernization are limited. They are no less important to emerging arms suppliers which rely on them as relatively inexpensive production inputs which often have the added advantage of being more readily available than equivalent products designed with military applications in mind. As dual-use items may be the products of firms and enterprises whose primary focus is not on serving the defence sector, their transfer may be much more difficult to identify, much less control. Components and sub-components may be exported for ostensibly civil purposes, only to be applied to military programmes, and platforms such as helicopters may be ordered by civil agencies only to enter service with defence establishments following their delivery, for example.

Arms transfers are strongly associated with arms production. Not only is it the case that new production is the principal source of arms that are transferred, but production requirements may underlie arms exports and imports. This issue is explored in detail elsewhere in this study, but it is important to note here that the arms production capacity of states plays a large part in determining the types and features of the arms which they are in a position to export or which they need to import. Arms transfers cannot be fully understood without situating them in the broader context of the defence-industrial landscape and considering the state/industry relationship.

Arms transfers usefully are conceptualized as a shared history between supplier and recipient. Arms transfer relationships are not necessarily restricted to a single transaction but often involve sustained if evolving interaction between the parties concerned. The nature of arms transfer relationships varies considerably. Relationships are determined by factors such as the type of arms transferred, the capacity of recipients to absorb arms, the nature of any industrial arrangements involved in the supply of arms, and the objectives of suppliers and recipients. The local production, co-production, or assembly of arms as part of the transfer process is common, though far from universal. It also is the case that arms transfers, particularly where these involve arms that represent a substantial advance on those in service with the recipient, may require short- or long-term support in the form of the provision of personnel capable of maintaining and operating the arms.

The analysis of arms transfers is complicated by the nature of the processes involved. It may be quite difficult to identify and trace arms transfers. Reported arms transfers should be considered provisional until such time as contractual details are finalized, which may take some time. It is important to distinguish between arms transfer agreements and deliveries and to recognize that the pursuit of negotiations, approval 'in principle' for the procurement of arms, selection of a preferred supplier, evaluation of arms by a prospective customer, or the signing of a letter of intent, memorandum of understanding, or similar instrument, does not represent an order and will not necessarily lead to a firm contract for the supply of arms. Even the signing of a contract may not constitute a final purchase agreement. In Indonesia, for example, arms contracts are 'subject to the necessary authorizations from the competent authorities'.[21]

Still less do these indicators signify the delivery of arms. Considerable time may elapse between the initiation of a procurement programme, the placing of an order, and its implementation, even where surplus arms are concerned. Reported arms transfers may be deferred or cancelled because of a recipient's changing operational requirements or payment difficulties or difficulty in securing formal approval. Suppliers also may suspend transfers where political relations deteriorate or they require the arms themselves, such as the United Kingdom's cancellation of the sale of the aircraft carrier *Invincible* to Australia following Argentina's invasion of the Falklands.[22]

Analysis also is complicated by the difficulties involved in quantifying arms transfers. The quantities of arms transferred may fall short of the numbers planned or contracted for and delivery schedules may change, with transfers accelerated or extended. Arms deliveries may extend over many years, and it may be some time before an operationally useful quantity are fielded by the recipient. Arms also may be delivered against unannounced contracts or supplied on a lease basis in advance of the delivery of arms that are on order. Orders for surplus arms may include examples that are intended as 'parts support' for sources of spares, rather than to be put into service. Purchases of older-model, often obsolete or obsolescent arms may be made for the sole purpose that they can be 'harvested' as sources of spares.

It is important to bear in mind as well that an apparent transfer of arms may represent another state operating its equipment under 'colours of convenience'. This occurs where a state is concerned to disguise its deployment of forces, most commonly in situations of conflict or heightened international tension where their participation is sensitive domestically or internationally or carries the risk of provoking intervention by rival states. Both Germany and Italy operated aircraft in Spanish markings during the Spanish Civil War, and the Soviet Union did so in the colours of several states at various times during the Cold War.

## *Arms Transfer Processes*

Arms transfer processes are quite varied and can be very complex. This may involve multiple states and sub-state actors. State and industry often collaborate in arms exports, though as noted above, their interests are not always compatible.

Institutional interests can play an important role, with the nature of bureaucratic processes contributing to the complexity of arms transfer processes in many states. This particularly is the case with arms exports. Arms exports may be the remit of multiple bureaucratic actors with conflicting parochial interests. Not only can a requirement for cross-agency review slow decision making on arms exports, as is the case with the United States, but the absence of a central authority with responsibility for arms exports can incur a high cost in terms of policy coherence and continuity. Assigning responsibility for arms exports to specific bureaucratic actors offers an advantage where they have particular expertise or have a capacity to effectively engage the intended recipient. In Iran, for instance, the Revolutionary Guards are responsible for transferring arms to foreign NSAGs such as Hamas and Hizbullah.[23] Decentralized bureaucratic processes are far less evident where arms imports are concerned, but the approval of multiple actors still may be required. This can include the military service concerned, which in some states has the final authority to determine the arms it will operate.

The arrangements under which arms are produced for export vary. Arms may be produced to a firm order or in anticipation of an order. Firms may extend production runs for arms, producing examples beyond those under contract in the hope that they eventually will secure buyers. The development of transnational arms production processes means that arms can be supplied and supported by offshore subsidiaries. It is not unknown for defence firms in states with restrictive arms export policies to circumvent controls through offshore production.[24] The complex arms production arrangements enabled by the transformation of the defence-industrial landscape are discussed in detail in Chapter 4.

Arms can be supplied under a variety of arrangements: they can be sold, donated, leased, loaned, traded through barter arrangements, or some combination of these. Arms may be transferred under lease-to-buy arrangements, for example. Arms also can be supplied on a reciprocal basis such as Russia's apparent exchange of Su-35 'Flanker' fighter aircraft for Iranian uninhabited aerial vehicles (UAVs) or the arms being replaced accepted by the supplier in partial payment.[25] Where arms are bartered, this can be for non-defence goods, under what are termed 'countertrade' arrangements. The donation of arms typically involves older equipment that is being phased out of service by the supplier, but newly produced and otherwise state-of-the-art systems have featured prominently in arms donated to Ukraine since 2022.

Countertrade arrangements are most attractive to developing states. Countertrade can be in full or part exchange for arms and can involve commodities ranging from foodstuffs to low value-added consumer goods, oil, and access rights for natural resources. Countertrade arrangements enable arms purchasers to overcome financial constraints while supporting the local economy. Countertrade typically reflects the needs of recipients but can be no less important to suppliers, particularly where this involves commodities which are in high demand and difficult to obtain. Countertrade arrangements are problematic in that they can limit the prospects for local defence-industrial development, however.[26] These also may prove counterproductive if the arms supplier seeks to maximize their profits by 'dumping' commodities on the international market, thereby depressing their value, as occurred with Soviet countertrade arrangements in the 1960s.[27] Despite this, countertrade arrangements remain popular and even have experienced something of a revival in Southeast Asia in the wake of the Coronavirus pandemic that erupted in 2020.[28]

Arms may be transferred directly from the service of one state to another under what is variously known as a 'hot' or 'warm transfer'. This practice typically is driven by security requirements, particularly the pressing need to supply arms to allied and friendly states that are threatened or which are engaged in conflict. Israel's predicament in the Yom Kippur War of 1973, for instance, prompted the United States to supply it with substantial quantities of arms taken from American units.[29] In some cases, however, this is a matter of expedience as it can be more straightforward and cost-effective to transfer arms such as naval vessels as they are being phased out of service than to reactivate them after maintaining them in reserve while awaiting transfer.

Arms may be operated by states at several removes from their original supplier. Arms may pass through the hands of multiple actors for a variety of reasons. Most often this results from the retransfer of arms that are surplus to an operator's requirements. There is a significant trade in obsolete and obsolescent arms, both to be operated by states facing substantial resource/capability gaps and to serve as a source of spares to sustain and recapitalize equipment fleets. Arms are on-sold directly by states and there are specialist arms brokers trading in surplus arms. Arms that no longer are effective in one operational environment still may be effective elsewhere, and their acquisition may in fact represent a substantial capability enhancement for their new operator. This helps to account for the longevity of outdated arms. In the 1970s, for example, the Philippines bought rifles that the United States had supplied to Germany in the 1950s, and which had subsequently been on-sold to Jordan, South Africa, and a private arms dealer in turn.[30]

Intermediaries may assist in the transfer of arms as a means of furthering their security agendas. This practice generally is driven by interest in supporting states or NSAGs with which they have common cause, and most commonly occurs where the provision of military assistance is a sensitive issue, either domestically or internationally. This may have the added advantage of facilitating the supply of arms that better meet the requirements of the states or NSAGs suppliers wish to support. The United States purchased Russian-produced helicopters from a variety of sources for supply to Afghanistan, whose air force was familiar with this equipment.[31] Saudi Arabia has provided crucial funding for arms procurements on the part of several Middle Eastern states, such as its 1973 purchase of French Mirage 5 fighters on the behalf of Egypt.[32]

States also may serve as intermediaries in an effort to enable other states to circumvent supply-side restrictions on the transfer of arms. In 1966, for example, Iran 'fronted' the purchase of surplus German F-86 Sabre fighters by Pakistan, which at that point was subject to an arms embargo by the United States.[33] States as diverse as Israel, Libya, and Pakistan supplied spares for American arms to Iran following its revolution.[34] Intermediaries have come to play a crucial role in circumventing arms controls where components, sub-components, and technologies are concerned. Russia is maintaining defence production in the wake of the strengthened controls generated by the outbreak of the Russo-Ukrainian War with semi-conductors transferred through other states.[35]

Security considerations can drive political authorities to conceal their role in transferring arms. States may elect to transfer arms covertly where they wish to disguise their support for a particular state or NSAG or in cases of great political sensitivity. During the Cold War the Soviet Union was careful to use intermediaries in supplying arms where it sought to avoid confrontation with Western states.[36] China supplied large quantities of materiel, ranging from small arms to tanks, to the Afghan *mujahedeen* in the 1980s through the United States.[37] This also was an important consideration in the provision of support to Middle Eastern states by the superpowers during the Cold War. Czechoslovakia served as the ostensible source of the initial Soviet supply of arms to Egypt in 1955 while the United States initially sought to disguise its role in supplying arms to Israel, with the Federal Republic of Germany providing the façade for deliveries of M48 tanks in the 1960s.[38]

Arms transfer processes can be particularly complex where states have only limited access to the mainstream international arms market or are excluded from it entirely. Clandestine and illicit procurement networks are particularly important to 'pariah states' that are situated on the periphery of the interstate system. The materiel concerned can range from small arms and light weapons (SALW) to combat aircraft and ballistic missile components and can include newly produced arms, surplus arms, decommissioned arms, or dual-use equipment. Transport aircraft and helicopters are particularly important in terms of the latter due to the relative ease with which they can be adapted for military service. States may go to considerable lengths to procure non-military equipment and then adapt this for military service. Despite the difficulties involved, this was a crucial means by which the Confederate States procured naval vessels during the American Civil War.[39] In some cases, the arms that are procured in this manner have been diverted from state stocks through theft.[40] Pariah states play an important part in this trade.

A number of states with limited access to the mainstream arms market have established sophisticated clandestine procurement networks as a means of circumventing arms export restrictions and embargoes. These may rely on 'front' or 'straw' companies to obtain arms clandestinely or legitimate firms to purchase dual-use items which then are shipped—often via circuitous routes—using false documentation.[41] North Korea has made extensive use of this approach.[42] Clandestine procurement also is pursued occasionally by states which do not need to resort to this as a means of mitigating international concerns about their arms imports. This was the case with China's acquisition of the uncompleted aircraft carrier *Varyag* from Ukraine in 1998. Because of the sensitivity of this acquisition, it was purchased through the Chong Lot Travel Agency, a suspected front company of the People's Liberation Army (PLA), ostensibly as a floating casino and entertainment centre.[43]

Arms transfer processes also can be very complex in conflict situations. Conflict requirements may force states to seek to procure arms wherever they can be found. Following Argentina's invasion of the Falklands, its agents were noted as 'scouring the world for black-market Exocets', a French anti-ship missile.[44] Conflict situations can compel states to procure arms which are obsolete or otherwise unsuited to their requirements from suppliers that they have not traditionally drawn upon, including black-market suppliers. During the Spanish Civil War, for example, the Republican government desperately purchased arms wherever it could, procuring a bewildering variety of often over-priced equipment of questionable utility from a broad range of suppliers.[45] The Russo-Ukrainian War has had a significant impact on arms transfers to Ukraine, but the degree of support provided by other states has meant that it has been spared the need to accept unsuitable arms. Ukraine is notable for the importance of commercial arms procurement alongside the extensive supplies of arms it is receiving as military assistance, and for the overlap between these processes.[46]

It is important to bear in mind that arms transfers can occur without the direct knowledge and sanction of political authorities in the states from which transfers are made. In the early 1960s, for instance, the United States was clandestinely purchasing Soviet small arms ammunition from Finland through a private firm.[47] Unauthorized exports of arms may occur despite the best efforts of political authorities. This may involve transfers of types of arms that are not approved for export or exports to states that are not approved to receive arms. Firms and enterprises may employ masking techniques with the aim of disguising the ultimate destination of arms, and tracking arms shipments can be a difficult exercise. Even authoritarian states may lack effective arms export control regimes. The slow pace of administrative reforms in China, which generally has lagged well behind the requirements generated by its economic liberalization, has provided considerable scope for firms and enterprises to operate independently of state direction, for example.[48] The Chinese government has had to contend with state-owned enterprises exporting arms without securing prior approval, most notably to Libya and North Korea.[49] For a time, the PLA was independently exporting arms as well.[50] Russia experienced similar issues following the end of the Cold War. In 1996 the general director of Sukhoi negotiated an agreement for the licensed production of Su-27 fighters in China without the prior knowledge or approval of the Russian government.[51]

Unsanctioned arms transfers also may represent diversions from state arsenals as a result of the unauthorized disposal of military equipment. This most frequently occurs in states with weak inventory control and where traffickers are able to exploit porous borders. Some 36 per cent of the one million small arms provided by the United States to Iraq between 2003 and 2008 'escaped official control', for example.[52] Some of the arms operated by insurgent groups in Africa's Sahel region originate from local states with 'weak state control of weapon stocks', as well as from Libyan stocks that were dispersed as a result of its civil war. NSAGs have been responsible for transferring these weapons.[53]

Illicit arms transfers are facilitated by suppliers which are prepared to disregard international arms transfer norms, such as Taliban-led Afghanistan.[54] This includes some sub-state actors. As noted above, firms and enterprises may have considerable scope to transfer arms independently of national authorities. Black-market arms dealers can play an important role in meeting the demands of combatants during conflict situations, particularly where major state suppliers seek to end a conflict by starving combatants of the means of waging it.[55] Illicit proliferation networks are particularly prominent in meeting the needs of insurgent movements, as these generally are excluded from the mainstream arms market. Several NSAGs have employed this approach with some success. The Liberation Tigers of Tamil Eelam (LTTE) purchased sixty tons of various types of explosives from Ukraine through a front company during their struggle against the Sri Lankan government in the 1990s, for instance. This effort succeeded as the Ukrainian government regarded the explosives as 'not for military use'.[56] Other prominent post-Cold War examples of such an approach include rebel groups in Sierra Leone and the Democratic Republic of the Congo (DRC).[57]

## Analysing Arms Transfers

Arms transfer analysis is rendered difficult by the complexity of the processes involved and by their sensitivity. Transfers of arms may only be apparent long after the fact and the details of arms transfer processes and terms of supply may remain obscure. It is not unknown for customers to request anonymity or otherwise conceal their arms acquisitions, with details remaining classified long after transfer has been completed. Considerable time may pass before the delivery of arms can be confirmed. The Dong Feng 3 ballistic missiles that Saudi Arabia received from China in 1988 were only publicly revealed in 2014, for example.[58]

To further complicate matters, those seeking to analyse arms transfers often are confronted by conflicting or unreliable information resulting from imprecise reporting and use of terminology, particularly where suppliers or recipients lacking transparency are involved. There is an important general distinction to be made between those states that are relatively transparent with respect to security matters and those that are not. The transparency of arms transfers tends to be most wanting in authoritarian states and states where authorities face what they regard as acute national security threats. Political authorities in these states generally are reluctant to release details of arms transfers. These are the states where arms transfers are most likely to be accompanied by confidentiality agreements at the request of the purchaser and where the non- or underreporting of arms transfers is most likely to occur.

Traditional narratives reflect a hierarchical understanding of the international arms transfer system. The dominant scholarly paradigm centres around analysing arms transfers on the basis of 'tiers' or levels of suppliers. The position of states within this analytical framework is determined by their arms production capabilities. Typically, this order is conceptualized as a pyramidal arrangement with a top tier comprised of those states where the defence-industrial base features original equipment manufacturers (OEMs) that are capable of producing a comprehensive range of advanced arms, with lower tiers comprised of progressively larger groups of states with decreasing arms production capabilities and higher dependency on imports.[59] The logic underlying this approach is analogous to that which informs thinking about 'ladders of production', under which arms production capabilities are assumed to develop in a linear manner. Andrew Ross was careful to note in his groundbreaking study of the subject that the progressive stages of development of an arms production capability in developing states was 'an ideal type against which actual developmental processes may be evaluated and measured',[60] but many scholars assume the general applicability of this framework.

Such a framework has considerable merit as a means of facilitating generalization and identifying developmental trends, but at the cost of considerable over-simplification. It is important to recognize that while certain states may be notable as innovators and early adopters of advanced technologies and are leading producers and suppliers of specific types of arms, states' capacities to supply arms differ greatly across categories and are not necessarily sustainable. The framework of tiers is relatively inflexible and has the effect of obscuring significant variation within and between suppliers. Analysis of defence trends and developments in developing and emerging industrial states, including where defence-industrial development and arms transfers are concerned, pays insufficient attention to the complexity of arms production in these states and the difficulties involved in developing and sustaining defence-industrial capabilities, and suffers from considerable over-generalization due to preconceptions about patterns of defence-industrial development.

The limitations of the framework of tiers have become more apparent as the ranks of the arms producing and exporting states have expanded in the post-Cold War period. Several emerging industrial states, where successful industrial development has propelled them past the general level of the developing states, have developed particular defence-industrial strengths and are contributing to the international arms trade in distinct ways, as discussed in Chapter 5. This has contributed to a global defence-industrial landscape that is far more complex than can be accounted for by a framework of tiers. Arms production in established and emerging arms suppliers alike increasingly is undertaken in collaboration with offshore industry, greatly complicating efforts to categorize the relative position of individual states. Some states possess more capable defence industries and thus are in a better position to transfer arms, but the international arms transfer system is dynamic. The sustainability of defence-industrial capabilities cannot be assumed, and the hierarchy of arms producers is far from static. A more nuanced approach that integrates the dynamics of contemporary defence-industrial processes is necessary to understand arms transfers.

The international arms transfer system is comprised of a complex mosaic of suppliers and recipients. Those states that are prominent in particular fields provide crucial developmental benchmarks. The nature of states' involvement in the arms transfer system reflects their industrial strengths and their security and economic requirements. The traditional distinction between levels of producers and suppliers no longer applies; states generally feature simultaneously as suppliers and recipients and there are important lateral as well as vertical flows of arms. Significantly, there now are important flows of arms from the emerging producer states to established arms producers. There is every reason to expect that the complexity of the international arms transfer system will increase as the ranks of the arms producing states expand and transnational defence-industrial ties deepen in an environment of heightened international security tensions.

# 2 The Imperatives of Arms Supply

The imperatives of arms supply define the international arms transfer system in critical respects. States occupy a privileged position in the arms transfer system and have an unrivalled structural capacity, including through their capacity to frame narratives of arms exports, but arms transfers are not the exclusive preserve of the state and it is important to consider the contribution of industry to the supply of arms. Arms exports might be initiated and fulfilled by states or industry, alone or in concert. The distinct basis upon which state and industrial actors engage in the supply of arms has important implications for the arms transfer system.

The terms under which individual states engage in the supply of arms reflect distinct sets of policy imperatives. It is constructive to distinguish between national security and economic imperatives in examining arms exports, bearing in mind, however, that these categories are not entirely mutually exclusive. Arms transfers may support national security even where they are driven by economic imperatives, while security-driven arms exports can provide important economic opportunities. The scope for political authorities to pursue security and economic objectives in tandem through arms transfers is considerable. The American provision of arms as security assistance at the height of the Cold War also served as an important means of offsetting the cost of stationing troops overseas, for example.[1] The Conventional Arms Transfer Policy of the United States announced in 2018 formally recognizes the importance of arms exports in economic as well as security terms.[2] Security and economic imperatives may conflict in important respects, however, compelling political authorities to prioritize or accept difficult compromises in arms transfer decision making.

Cursory examination of the international arms transfer landscape suggests that it is relatively static but in fact it is subject to considerable change. New suppliers continue to emerge while others decline in importance or depart the field altogether, while arms exporters' profiles evolve in concert with internal and external trends and developments such as their industrial progress and changes in the international security environment. International, and in many cases domestic, arms supply norms also are evolving, influencing export policies. There are important differences between suppliers in the arms they supply, their objectives in supplying arms, and the terms under which they supply them.

## States and Arms Exports

Many states export arms to some extent and at some point, but the arms supply landscape is highly uneven. Those states which export arms on a more sustained basis and on a large scale generally have a far greater impact on the arms transfer system than those which export intermittently or on a smaller scale and those whose engagement of the market is limited to the retransfer of surplus arms.

The importance political authorities attach to arms exports often is demonstrated by the level of institutional support. Defence attachés often facilitate arms exports and a number of states maintain dedicated arms export agencies, such as Russia's Rosoboronexport. Other states assign this function to the defence or commerce ministry or a procurement agency such as the Republic of Korea's (South Korea's) Defense Acquisition Program Administration. In the United States the Defense Security Cooperation Agency (DSCA) is engaged in the supply of arms as part of its mandate to support capacity-building in foreign security forces. States may establish specialized institutional frameworks to facilitate transfers to particular states, as with the Ukraine Defense Contact Group (UDCG) discussed below. The regulatory role of the state notionally enables political authorities to determine the qualitative and quantitative parameters of arms exports and the recipients to which they may be supplied. In practice, however, state control over arms exports may fall far short of this.

State involvement in arms exports is well established in many cases but may be inconsistent and does not necessarily develop in a linear manner. Arms export policy trends often reflect changes in the perceived requirements of national security and economic success. This is demonstrated by the impact of heightened international tension and conflict, which generally engender more strategic approaches to arms transfers. The state may play a crucial role in the development and production of arms that are exported, even where these functions are not state monopolies. State support can be crucial to the export of arms due to its regulatory and marketing roles, particularly where state-associated enterprises are concerned as these generally are less dynamic and the profit incentives that drive their private-sector counterparts generally are not as strong.

The means by which states support arms exports are many and varied. This can take the form of credits and financial guarantees and inducements such as the surrender of delivery positions to allow export customers to receive arms more quickly. In 2008 Russia offered to write off Libya's substantial Soviet-era arms debt in exchange for the placing of new arms contracts.[3] States also can demonstrate the effectiveness of arms under combat conditions. Russia's deployment of advanced arms in the civil war in Syria can be seen in this light. States may go so far as to seek to undermine the sales prospects of arms offered by rival suppliers. The United States has promoted American arms by withholding export approval for technologies of American origin incorporated in competing products and is promoting the F-35 Joint Strike Fighter to India in an attempt to wean it from its traditional reliance on Russian combat aircraft.[4]

State intervention in commercial arms exports generally strengthened in the interwar period. This trend was the product of increasing concern over the security implications of arms transfers and changing norms resulting from heightened public concern over the consequences of arms exports. On occasion domestic pressure led political authorities to block arms exports to states such as Spain that were sites of internal conflict.[5] The interwar period was notable for the introduction of the first formal arms export licensing requirements. This trend also reflected the changing industrial landscape. The significant expansion of arms production by offshore subsidiaries between the First and Second World Wars generated an unprecedented policy challenge, compelling political authorities in some states to intervene in an effort to control their arms exports.

The trend of increasing state involvement strengthened following the Second World War. This was in part the product of changing popular expectations.

In many states the domestic environment for arms exports gradually became much more contested as arms transfer norms evolved, as discussed below. Arms exports attracted increasing popular attention as a result of growing concern over their potential to exacerbate conflict situations and facilitate human rights abuses. This testifies to the success of civil society groups in highlighting the negative effects of the arms trade as they sought to generate public opposition to arms exports. The increasing sensitivity of arms transfers contributed to the general trend of states subjecting exports to greater oversight and tighter control. Evolving domestic norms are influencing the development of broader international norms.

While both security and economic imperatives represent important drivers of arms transfer policy, the emphasis can vary considerably between states and over time. There has been a noteworthy general trend under which economic imperatives have assumed increasing importance in arms export decision making. Not only is there greater recognition of the economic contribution of arms exports, and in the case of developing states, their contribution to industrial development, but production for the export market is valued as a means of reducing arms procurement costs. It was recognized, for example, that exports of the Popeye air-to-surface missile were crucial to ensuring its affordability by Israel.[6]

The increased focus on economic objectives generally has not come at the expense of attention to security imperatives in arms export decision making. The rivalry between the United States, the Soviet Union, and China and the blocs of states that they led that defined the Cold War led to sustained official attention to the security implications of arms exports. There was extensive resort to arms exports as a means of attaining security objectives and strengthened efforts to ensure that arms transfers did not undermine national security. In many cases arms transfers were heavily subsidized or facilitated by long-term loans with highly favourable repayment terms or were outright grants.[7] It was noted at one point, for example, that where the United States was concerned, 'If no country showed interest (or had insufficient funds), the United States effectively gave the equipment away … at prices one-tenth to one-hundredth the initial cost.'[8]

The challenges and opportunities presented by deepening industrial globalization have contributed to increasing state intervention in arms export processes. Globalization in the context of defence industries is discussed in depth in Chapter 4, but it is sufficient to note here the development of extensive general transnational industrial integration. This has significant implications for arms exports. Increasing flows of components, sub-components, and technologies render management of arms exports simultaneously much more important and much more difficult. The asymmetrical effects of globalization on industrial processes translate into significant differences in how political authorities may feel compelled to approach the supply of arms. States whose qualitative technological advantages are threatened by the potential levelling effects of transnational industrial processes have been at the forefront of efforts to limit the extent to which arms exports contribute to the development of defence-industrial capabilities in politico-military adversaries.

This evolving industrial landscape provides the context for contemporary arms exports. Security and economic imperatives generally are producing much more complex policy requirements in this environment. This particularly is the case where the importance attached to security and economic objectives is sufficient to drive political authorities to pursue them in tandem.

## The Security Imperatives of Arms Exports

The national security imperatives driving arms exports may concern the supplier, the recipient, or international security more broadly. These are not entirely mutually exclusive, but the focus of concern can influence the nature and quantity of arms transferred and the terms under which they are supplied. Arms may be transferred with a specific objective in mind, such as enabling the recipient to counter a particular military threat, or with a more general purpose. Arms may well be supplied in response to a crisis, which might be political rather than military in nature.

Arms transfers represent a key means by which political authorities promote national security. The transfer of arms enables suppliers to indirectly strengthen their military position by contributing to the capacity of allied or friendly states to deter and, if necessary, combat a common opponent and to support the supplier in the event of a conflict. Arms transfers can be crucial where recipients lack the industrial base required to produce arms that are sufficiently advanced or in sufficient quantities. Security imperatives may drive supplier states to donate or supply arms on concessionary terms by providing them at reduced-cost 'friendship' prices. States may reverse arms export decisions where political circumstances or security requirements change. The United States, for example, suspended Turkey's involvement in the Joint Strike Fighter programme following its procurement of S-400 surface-to-air missiles (SAMs) from Russia but offered this aircraft to the United Arab Emirates in return for its normalization of relations with Israel.[9]

The importance of supporting allied and friendly states through arms transfers increases in times of conflict or heightened international tension. This is demonstrated by the United States where in 1941, in the face of determined opposition from isolationist members of Congress, President Franklin Roosevelt obtained the power to supply arms without Congressional approval to any state whose defence he regarded as vital to American interests, without payment.[10] Some US$48.5 billion of military equipment ultimately was made available to forty-eight states under the Lend-Lease programme.[11] The provision of arms as military assistance remained a pillar of American security policy throughout the Cold War, with the United States transferring substantial quantities of arms to a broad range of states under arrangements such as the Military Assistance Program (MAP).[12] Arms transfers remain a key instrument of American security policy. The American government is helping to sustain Ukraine's defence by providing arms under the Ukraine Democracy Defense Lend-Lease Act of 2022.[13]

Many states export arms to further their security agendas. The Soviet Union and China transferred arms on a large scale during the Cold War and this remains an important instrument of security policy for Russia and China. While major powers are far more prominent because of the scale and global scope of their security-driven arms transfers, the role of other suppliers is no less important. Even where they only are able to supply arms in relatively modest quantities, the impact can be decisive on a local or regional scale.

The Russo-Ukrainian War demonstrates the importance of arms transfers to the security of supplier states as well as Ukraine. The perceived importance of Ukraine's defence to their own security has encouraged concerned authorities in European states and elsewhere to provide military assistance. While many of the arms being supplied to Ukraine are older models scheduled for replacement or held in reserve, many states are transferring arms that are in first-line service and in some cases the subject of ongoing procurement programmes. Significantly, security concerns have encouraged political authorities in some states to ease long-standing restrictions on the transfer of arms to conflict areas.[14]

The importance attached to supporting Ukraine through the provision of arms is engendering unprecedented transfer arrangements. Following the Russian assault in February 2022, states began to collaborate on the supply of arms to Ukraine. The UDCG, which has expanded to a fifty-nation 'coalition of the willing', provides a crucial mechanism for addressing Ukraine's arms requirements, not least by coordinating the supply of arms.[15] As well as coordinating their arms transfers to Ukraine, states are facilitating arms transfers by third parties and collaborating to enable the supply of arms that Ukrainian personnel are familiar with. Several states are refurbishing arms being donated by other states or leading multi-state transfers of arms to Ukraine.[16] This extends to compensating Eastern European operators of Soviet-era arms for transferring arms to Ukraine.[17] The United States has been approaching states with stocks of Soviet-era arms to supply these to Ukraine.[18] The United Kingdom, the United States, and Germany with its *Ringtausch* ('Ringswap') programme are providing arms to these states in return.[19]

Arms transfers offer certain advantages as a means of military assistance. Arms transfers generally are both less expensive and less domestically and internationally sensitive than direct military intervention. This was appreciated by American authorities as they sought to limit the international security obligations of the United States and reduce its overseas military commitments in the wake of shifting popular sentiment in the late 1960s. Increased arms transfers were central to the programme of 'Vietnamization', which was intended to allow American disengagement from that conflict.[20] Arms transfers were a key pillar as well of the Nixon Doctrine. This emphasized the importance of self-defence by friendly and allied states, which the United States would support through military assistance.[21] Similar advantages apply to arms exports as a means of enabling proxy states and NSAGs to engage the enemies of supplier states. As well as being more cost-effective, this reduces the risk of open conflict between rival states. The Soviet Union, the United States, and China were notable for arming proxy forces during the Cold War, and this remains important to the security strategies of a number of states.

Political authorities may endeavour to ensure that the arms they supply effectively support and do not undermine their security interests by setting conditions on their transfer. Arms exporters may seek to minimize the risk that arms transfers prove counterproductive by imposing conditions on their deployment or operation. The United States, for instance, stipulated that F-16 Fighting Falcon fighters sold to Pakistan be used exclusively in the counterterrorist role,[22] while some air defence systems exported by Russia are modified to prevent them from engaging aircraft of Russian origin, thus ensuring that they cannot be used against Russia.[23] Concern over the potential of transferred arms to exacerbate the Russo-Ukrainian War has led some suppliers to impose limits on how arms supplied to Ukraine are employed.[24] Suppliers may be concerned as well over the potential for exports of advanced arms to result in technology transfers to rival states. Such concerns were much in evidence following thc Iranian revolution of 1979 due to the level of sophistication of some of the arms supplied by the United States and this consideration also is influencing decision making on arms transfers to Ukraine.[25]

Arms transfers represent an important instrument for promoting international security in general. This stems from their perceived contribution to regional stability. The United States, for example, long has sought to maintain the stability of the Middle East though arms transfers and the Japanese government is approaching arms exports as a means of enhancing regional security through the development of a network of 'like-minded' Asian states.[26] The promotion of international security represents something of a moving target, however, as arms transfers may drive other states to procure or transfer arms, potentially generating a classic interstate 'arms race'.

Arms transfers are an important instrument for building interstate relationships. They represent a useful means of signalling commitment to the security of allied or friendly states. A desire to demonstrate such a commitment may encourage the transfer of arms even in the absence of a pressing security threat. Such 'arms diplomacy' is a tangible expression of support as well as enhancing their defence capabilities. The very act of transferring arms represents an important political statement by the supplier, particularly where this occurs in the face of international opposition.[27] Arms exports can have a significance disproportionate to the military capabilities they provide as a result. Institutionalized arms transfer processes, where arms are transferred as part of a formal security commitment, often on a sustained basis, demonstrate political commitment far more effectively than discrete transfers of arms.[28] The supply of arms often is provided for under formal defence assistance agreements and also often accompanies informal security commitments. The strengthening of relationships can be indirect as well as direct. A desire to reinforce its security relationship with the United States was one of the factors underlying Japan's 2011 decision to overturn its long-standing ban on arms exports.[29]

As well as serving as a means of strengthening bilateral ties, arms transfers can provide an effective and relatively inexpensive vehicle for developing international influence. The importance of arms supplies may be such that their supply will render political authorities in recipient states favourably disposed to the supplier, potentially offsetting the influence of rival states. Seeking political advantage through the transfer of arms is a well-trodden path. This can be pursued as a means of enhancing the general level of influence over a state or in an effort to influence its position on a particular issue.

So important are arms transfers as an instrument for projecting political influence and such a time-honoured practice is their use in this manner that a supplier often is assumed to exert some level of influence where a state is substantially dependent on it for arms. The inclination to view arms transfers in these terms is strongest where there is a predisposition to suspect the motives of the supplier. This helps to account for the depth of concern demonstrated over arms exports by politico-military rivals. It is misleading to regard the presence of arms from a particular state as necessarily indicating close political or security relations, much less influence, but interest in enhancing influence may form at least part of the rationale for arms exports and arms may serve as an important vehicle for influence in many cases.

The leverage provided by arms transfers can be considerable. The scope for arms transfers to serve as a useful means of managing other states' behaviour derives from the importance of arms and the dependency produced by the requirement for post-transfer technical and material support. Without maintenance, repair, and overhaul (MRO) services and sustained access to spares, it is difficult, if not impossible, to operate arms for long. This particularly is the case with maintenance-intensive arms such as aircraft and naval vessels. This was demonstrated by Iran's difficulties in operating its American-made arms without the support of the United States as it fought Iraq in the 1980s.[30] The scope for third parties to supplant the original supplier in providing post-transfer support varies but often is relatively limited. Suppliers may seek to maximize their leverage by limiting the capacity of the recipient to operate the arms they provide without ongoing assistance. The Soviet Union, for example, initially sought to keep China's armed forces dependent on its support by withholding 'schematics or any type of production information' from the arms it supplied.[31]

Arms transfers can in exceptional cases produce reverse leverage. This occurs where the recipient exercises greater influence than the supplier. Should a supplier become dependent on the custom of a particular export client, this may provide it with a capacity to influence the supplier contrary to its best interests. The post-Cold War importance of arms exports to China to Russia's efforts to fund defence R&D has led Russia to agree to supply advanced arms despite concerns that China will reverse-engineer their designs and produce unlicensed copies.[32] The Russian government has sought to address its concerns by pressing China to respect intellectual property rights and by requiring it to provide legally binding guarantees that it will refrain from copying Russian arms.[33] For most arms exporters, limited dependence on particular export markets leaves little scope for reverse leverage.

Arms transfers can provide an important means of obtaining specific political and military benefits. Arms may be supplied under transactional arrangements in the pursuit of a variety of objectives. At one point the United States offered Israel Joint Strike Fighters in return for its agreement to suspend the construction of new settlements on the West Bank for ninety days.[34] Arms transfers have been used to secure access to military facilities, such as the American arms package provided to Spain in return for the lease of air bases in the 1950s.[35] Arms also may be supplied as means of securing more limited forms of access to military facilities, such as for the replenishment and repair of naval vessels. The potential for deployed military personnel from the supplier state to facilitate the introduction of arms into service and provide logistical support can represent an additional inducement for states to provide access to facilities in return for arms.

Arms transfers can be employed as an offensive instrument of statecraft. They can be approached as a means of undermining the security of another state. The Cold War saw extensive competitive arms transfers by politico-military rivals such as the United States and the Soviet Union. This has been less evident following the Cold War, but the United States has sought to 'contain' Iran through supplying arms to its regional rivals such as Israel, Saudi Arabia, and the United Arab Emirates.[36] Chinese opposition to American arms transfers to Taiwan likely reflects residual concern that the United States is pursuing a strategy of 'containment' against China.

Political authorities with much more limited agendas and means than the major powers appreciate the strategic potential of arms exports. This is manifest in the range of states that provide military assistance through the supply of arms. Sometimes these efforts are undertaken in conjunction with major powers, as has been the case with many of the states supporting Ukraine. More generally, states transfer arms independently in the pursuit of their respective security agendas. Israel, for instance, has supplied arms as a means of encouraging states such as China to cease providing arms to Iran. Israel hoped that the sale of Phalcon airborne early-warning aircraft would help to influence Chinese thinking about its support for Israel's adversaries.[37]

The importance attached to arms exports as policy instruments is demonstrated by the lengths that states may be prepared to go to expedite their delivery. States may transfer arms directly from their active inventory as well as from surplus stocks, and in some cases have accelerated their transfer by forgoing delivery positions or by airlifting arms to states engaged in conflict. It is common practice to grant preferential treatment to allied and friendly states. The United States, for example, expedites arms transfers to the members of the North Atlantic Treaty Organization (NATO) and to states designated 'Major Non-NATO Allies' and 'Major Defense Partners'. Presidential Drawdown Authority allows the American president to authorize the transfer of excess arms from national stocks without Congressional approval as a means of providing immediate assistance and the Excess Defense Article programme provides a mechanism for transferring surplus arms to allied states.[38]

The scope for exploiting the potential of arms transfers to further national security interests can be considerable, depending on the resources available. Some states with large defence establishments can draw on substantial stocks of arms. The major powers demonstrated a capacity to transfer substantial quantities of arms at short notice during the Cold War. Even China, which could not match the resources of the United States or the Soviet Union, supplied arms on a massive scale to some of the states it supported.[39] A number of states have demonstrated this capacity in supplying arms to Ukraine following the outbreak of the Russo-Ukrainian War. Some states maintain strategic stockpiles of arms that have been retired from service which can be transferred on short notice. The Soviet Union reportedly maintained a substantial stockpile of arms in Lebanon that were available for transfer to Middle Eastern states, while the United States maintains a stockpile of arms in Israel, which it has granted Israel access to on multiple occasions.[40] Suppliers in a position to draw on the output of state-run defence-industrial establishments also may be able to provide arms in large quantities on relatively short notice. The Soviet Union demonstrated this in supplying arms to Middle Eastern states during the Cold War. It had largely replaced the vast quantities of arms lost by Egypt and Syria during the Six-Day War of 1967 by the second half of 1968, with many of the arms supplied more modern than those they replaced.[41]

International and domestic norms can impose serious constraints on arms exporters. There are international norms against the supply of arms to states engaged in conflict, particularly where they are aggressors, and against supply to states which employ their defence establishments as instruments of repression. There also is a norm against supplying arms to non-state actors. These norms are far from absolute, however. Their strength varies considerably across the international system as arms transfer norms are not universally accepted and political authorities may elect to export arms in defiance of norms even where they are. Quite often, the strength of norms reflects the relative influence of civil society. Civil society groups have figured prominently in promoting domestic norms that constrain arms exports, in some cases compelling political authorities to forgo particular arms exports or to resort to the surreptitious delivery of arms. The strength of norms restricting the export of arms generally is greatest in liberal democratic states. The American government was forced to develop an elaborate scheme involving the supply of arms of East German manufacture that were paid for by South Africa as a means of arming the Nicaraguan 'Contra' rebels in 1985 after Congress barred it from providing support.[42] American norms restricting the export of arms strengthened under President Joe Biden, who broadened the threshold to block exports on human rights grounds.[43]

The Russo-Ukrainian War is having a significant impact on arms transfer norms. This conflict is generating popular pressure on political authorities in many states to supply arms to Ukraine. This effect is most marked in states which traditionally have barred arms transfers to conflict zones. This is complemented by developments at the international level as states which traditionally have refrained from transferring arms to conflict zones are under increasing pressure from other states to transfer or at least support the retransfer of critical items such as ammunition to Ukraine.[44] The enduring strength of norms restricting the transfer of arms helps to account for the incrementalist approach to the supply of arms such as tanks and fighter aircraft to Ukraine, which political authorities in key states have become more willing to transfer as the domestic and international ground has shifted, despite the perceived escalatory potential.[45]

The contribution of arms transfers to security varies considerably. Arms transfers do not necessarily enhance the security of suppliers or recipients. Their impact may be offset by arms transfers to rival states or by local arms production in these states. The benefits of arms transfers also may be undermined by the inability of recipients to effectively operate the arms received. The absorptive capacity of states most often is found wanting where advanced arms are concerned, particularly where these represent a generational advance over those they are intended to replace. There is no guarantee as well that arms transfers will generate any political capital as authorities may be prepared to accept the consequences of a loss of access to arms and arms related support or identify an alternate source of support. Some states strive to maintain their policy independence by diversifying sources of arms. North Korea managed this quite successfully during the Cold War, drawing on China and the Soviet Union for arms.

Arms transfers can generate as well as help to address security concerns. This particularly is the case where advanced arms are concerned. An important arms recipient may come to be regarded as an adversary, as was the case with Iran following the revolution which toppled the pro-American Pahlavi monarchy in 1979. There also is the danger that arms that have been supplied to one state or NSAG might be retransferred to the detriment of the security of the original supplier. The potential for uncontrolled technological diffusion can render arms exports problematic from a security perspective. The advanced technologies embodied in arms may be intentionally retransferred or may proliferate unintentionally through battlefield capture or illicit diversion. North Korea has demonstrated considerable aptitude for exploiting surreptitiously obtained arms, in some cases of American origin, as sources of technology.[46]

Recognition of the potential dangers of arms transfers is manifest in efforts to exercise post-transfer arms control. There is growing attention to this issue, particularly where advanced arms are concerned. Political authorities in supplier states may restrict the quantities of the arms that they export to limit the prospects for their retransfer. Some states prohibit the retransfer of the arms they export without their express approval, and some go so far as to strive to retrieve arms they have supplied following changes in the circumstances that prompted their transfer. The United States sought to recover Stinger man-portable SAMs that it supplied to the *mujahedeen* fighting the Soviet-backed government of Afghanistan in order to prevent them from falling into the hands of terrorist groups, for example.[47] Securing sensitive technologies is the subject of sustained attention in the United States. The American government has developed an array of end-use monitoring and other arrangements to ensure that arms transfers do not lead to uncontrolled technological proliferation and this issue figures prominently in American arms export decisions.[48]

Some suppliers seek to limit the potential of arms transfers to undermine their security by providing lower-performance export models of arms produced to less demanding technical standards. Such 'sanitized' equipment may represent an effort to tailor arms to the less demanding requirements of particular export customers, but more commonly this is pursued as a means of safeguarding sensitive technologies. For similar reasons states may strip surplus arms of sensitive components prior to their transfer.

The national security implications of arms transfers can lead political authorities to seek to counteract transfers by other states. States may intervene to prevent a particular transfer or disrupt an arms transfer relationship altogether. The scope for this often is quite limited, but the United States successfully pressured Israel to limit transfers of advanced arms to China by denying it access to some critical technologies.[49]

While the scope for intervention is growing in concert with deepening transnational industrial integration, political authorities more commonly focus on the negative security implications of their own arms transfers. This is demonstrated by the evident care with which the American government seeks to minimize the extent to which arms transfers exacerbate regional tensions. Where arms transfers to Taiwan are concerned, this has involved limiting the capabilities of some of the more advanced arms supplied and lowering the profile of transfers by considering them separately instead of grouped together as 'bundles'.[50] Such a strategy has been adopted by states supplying arms to Ukraine, where a desire to avoid escalating tensions with Russia initially discouraged the supply of longer-range arms such as certain artillery systems and combat aircraft.[51]

## *Arms Transfers and the Economic Basis of Defence*

Arms exports represent an important means of supporting the national defence-industrial base. Exports can be crucial to efforts to render arms development and production economically viable. As Israeli Prime Minister Yitzhak Shamir noted, 'countries that manufacture arms also must export arms. Otherwise, they are incapable of maintaining a weapons industry'.[52] Exports represent a viable alternative to heavy state subsidization of defence firms and enterprises where limited domestic requirements cannot generate the production rates necessary to sustain domestic manufacture, support the modernization of industrial facilities, and fund R&D. For some states, exports can mean the difference between artisanal and mass production. Exports may be particularly important to state-run defence industries, which often are less efficient and may operate at a loss.[53] Arms exports generally are important to defence industries in emerging arms producers, which initially were established for security rather than economic reasons.[54]

The importance of exports to established arms producers derives from the struggle firms and enterprises face in contending with procurement cycles that produce dramatic shifts in orders. Defence firms and enterprises must contend with the so-called 'valley of death' that occurs when research funding nears its end and procurement funding has yet to build up or where there is a gap between production contracts. Without exports, firms and enterprises could be forced to retrench or to close production facilities. Arms exports enable states to maintain a regular 'drumbeat' of production that maintains critical industrial capabilities, helping to sustain a critical industrial reserve capacity for wartime.[55] Arms exports provide a means of insurance against the vicissitudes of domestic procurement by keeping production lines active or 'hot' so that they are available in the absence of substantial national orders, and by helping to maintain a cadre of qualified production personnel.[56]

Interest in exploiting the potential of arms exports to support the defence-industrial base increased in many established producers following the precipitous decline in orders that accompanied the end of the Cold War. In an important shift for American arms export policy, in 1995 President Bill Clinton formally recognized the economic importance of arms transfers in Presidential Directive 41, which instructed all concerned departments to promote arms exports.[57] The objective of 'exportability' was formally confirmed as a consideration in American arms programmes in 2012.[58]

Reducing the economic burden of the materiel requirements of defence is an important consideration in many states. Arms exports represent an important means of funding or recovering the cost of developing arms. Some states impose a levy on export sales to recoup developmental costs and higher production rates resulting from exports translate into lower unit costs through economies of scale. This can be an important consideration where political authorities are confronted by significant resource/capability gaps. The American Joint Strike Fighter programme takes this a step further. This was structured from the outset to encompass export customers whose contributions to the development and production of the aircraft would help to offset the high costs of the programme.[59] The precedent set by the integration of development, production, and export considerations may represent the future for advanced arms as their capital costs continue their apparently inexorable rise.

The need to reduce the economic burden of defence also encourages states to export surplus arms. The export of arms which are approaching the end of their intended service life, or which otherwise are being retired from service is a common means of generating revenue, even on the part of states which have little apparent requirement to do so. There is a ready market for surplus arms, which may be more affordable and often are available on a far quicker timescale than newly produced arms, even if they do not represent the state of the art.

Arms exports provide other important defence-industrial benefits. The need to offer products that can secure customers in the highly competitive international market can spur innovation that contributes to the development of arms required by the national defence establishment. Defence firms and enterprises may offer national procurement authorities improved versions of existing models which are influenced by arms produced for export or new models developed specifically for the export market. This is particularly important where the national market for arms is relatively limited and developing the arms required represents a significant burden but can benefit even major powers. The United States, for example, is pursuing the acquisition of an airborne early-warning aircraft that originally was developed to meet the needs of the export market.[60]

Security objectives often are pursued alongside economic objectives in the export of arms. While not necessarily mutually exclusive, these potentially conflict in important respects. The distinctive features of arms exports where economic imperatives are concerned and the intersection with security imperatives are discussed below.

## The Economic Imperatives of Arms Exports

The economic imperatives that are the focus of this section are distinct from those associated with the requirements of national security. These economic imperatives represent facets of economic security and are distinguished by their general economic focus, though the export of arms as a means of supporting the defence-industrial base potentially generates important incidental economic benefits. The defence-industrial sector can be approached as an economic sector able to provide general benefits such as employment and which contributes to economic growth and development. This perspective is informed by an appreciation of the capacity of industrial progress to drive economic development. This highlights the value of arms exports as a means of generating revenue that can support qualitative industrial development as firms strive to progress up the product chain.

The issues surrounding the economic imperatives of arms exports are more complex than those associated with security imperatives. This is due in part to the more prominent role of industry in the processes involved and the exogenous pressures, including those of the international arms market, to which commercial arms exports are subject. States play a key role, but the requirements of industry help to define this role. Market-based arms export approaches involve different considerations than state-dominated approaches. These factors can greatly complicate arms transfer decision making.

Private firms play a crucial role in the development, production, and marketing of arms in most states. The notable exceptions are the small body of states with a strong tradition of central economic planning, such as Russia, China, and North Korea. Here, the defence-industrial landscape is dominated by the state and its institutions, including state-run research facilities and state-owned enterprises, and the state generally is responsible for marketing arms. In China, this extends to mounting regional campaigns to promote arms exports.[61]

The economic importance of arms exports varies considerably between cases and over time. A focus on the economic benefits of arms exports may be contingent upon the necessary political space. An economic focus generally is strongest where security imperatives are relatively weak. For many states, this corresponds to periods when there are no pressing national security threats. Even states that maintain a policy of neutrality are more likely to focus on arms exports in security terms in times of conflict or heightened international tension. There often is strong interest as well in the economic benefits of arms exports in states which otherwise have limited export options, as is the case with North Korea. The importance attached to arms exports by its government is demonstrated by the determination with which it pursues this trade through intermediaries in order to circumvent UN sanctions.[62] North Korea even has imported arms for the express purpose of reselling them for a profit. North Korea supplied Chinese 'Silkworm' anti-ship missiles to Iran at 'a considerable profit' during its war with Iraq, for instance.[63]

There was a general strengthening of economic imperatives following the end of the Cold War, with arms exports seen as a means of offsetting declining domestic demand in an environment of defence-industrial over-capacity. Between 1990 and 1998, for example, employment in the German arms industry fell from 280,000 to 100,000.[64] Comparable drops in defence-industrial sector employment also were experienced by major arms producers such as France, Russia, the United Kingdom, and the United States.[65] Reduced international security tensions resulted in precipitous declines in demand for arms in NATO states and those which had constituted the rival Warsaw Treaty Organization (WTO). Domestic orders generally were more intermittent and for much more modest quantities of arms. This compelled many producers to pursue increased exports as the price of maintaining industrial employment levels.

There was some interest in having defence industries use their excess capacity for civil production and in 'defence conversion', under which firms and enterprises would refocus on the requirements of the civil market. The limitations of these approaches soon became apparent, however. There proved to be less scope to offset declining national arms orders than initially was expected due to the high cost of defence conversion and the distinct requirements of defence and civil industries.[66] This highlighted the importance of arms exports as a means of supporting industry and generating employment. The strength of economic imperatives remains strong in many states despite the security concerns generated by the present environment of heightened strategic competition.

Interest in providing employment is a common economic driver of arms exports. It is possible to distinguish between those states where this is the principal objective and those where this is pursued alongside the objective of providing a basis for industrial development. The economic value of arms exports to developed industrial states derives largely from their provision of employment and contribution to prosperity.[67] While the developmental potential of arms exports is not unimportant to political authorities in these states, it is far less crucial.

Interest in the developmental potential of arms exports largely is limited to developing states and emerging industrial states which have reached an intermediate stage of industrial development. Industrial underdevelopment in some of these states renders defence- and civil-industrial progress dependent on high levels of state support, which may prove difficult to sustain. Elsewhere it is the case that industrial development is uneven, with civil-industrial development failing to keep pace with defence-industrial development. What these states have in common is a strong incentive to exploit the potential of arms exports to support industrial development. Political authorities typically approach defence-industrial development as a means of industrial upgrading in critical high-technology sectors such as aerospace.[68] Many emerging arms suppliers pursue defence industrialization in tandem with civil-industrial development and approach arms exports as a means of furthering both.

The distinction between developed, emerging industrial, and developing states where the economic importance of arms exports is concerned is eroding as the former are confronted by spiralling arms R&D and production costs that encourage multinational industrial collaboration. The approach of the Joint Strike Fighter programme testifies to the daunting challenge facing even major arms producers such as the United States. Arms exports can be expected to figure more prominently in the industrial development strategies of established producers as arms costs continue to spiral.

Political authorities in many states are responding to this challenge by placing greater emphasis on exports and industrial collaboration. Where there is interest in exploiting the potential of arms exports to support industrial upgrading, this is generating close attention to defence-industrial arrangements. As well as encouraging exports of complete systems where possible, political authorities in many states pursue local industrial participation in arms exports led by offshore industry.[69] This has been supported through the industrial offsets provided for under arms procurement contracts, which often include provisions for local firms and enterprises to contribute to suppliers' exports through the supply of components and sub-components. This has contributed to the emergence of a transnational arms industry and the development of emerging arms suppliers, as discussed in Chapter 4.

An economic focus generates pressures that encourage a less restrictive approach to arms exports. Political authorities may be subject to strong domestic pressure, including from industry, to approve arms exports. Typical is the view that exports are critical to firms' long-term competitiveness and profitability, including in terms of their capacity to undertake R&D. In their campaign to have it overturned, defence firms in Japan argued that its long-standing ban on arms exports prevented collaboration with foreign firms.[70] Domestic pressure for arms exports increased in many states following the Cold War when deep cuts in the arms orders that firms and enterprises had been accustomed to rendered exports more critical to their survival.[71] This is reinforced by industrial globalization. The integration of firms and enterprises into transnational supply chains exposes political authorities to pressure to export from partner states with less restrictive export policies.

The pressure exerted by industry and foreign authorities is exacerbated by the intense competition that characterizes the contemporary international arms market. Competition for export orders increased noticeably in the latter part of the Cold War. The first two decades of the Cold War saw arms exports dominated by a relatively small group of major suppliers, namely the United States, the Soviet Union, the United Kingdom, and France. The dominance of these states eroded over time. This was demonstrated by the declining market share of the United States, which was responsible for only 33 per cent of international arms deliveries in 1985, compared to about 60 per cent in 1969.[72] Competition increased following the end of the Cold War for the reasons outlined above, and continues to grow as new exporters emerge and their defence-industrial capabilities mature.

Economic imperatives have important implications for arms exports. There are several features that characterize arms exports where these are driven primarily by economic imperatives. Such a focus often produces less consistent patterns of supply as the secondary importance of security considerations results in fewer restrictions on the arms that may be exported, the quantities that may be supplied, and the customers that may be supplied. An economic focus on arms exports can impact significantly on the terms under which they are transferred. The focus on commercial terms with respect to price and delivery can result in the supply of arms to states regardless of the security implications. Such pragmatic arms export decision making is evident on the part of many suppliers. This tends to be most readily apparent in the transfer of advanced arms due to their perceived impact in security terms and the international attention this generates. This pragmatism also is demonstrated by the readiness of suppliers which have no security commitments to supply advanced arms to combatants at war. Some states even simultaneously supply arms to rival states engaged in conflict. China and the Soviet Union supplied arms to both Iran and Iraq when they were fighting in the 1980s, for example.[73]

The economic contribution of arms exports varies greatly. Some suppliers are far more successful at exporting arms than others and some succeed in deriving significant industrial benefits from exports while others do not. The economic contribution of exports is determined in part by states' industrial strengths. Arms exports provide economic benefits to many states in terms of providing employment, but the qualitative industrial benefits often prove far more elusive. The prospects for arms exports contributing to industrial development in states where defence R&D and production are restricted to low value-added product sectors are quite limited, but where defence firms and enterprises figure prominently in high-technology product sectors such as aerospace and information and communications technology (ICT), the prospects are much better. Emerging arms producers such as South Korea have considerable potential to exploit the opportunities provided by arms exports to support industrial development as well as to advance their defence development programmes.

This has important implications for the international arms market. Traditionally, the industrial limitations of emerging arms producers restricted them to supplying states with less demanding requirements. Their defence industries generally were characterized by relatively limited product ranges and they were unable to supply complete systems that could compete in qualitative terms with those offered by established producers. This is changing as the progressive development of defence-industrial capabilities on the part of the expanding class of emerging arms suppliers enables them to offer arms that meet the needs of developed states as well. Israel led the way in this. It is noteworthy that the American government, which agreed to fund some 40 per cent of the cost of the development programme of Israel's Lavi fighter in the 1980s, maintained the right to veto any export sales of the aircraft.[74] Emerging suppliers such as South Korea and Turkey, which are supplying a growing list of developed states, represent an important trend which will strengthen as arms exports continue to promote defence- and civil-industrial development.

## Arms Transfers Between Security and Economic Imperatives

Arms export decision making often is far from straightforward. States are not unitary actors and arms transfer issues can generate intense policy debate. There may be deep divisions within the policy community over the wisdom of supplying arms to a particular customer or over the quantity or quality of arms or the terms of supply. These tensions may occur within as well as between bureaucratic actors whose responsibilities encompass arms exports. States' arms transfer policies often strike some balance between conflicting imperatives. Policy debates may not be readily apparent, however. This particularly is the case in states with limited policy transparency, where the sensitivity of security issues generally discourages open discussion. Understanding arms export policy often requires reading into general trends or the particulars of specific export decisions as a result.

Tensions between conflicting policy interests can greatly complicate arms transfer policy. Often the fault lines are defined by security and economic interests, with tension between interest in securing the economic benefits of arms exports and concern over their security implications, as is the case with Russian exports to China.[75] This tension is most readily apparent where the issue of arms transfers to states that represent actual or potential politico-military adversaries arises. The attractiveness of the Chinese defence market has generated a dilemma for many arms suppliers. While there is strong interest in meeting China's demand for products and services that would offset its defence-industrial weaknesses, potential suppliers have had to balance this against concerns over the security implications of exporting arms to China. This has produced considerable strain on efforts to maintain the European Union (EU) arms embargo that was imposed in the wake of the Tiananmen Square Incident of 1989.[76] How states approach the complex issue of arms exports reflects their distinct economic and security agendas.

The tension between security and economic imperatives greatly complicates efforts to manage the arms trade. As discussed in detail in Chapter 7, concerned authorities responsible for developing and implementing arms transfer controls often must balance conflicting security and economic requirements.

## Industry and Arms Exports

Firms and enterprises are key actors in the international arms transfer system and contribute to arms exports in a variety of respects. The important role of industry in producing and exporting arms as a means of generating profits is of long standing. The contribution of industry has changed over time. Sub-state actors grew in importance as the expansion of European armies generated arms demands that could not be met through artisanal production. This created an international demand for arms related expertise as well as for arms themselves that stimulated the development of larger and more capable firms and enterprises. Their role in the international arms transfer system grew in concert with the development of a (relatively) liberal economic order from the nineteenth century.[77] The importance of industry continued to expand following the Second World War as it evolved to meet increasing domestic and international demand for arms.

The interests and relative independence of industry have important implications for arms transfer processes. Firms and enterprises generally are highly self-interested and entrepreneurial as they strive to secure export contracts that generate profits and keep production lines open. The importance attached to exports by industry is demonstrated by willingness to develop arms in response to client-specific requirements. Firms and enterprises cater to the needs of export customers which do not require or are not able to afford arms developed with national requirements in mind. In some cases, these are 'austere' versions of arms intended to satisfy less exacting requirements, these being the modern equivalent of the poor-quality 'trade guns' produced for Asian and African markets in the pre-colonial period, which were 'far below the standard required for the European market'.[78] Many arms developed for export customers are no less or even more advanced than those produced for the domestic market, however. A focus on the export market can prove self-reinforcing if the requirements involved differ significantly from those of the national market.

Industry is a key driver of arms exports in many states, with firms and enterprises actively pursuing export opportunities. Firms and enterprises generally enjoy considerable freedom of action and pursue their commercial interests to the extent that they are able. Even state-owned enterprises may seek to export arms without prior official approval. This generates a substantial international arms trade that is relatively independent of political interests. Firms and enterprises generally must contend with politically imposed barriers which reflect security considerations, but they do not necessarily respect such barriers; while many comply with restrictions on arms exports, others do so only to the extent that they must or disregard them altogether. Questionable export activities by firms and enterprises can result from differing interpretations of export guidelines or from deliberate efforts to circumvent export controls. Despite numerous examples of unsanctioned arms exports, it commonly is assumed that defence firms and enterprises remain under effective national control and that they export with at least the tacit acquiescence, if not under the direction, of political authorities.[79]

There can be considerable tension between industry and political authorities in the states in which it is based and in which it operates, even where firms and enterprises are not exporting arms illicitly. Political authorities in many states recognize the impact of market imperatives and the scope for firms and enterprises to act independently of official direction and contrary to national interests. The struggle to exert effective control over arms exports in many states testifies to the depth of official concern over industry's inclination to export without due regard for national interests as well as the difficulties inherent in this exercise. The state/industry relationship in many states is growing more complex as transnational industrial integration deepens and firms and enterprises develop functional relationships with offshore capability partners.

It is important to differentiate between those sub-state actors that are legitimate from the perspective of most political authorities and those that are not. The former, which include state-owned enterprises and privately owned firms, far outnumber the latter. The considerable freedom of action in developing export markets generally granted by political authorities reflects the common expectation that industry is best placed to pursue export opportunities, and that the importance of exports to the success, and indeed survival, of firms and enterprises will drive them to export. This perspective now is evident even on the part of Chinese authorities. The progressive commercialization of its defence-industrial sector as economic reforms deepen has extended to state-owned enterprises. Profitability now is encouraged in state-owned enterprises, and those that produce arms are expected to exercise considerable initiative in pursuing export opportunities.[80]

Considerably more problematic from the perspective of political authorities in most states are those sub-state actors which operate at the margins of the mainstream arms market or outside it altogether. These actors are more likely to operate with little or no regard for the interests of the states in which they are based. Of particular concern are some of the brokers specializing in the sale of arms that for reasons of obsolescence or redundancy have been declared surplus. Their stock in trade often includes, or may consist entirely of, arms components. These dealers are notable for serving the market provided by operators which lack the means or the opportunity to procure more modern arms. This may include states which are subject to formal supplier restrictions.

Unscrupulous arms traffickers long have been a subject of official concern. It was arms dealers such as Sir Basil Zaharoff and firms such as Remington and Du Pont, which rose to prominence in the nineteenth century and which were prepared to export arms indiscriminately and even sought to generate demand for arms, that gave the international arms trade its notorious reputation.[81] Zaharoff, who served as an agent for a number of European firms prior to the First World War and sold arms to rival sides in the Balkan Wars, provided the benchmark for this perspective.[82] Such actors often are viewed with suspicion even where they are not engaged in illicit arms transfers, due to their perceived opportunism and lack of principles. Their antithesis is provided by Count Carl Gustav von Rosen of Sweden, who supplied armed Minicon training aircraft to the rebel state of Biafra in 1969 out of his personal commitment to its fight for independence.[83] The image that persists, however, is that of arms dealers who are prepared to export without restraint.

Arms traffickers operating around the margins of what is from the perspective of the international community the legitimate arms trade remain a fixture of the arms transfer system, though they are less prominent than formerly. Their postwar heyday was in the 1950s and 1960s. This resulted from a unique combination of factors. Stocks of arms rendered surplus by the end of the Second World War or through states replacing earlier generations of arms with arms of that vintage remained high, providing ample product for export. Numerous arms dealers sought to profit from this by supplying states and NSAGs in conflict zones in Latin America, Africa, and the Middle East. The importance of such traffickers derived also from the heavy demand in the high Cold War period for the services of intermediaries which could supply arms discreetly and with plausible state deniability. A number of states engaged the services of arms dealers to undertake 'gun-running' on their behalf. The overall importance of these actors gradually declined as the Cold War progressed, however, as states increasingly undertook this role themselves.

The services provided by arms traffickers remain important where international sanctions limit states' access to arms. Often arms dealers such as Viktor Bout, who until his arrest in 2008 was a major trafficker, serve the market generated by internal conflict situations which arms transfer norms discourage many states from supplying.[84] Individual arms traffickers have been supplanted to some extent by transnational criminal organizations.[85] The importance of these actors can be expected to increase in tandem with heightened geopolitical competition and growing interest in some states in providing arms outside of formal arms export processes.

The scope for one category of sub-state actor is increasing in concert with deepening transnational defence-industrial ties and the emergence of new arms producers. There is considerable demand for independent experts or 'technological mercenaries' in this environment. This is of great concern to political authorities in some established arms producers, but it has proven quite difficult to develop a clear understanding of this facet of the international arms trade, much less control it, due to the nature of the activities of these actors. Both the individuals themselves and the states that draw on their services have strong incentives to avoid publicizing their contribution. As a result, the nature of this may not be apparent until long after the fact.

# 3 The Imperatives of Arms Imports

The imperatives driving arms imports shape the international arms transfer system in important respects. Arms imports in most cases are a substitute for indigenous arms production and the demand driving imports often reflects the requirements of states which lack the necessary resources or where political authorities do not support defence R&D and production. The development of comprehensive defence-industrial capabilities does not necessarily free a state from the requirement to import arms, however. It is misleading to conceptualize mutually exclusive categories of arms exporters and arms importers; with notable exceptions, even major arms exporters import arms.

Complex imperatives drive arms imports in many states. As is the case with arms exports, it is constructive to distinguish between security and economic imperatives. These categories are not entirely mutually exclusive but capture the key rationales underlying arms imports. The tension between security and economic imperatives can be considerable, potentially complicating arms import processes. The balance between security and economic imperatives varies between states and may shift within states over time in concert with evolving security and economic agendas, the development of industrial capabilities, and changes in the security environment.

Security and economic imperatives determine what arms are procured and the terms and arrangements under which they are imported. Increasingly, arms imports comprise production inputs in the form of components, sub-components, and technologies as well as complete arms. This reflects strengthening demands for local participation in the production of imported arms as well as the structural transformation of the global defence-industrial landscape. Arms exports increasingly depend on imports of production inputs.

## The Security Imperatives of Arms Imports

Security imperatives generally represent the principal determinant of arms imports. Arms imports may be regarded as crucial to national security in peacetime as well as wartime. The scale of arms importation increased in concert with defence development in European states and the expansion of the Euro-centric world through the emergence of post-colonial states beginning in the nineteenth century. Arms imports were crucial to the emergence of mass armies in many European states and to the development of the defence establishments of non-European states which generally were modelled on those of European states.[1] International demand for arms expanded with the postwar wave of decolonialization, which saw the emergence of numerous independent states with little capacity to develop and produce the arms they required.

The security imperatives driving arms imports are many and varied and the focus of official concern may shift considerably over time. Fundamental to most states is the imperative to equip the national defence establishment. This may involve arms required as part of general programmes of defence development or which are required to respond to particular security threats. The inability of a state to satisfy the materiel requirements of its defence establishment, particularly in times of heightened international tension or interstate conflict, undermines national security. No less significant are the implications for states which are confronted by armed insurgencies. So fundamental is the capacity of states to field arms that this represents an important expression of domestic legitimacy and international status, as discussed below.

National arms requirements vary considerably. These are determined by factors such as military doctrine, levels of defence and defence-industrial development, and the prevailing external or internal threat environment. Arms import requirements can evolve gradually over time or emerge quite suddenly in concert with trends and developments in any of these areas. Operational requirements stemming from conflict situations may develop at quite short notice and may generate arms demands which can be met only through imports. The emergence of unanticipated threats may compel political authorities to bypass normal procurement channels. Arms procured on an urgent operational requirement (UOR) basis often are sourced offshore. Periods of heightened international tension can have a similar effect on demand for imports, albeit often in a less immediate time frame. The defence transformation involved in a shift in focus from internal security to a focus on external territorial defence generally has a significant impact on arms import requirements, but the shift involved can be quite protracted.

Operational considerations can influence the general level of imports and can have the effect of increasing or decreasing demand for specific categories of arms. These can even influence the arms that are available for import by encouraging suppliers to develop new models of arms for export, including in an effort to circumvent restrictions imposed by suppliers contributing key components. The general trend has seen states procure more advanced arms as defence modernization progresses, with requirements being satisfied through imports in many cases. States typically become more discriminating arms importers over time. This often manifests in more rigorous evaluation processes, more careful consideration of competing arms offers, and the negotiation of terms that better support industrial or defence-industrial development.

Operational considerations deriving from the military capabilities of actual or potential politico-military rivals can impact significantly on arms imports. Concern over the threat posed by adversaries typically is reflected in close attention to their arms programmes. Arms imports can prove mutually reinforcing in the sense that procurements by one state potentially encourage reciprocal imports by a rival due to the perceived security threat this represents. This is reinforced by the tendency to engage in 'mirror imaging' or 'mirror thinking', the practice of assuming that other actors perceive and approach an issue in a similar manner to oneself.[2] This encourages political authorities to assess arms import trends in rival states in terms of the potential threat they represent.

Where this involves an action-reaction cycle, producing a sustained dynamic of rival arms procurements as political authorities strive to establish a decisive quantitative or qualitative advantage, this can be termed an 'arms race'. The process involved in such highly focused, competitive arms procurements is complicated by the seemingly inexorable advance of technological frontiers.[3] The capability advances offered by successive generations of arms often provide a focus for efforts to achieve and maintain qualitative military superiority. The concept of arms race may be most familiar in a strategic context, particularly that of the nuclear arms race of the Cold War, but is no less relevant to the field of conventional arms. Arms races can be confined to specific categories of arms such as combat aircraft or may encompass a broad range of arms. Arms races may stem from long-standing interstate rivalries or conflicts that have arisen relatively recently. They may be restricted to particular rivals such as the United States and the Soviet Union or India and Pakistan, or can be regional in scope, such as the long-posited East Asian arms race.[4]

Developing states figure prominently in considerations of conventional arms races. This reflects the more conspicuous nature of their arms procurements; a far greater proportion of the arms fielded by these states are obtained through imports than is the case in the developed states. This focus also demonstrates the extent to which the competitive acquisition of conventional arms by major powers such as the United States and the Soviet Union and their allies was overshadowed by the nuclear arms race of the Cold War.

Competitive arms procurements are the subject of considerable attention within the states concerned and more generally. This reflects the depth of concern over the domestic and international implications of arms imports. With their effect of driving the procurement of more advanced arms, arms races commonly are regarded as increasing the likelihood of conflict and as potentially destabilizing.[5] While arms racing does not necessarily produce these effects, its potential to generate sustained demand for arms which offer a qualitative advance over those in service has important implications for the international arms market and for efforts to control arms transfers.

The term 'arms race' must be applied with caution, however, to avoid undermining its conceptual value. It is important to distinguish arms import trends sustained by particular competitive interstate rivalries from those that are not. An arms race is not always perceived as such and reflects political as much as military considerations, with the process that defines an arms race driven as much by concern over the intentions of rival states procuring arms as concern over the type or quantity of the arms procured.[6] Arms import patterns in most cases do not suggest a sustained response to specific procurements in a manner characteristic of an arms race. In importing arms, political authorities are contending with the demands generated by the progressive advance of technological frontiers, the pace of which accelerated following the Cold War. Interest in realizing 'transformational' military capabilities through the introduction of advanced arms is general. This is the case even where defence development lags far behind that of the states at the forefront of the Revolution in Military Affairs (RMA). The state of defence capabilities in rival states, which arms imports may play a key role in determining, still helps to inform arms import decision making, however.

Political considerations can impact significantly on arms imports. States might not be in a strong position to import arms from some suppliers due to the state of their relationship, even where they are not subject to formal arms sale restrictions. Political distance with a supplier may impede efforts to obtain arms or preclude this altogether. Some arms producers demonstrate considerable reluctance to supply advanced arms in particular to states that they do not share a close relationship with. While the acquisition of arms from a particular supplier does not necessarily signify a close political or security relationship, close ties facilitate access to arms. There are several long-established arms transfer relationships where particular suppliers play prominent roles in meeting the arms import requirements of particular states. Notable supplier–recipient relationships include those of the United States and Israel, Russia and India, and China and Pakistan. Political authorities may be proactive in requesting military assistance in the form of arms from their international supporters. This particularly is the case where financing represents a major obstacle to the purchase of arms.

Political authorities often are forced to compromise in deciding what arms to import. It is axiomatic that security requirements encourage procurement of the arms that offer the best capabilities on the most favourable terms possible. These requirements may be, but are not necessarily, satisfied by the most advanced arms available. Other considerations such as suitability for the intended operational environment in terms of ruggedness and maintainability also may factor into arms import decision making. Political authorities do not necessarily select arms based on these criteria, however. They often are confronted by cost versus capability and quality versus quantity dilemmas for which there are no straightforward solutions.

States may not possess the financial resources needed to import the arms dictated by their operational requirements. Affordability considerations can prove decisive in arms import decision making. In extreme cases, states may be forced to retire and sell arms in their inventory in order to afford newer generations of arms. This was the case with Egypt after 1967, when it sold its MiG-17 fighters to pay for newer MiG-19s and -21s from the Soviet Union.[7] Similar considerations are manifest in countertrade practices involving commodities such as foodstuffs and natural resources. The continuing importance of countertrade to developing and even some emerging industrial states is noteworthy. Countertrade arrangements may be crucial to NSAGs which lack access to legitimate revenue streams.

The need to strike a balance between cost and capability and quality and quantity can compel states to import less-advanced arms alongside arms offering superior capabilities. The high cost of advanced arms can force political authorities to settle for models that do not best meet their needs. There is a substantial market for arms designed to less demanding standards that are intended to meet the requirements of export customers, as well as austere models of arms originally developed with more exacting requirements in mind. These have the advantage of being less costly but rarely are these the arms of choice for states. This provides an important niche for suppliers such as China which can provide relatively inexpensive and yet relatively advanced arms. Affordability issues ensure that there is a ready market for surplus arms and may mean that arms such as naval vessels are delivered without their full complement of systems such as armament or that states are forced to lease arms. This reinforces the role of external state supporters which are prepared to supply arms at concessionary rates or at no cost in pursuit of their policy agendas.

The operational record of arms can influence arms import decision making. The service history of arms is important for its effect in demonstrating their strengths and weaknesses. The successful employment of particular equipment types or models in conflict situations highlights their capabilities, for example. The effectiveness of some of the aircraft and air defence systems operated by Western states in the Gulf War of 1990–91 had such an effect in Saudi Arabia.[8] The Russo-Ukrainian War similarly is encouraging states to procure the artillery, missile systems, and UAVs that Ukraine has operated to great effect.[9]

Arms import decisions also can be influenced by shared state requirements, either in the interest of the economies of scale produced by collaborative procurement or in the interest of interoperability, logistic compatibility, and operational cost savings. The collective decision of the governments of Belgium, Denmark, the Netherlands, and Norway to purchase the F-16 Fighting Falcon fighter in 1975's 'Sale of the Century' is a noteworthy example of the pursuit of economies of scale through collaborative procurement. Collaborative procurement processes can be institutionalized through joint purchasing groups and mechanisms such as NATO's Smart Defence working group, which oversees joint procurement of precision-guided munitions by member states.[10] Interoperability and logistic compatibility tend to be considered where there is interest in facilitating operations with close military allies. Interoperability with American forces has been an important factor in South Korean arms import decision making, for instance.[11] The potential for interoperability is contributing to export demand for the American Joint Strike Fighter.[12]

Arms import decisions also may be the product of interest in influencing the supply of preferred arms from other suppliers or in obtaining arms on better financial terms. States may announce their intention to procure an equipment item as a means of persuading other suppliers to provide advanced arms which they have been reluctant to export. The announcement by the United Arab Emirates of its intention to procure the Su-35 'Flanker' from Russia may have represented an effort to leverage export approval for the Joint Strike Fighter from the United States, for example.[13] Arms have been imported to leverage better terms from local industry. Russia's order for Lince armoured vehicles from Italy, when development of such a vehicle was well within local industrial capabilities, was pursued with a view to driving down the cost of Russian-produced arms.[14]

Arms import options may be limited. This particularly is the case during times of conflict or heightened international tension, when demand can outstrip supply and established arms suppliers may be unable or reluctant to export. In such an environment, production lines tend to be 'crowded' and competition for available arms supplies may be intense, with less strategically important states forced to make sub-optimal arms import decisions in terms of the suitability of arms and their delivery time frame. More limited options may lead to the import of older equipment that is uneconomical to maintain and operate, at patently inflated prices. In 1940 the British government considered itself fortunate to secure First World War-vintage small arms and artillery from the United States to re-equip its army, as well as fifty obsolete destroyers in exchange for granting the United States naval bases in various parts of the Empire.[15]

Rationality in arms imports is not always apparent. Security requirements can compel the importation of arms that are unaffordable or which states are unable to operate effectively. Both features characterized the arms procurement programme pursued under President Sukarno of Indonesia in the 1960s.[16]

Some states base arms import decisions strictly on availability and price considerations, regardless of any operational and logistical implications. Such an approach can compensate for limited procurement budgets but potentially comes at the cost of a heterogenous arsenal of unsuitable arms. Apparently irrational arms import decisions also can result from the procurement of what are regarded as high-prestige items, as discussed below.

Arms import requirements are influenced by the level of defence-industrial development. The elusive objective of sustainable defence-industrial development has important implications for arms imports. Many states undertake some level of arms production, which generally requires the import of at least some production inputs in the form of components, sub-components, and technologies. The trade in production inputs is growing as more states seek to develop their defence-industrial capabilities and as they initiate more ambitious projects which are more difficult to sustain in the absence of sustained offshore support.

There are two facets to this issue. The import of production inputs is discussed in detail below, but it is important to note that this often is pursued in conjunction with the import of complete arms. Many states base arms R&D and production programmes on foreign designs. This is reflected in the contribution of licensed production and co-production arrangements. Arms imports may involve limited numbers of complete systems and transfers over time may involve decreasing amounts of production inputs as the local industrial contribution grows. The second facet is that of transnational arms production, which is structured around the transfer of production inputs between spatially dispersed capability partners. This can require the importation of production inputs which will ultimately be re-exported in some form.

The importation of components, sub-components, and technologies is an important feature of arms imports by established as well as emerging arms producers. This trend is likely to survive the strengthening focus on supply-chain security evident on the part of many arms producers that has been generated by concern over the reliability of suppliers of critical production inputs. The factors driving reliance on offshore capability partners remain and concerned authorities are responding by working with trusted partner states under what is referred to as 'friendshoring' or 'ally shoring'.[17]

Even established arms exporters with comprehensive defence-industrial capabilities cannot easily escape the requirement to import arms. States' defence industries are characterized by sectoral strengths and weaknesses. This may render states unable to readily produce the full range of arms required by their defence establishments or result in a situation whereby doing so would not be cost-effective. It also may be necessary to import arms to address equipment gaps resulting from delays in production programmes or to offset shortages and regenerate defence capabilities during and following conflicts. Conflict situations can transform arms exporters into arms importers. Major European arms producers such as France and the United Kingdom imported arms on a large scale as the Second World War approached and many European states, including Russia, are placing large import orders for arms following the outbreak of the Russo-Ukrainian War.[18] In many cases these states are importing arms using urgent or 'emergency' procurement mechanisms with short delivery timelines.[19]

The East Asian emerging industrial states in which general industrial development is providing a strong foundation for sustained defence-industrial progress also have not been able to escape the need to import arms. While states such as South Korea have demonstrated an impressive capacity to develop and produce the arms that they require and have emerged as important arms exporters, they continue to import arms on a large scale. The difference is the degree of dependence on arms imports and the form that they take. In many emerging industrial states, imports of production inputs have assumed increasing importance even as the importation of complete systems continues. Importation generally remains a more cost-effective means of procuring arms and generally delivers arms more rapidly than local R&D programmes. While these states are far less dependent on arms imports than in the past, they are far from completely independent arms producers.

Arms imports are particularly crucial to the security of developing states, even if these do not necessarily enable them to close what can be enormous capability gaps with their adversaries. Most developing states are characterized by weak arms production capabilities and an even weaker basis for arms R&D, with industrial bases that are relatively underdeveloped. Defence-industrial development in these states is typified by limited and sporadic progress. Many developing states have ambitious defence-industrial visions, but their arms programmes often fall short, resulting in 'enclave' industries that are effectively isolated from the civil-industrial sector.[20] Defence firms and enterprises may possess R&D and production capabilities well in advance of their civil counterparts, but arms programmes often prove unsustainable in the absence of ongoing substantial state support. Defence-industrial underdevelopment is a subject of concern in many developing states, not least because of its implications in times of conflict or heightened international tension. A senior Egyptian official once declared that his country favoured local arms production 'even if the cost of production is double the price of imported arms', for example.[21]

Arms imports potentially represent a double-edged sword where security is concerned. The prospect of strengthening security through arms imports may be tempered by concern over the dependence which may be a corollary of this. While arms imports enable states to overcome defence-industrial resource constraints and meet operational requirements, they can simultaneously maintain or strengthen a dependency relationship that provides the supplier with considerable leverage. Dependence is such an issue in arms imports because of the importance of security of supply. Security of supply concerns stem from the difficulties inherent in compensating for the loss of access to arms from established suppliers. Recipients are vulnerable to supply disruptions in the form of formal arms embargoes or informal supply restrictions. There is particular concern over the potential loss of access to arms during periods of conflict or heightened international tension. A crucial factor is how prepared political authorities are to face the consequences of a loss of access to arms and post-transfer support in the form of the supply of spares and the provision of MRO services.

The development of a dependency relationship depends on several factors. These include the nature of the general relationship between the arms supplier and the recipient, the importance of arms from that supplier, and the scope that exists for drawing on alternative sources of arms and support for arms that are in service. The operation of arms can prove difficult, if not impossible, in the absence of ongoing support from the OEM. Political authorities in arms importing states recognize the scope for arms transfers to be employed as an instrument for political leverage and may consider it important to minimize the potential for the exercise of coercion through restricting or denying access to arms. Dependence is less a subject of concern where this involves a supplier with which the recipient enjoys a relationship of trust.

The reliability of arms supplies tends to be a particularly sensitive issue in developing states. Not only are these states generally rendered far more vulnerable to interruptions in the supply of arms by their defence-industrial limitations, but also it is the case that arms suppliers generally face fewer political and economic constraints in restricting the supply of arms and the provision of post-transfer support. Suppliers may be less reliant on the market provided by developing states and there generally are fewer repercussions from restricting arms supplies and support. Concern on the part of political authorities in developing states is grounded in a long history of politically driven restrictions on the supply of arms. Political authorities in developing states generally are wary of what they regard as undue dependence on the developed industrial states, of which dependency for arms is an important facet.[22]

Concern naturally trends to be strongest in states which have been subject to arms embargoes, or which otherwise have been confronted by daunting political obstacles in their efforts to import arms. The lasting impact of negative experiences with arms suppliers is demonstrated by the arms acquisition strategies of diplomatically isolated 'pariah states' such as Iran, North Korea, and Taiwan. Iran's difficulties in supporting American-made arms have produced a marked reluctance to depend on OEMs for long-term support, even where there is no apparent cause for concern. This is manifest in a preference for unofficial networks for the supply of spare parts required to maintain aircraft that it operates. While this approach was necessary to support aircraft such as the F-4 Phantom II and F-14 Tomcat following the imposition of an arms embargo by the United States, this is not required for the arms of non-American origin that it has procured in recent decades.[23]

Security of supply concerns in developed industrial states tend to be less acute than in developing states. The focus of concern in these states reflects their level of defence-industrial development. Concern here tends to be over threats to the supply of production inputs rather than dependence on complete systems or post-transfer support. The grounds for concern in these states expanded as transnational arms production became more the norm, with local industry increasingly reliant on production inputs from offshore capability partners. Foreign firms and enterprises may refuse to transfer critical technologies, either for commercial reasons or at the direction of political authorities. Cases such as that where the Japanese government apparently pressured Kyocera to cease supplying missile components to the United States through its American subsidiary highlighted the potential lack of reliability and accountability of foreign firms, even when they are based in friendly states.[24]

Supply-chain security concerns resulting from heightened geopolitical competition are strengthening attention to this issue. Political authorities in a growing number of developed states are concerned to limit their dependency on offshore industry in arms R&D and production programmes. This is being conceptualized in terms of 'technological sovereignty' and 'technological independence'.[25] Concern is most marked in the United States, where this is driving efforts to limit reliance on Chinese industry and to strengthen American production capabilities in key areas.[26]

Various strategies are employed by states to mitigate the risks involved. In some states political authorities are wary of purchasing from suppliers of particular concern. Political authorities may signal their concern by abrogating contracts with suppliers that are the subject of concern, but this is exceptional. More commonly, arms suppliers are supplemented rather than supplanted. Egypt continued to import arms from the Soviet Union despite its growing disquiet over the arms supply relationship, for instance.[27] States may seek to limit dependency by diversifying their arms suppliers. At one point Malaysia required that ammunition be available from at least three independent suppliers, while Indonesia sought to diversify its range of sources following the imposition of an arms embargo by the United States in the 1990s, even drawing on China.[28] India has relied for some time on the Soviet Union and subsequently Russia for most of its arms imports, having been subject to American arms sanctions, but concern over Russia's reliability now is leading it to diversify its arms suppliers, with the United States figuring prominently in these efforts.[29] Diversification can be a difficult exercise, particularly where this comes at the expense of a long-standing arms supply relationship.

The depth of concern over dependence is demonstrated by the commitment to the development of indigenous defence-industrial capabilities. Despite the daunting obstacles involved, particularly for states where the defence-industrial base is comprised of 'enclave' industries, political authorities generally set great store by indigenous arms R&D and production. Interest in developing states, which generally are the most dependent on arms imports, remains strong despite their mixed record, particularly where advanced arms are concerned. It is noteworthy that strong interest is not limited to states such as Iran, North Korea, and Taiwan which have experienced significant security of supply difficulties.

There is widespread interest in the 'localization' of arms production as an alternative to the importation of complete systems. This can take the form of the licensed production of complete arms, their co-production, where a significant proportion of the components are provided by the supplier or otherwise sourced offshore, or local assembly, where all or nearly all of the components are imported. Security of supply concerns similarly drive efforts to develop local MRO capabilities for the support of imported arms. These efforts are pursued notwithstanding the higher overall costs and the daunting challenges that generally are entailed, particularly for developing states.

In most states security of supply concerns can be addressed only in part by defence-industrial development. The potential of defence-industrial development to free states from the need to import arms particularly is limited where licensed production is restricted to co-production or assembly. This is because production at these levels does not free a state from a reliance on imports, albeit of a different sort. This represents a transition from dependency on the import of complete systems to dependency on inputs in the form of components, sub-components, and technologies required for local arms production. What is more, the need to order critical long-lead time materials required for production provides states with little scope for accelerating production on short notice in response to heightened international tension or conflict situations. This particularly is the case where advanced arms are concerned. The local production of foreign arms designs generally is recognized as only partially offsetting security of supply concerns and for this reason often is approached as an intermediate stage in the process of lessening dependence.

Security considerations of an altogether different nature factor in arms imports in some cases. Arms can be procured for the political benefits they confer as well as their military value. This reflects the importance of arms procurements as political statements. Arms represent important prestige items, the acquisition of which is symbolically significant both domestically and internationally. Advanced arms can represent a powerful symbol of modernity in developing states, with the procurement of high-prestige arms which are available for conspicuous display regarded as symbolizing a country's progress and conferring membership in an exclusive community or 'club'. The fact that such communities are 'imagined' in the sense that they are cultural artefacts does not detract from the importance that may be attached to membership through the possession of advanced arms.[30]

The particular arms that are regarded as objects of prestige are context-specific, but generally are distinguished by offering exceptional capabilities that are highly coveted. During the civil war which raged in China following the First World War, artillery systems served as important status symbols.[31] At the present time, advanced combat aircraft and ballistic missiles are conspicuous as prestige acquisitions, as well as for their value as weapon systems. One observer noted that Algeria's procurement of Su-30 'Flanker' fighters from Russia in 2008 would 'show that Algeria is far from a backward state', for example.[32] The prestige attached to particular types of arms can be influenced by procurement trends on the part of major military powers, the exclusivity of the group of states operating the arms, and their demonstrated effectiveness in combat. Arms that are important in symbolic terms do not necessarily contribute to the development of military capabilities.

The act of importing high-profile arms has been regarded in many states as enhancing their international status. Arms transfers are highly symbolic in this respect. As one study noted, 'Developing countries frequently portrayed U.S. willingness to sell them advanced fighter aircraft as a symbol of U.S. intentions and friendship.'[33] In Afghanistan, a strong arms supply relationship with the United States was valued as a demonstration of American commitment to the ruling regime.[34] This is particularly important where the international status of a political entity is disputed. The procurement of arms helps to confer legitimacy in the international system, with transfers demonstrating recognition of the state status of the recipient. Political authorities seeking to establish or reinforce the legitimate status of their states strive to procure arms from foreign suppliers. This consideration is most salient in states that might be considered quasi- and proto-states which struggle to secure formal diplomatic recognition. Taiwan represents a prominent example of this.

Domestically, the acquisition of arms also enhances the prestige and legitimacy of the ruling regime. The leadership of the Sudan People's Liberation Movement ordered Mi-17 'Hip' helicopters from Russia prior to the 2011 referendum which paved the way for the independence of South Sudan as a means of establishing its domestic as well as its international legitimacy.[35] In Taiwan, the procurement of advanced arms, which effectively means importing from the United States, is considered to strengthen the position of the president.[36]

The symbolic importance of arms helps to explain the general disdain with which 'sanitized' export models of arms with downgraded capabilities are held in developing states, despite the fact that they are more cost-effective and export approval is more likely to be forthcoming.[37] While states with limited options may have little choice but to accept downgraded export models, those that are able generally seek to import more capable equipment. The symbolic importance of arms similarly helps to account for interest in importing of arms of little apparent or immediate utility.

It also is important to consider the role arms imports play as diplomatic instruments, as distinct from their role in establishing and maintaining the international status of a state. As is the case with arms exports, arms imports can serve as an important means of establishing or reinforcing interstate ties, in this case with supplier states. Prior to the First World War, for example, the Ottoman Empire sought to order warships from Germany, France, and the United Kingdom to avoid isolating itself from any of these 'great powers'.[38] More recently, interest in strengthening ties with Japan in the face of what is perceived as a growing threat from China led the Indian government to approach Japan about the supply of submarines.[39] States may place arms orders strategically as a means of demonstrating the strength of their relations with particular suppliers. As one observer noted, the government of Qatar views arms imports such as fighter aircraft as an opportunity to 'purchase a strategic relationship' with supplier states.[40]

No case at the present time better demonstrates the importance that can be attached to arms imports as a diplomatic instrument than that of Taiwan. Taiwan approaches American arms as a means of maintaining the bilateral relationship as well as a means of maintaining its independence.[41] Contrary to what might be expected given Taiwan's defence requirements and its past and present difficulties importing arms as a marginal member of the international community, imports are prioritized over local manufacture. Production of the largely locally designed Ching Kuo fighter was cut from the planned 250 to 130 after the American government agreed to supply the F-16 Fighting Falcon, and the order for the indigenous Sky Bow SAM system was reduced to six from nine once the United States agreed to supply the Patriot.[42] These American arms were prized for reinforcing ties with the United States as well as confirmation of continuing American recognition of Taiwan's state-like international status.

Conversely, states can place arms orders strategically to signal their political distance from particular states. Political authorities are most likely to resort to this where a political relationship of long standing comes to be regarded as a liability. In the 1930s, for example, Belgium sought to distance itself from France and demonstrate its neutrality by ending its reliance on French aircraft. Belgium placed orders with the United Kingdom and elsewhere instead.[43] Turkey's recent interest in procuring Russian and Chinese arms may represent an effort to distance itself from the United States, which has been highly critical of several aspects of Turkish domestic and foreign policy.

## *Arms Imports and Defence-Industrial Development*

The security and economic imperatives of arms imports overlap considerably where defence-industrial considerations are concerned. Offsets mechanisms are discussed in the following section, but it is important to note the role of defence-industrial considerations in the security imperatives of arms import decision making. Arms imports can be closely linked to defence-industrial interests in a number of respects. As well as interest in offsetting the dependency associated with arms imports, arms imports can figure significantly through their potential contribution to defence-industrial development.

Arms imports can facilitate defence-industrial development by providing examples of equipment to serve as a template for new arms designs. Some states import limited quantities of arms for the express objective of obtaining a pattern for reverse-engineering or copying. Even where arms are not imported with such considerations in mind, they still can serve as vehicles for technology transfer. It is common for the first generation of designs of emerging arms producers to be derived from imported models. This was the case with China following the deterioration of its relationship with the Soviet Union during the Cold War. China undertook to produce the full range of arms that it had received from the Soviet Union as a matter of some urgency. Over the course of the 1960s China put into production numerous models based on Soviet designs, from fighter aircraft to armoured vehicles, artillery, and submarines. The reverse-engineering of arms and the development of derivatives can continue long after the initial transfer. 'Scud' missiles of Soviet origin that were received from Egypt in the early 1980s have provided the basis for an expanding North Korean family of more advanced, longer-range ballistic missiles, for instance.[44]

## The Economic Imperatives of Arms Imports

The economic imperatives driving arms imports may be less obvious and generally are subordinate to those of national security but figure in arms import decision making in many states. The arms trade long has been recognized as an important vehicle for technology transfer that supports industrial modernization.[45] The importance of arms transfers has grown in concert with recognition of their potential contribution to economic security, particularly in developing and emerging industrial states. Arms imports can contribute to prosperity by providing employment and accelerating economic growth through the 'spin-off' effect of defence technologies facilitating civil-industrial development. Arms imports may be approached as a means of supporting local industry, either in terms of advancing the capabilities of established local firms and enterprises or launching new industries.

The scope for offsets provides the means for arms imports to contribute to industrial development. Offsets are legally binding provisions for industrial participation or other specific obligations that can be stipulated in procurement contracts. Offsets can involve the reciprocal supply of arms but more commonly provide for industrial and commercial arrangements. Offsets of this nature, which variously are referred to as 'industrial offsets', 'economic offsets', 'industrial participation arrangements', and 'industrial benefits', can take different forms. This includes direct offsets, indirect military offsets, and indirect civil offsets. Direct offsets involve local participation in the arms procurement programme. This may take the form of the production of components or subcomponents, local assembly, or R&D for modifications to adapt the arms design to local requirements. Indirect military offsets are defence-related but do not concern the programme in question. Industrial participation agreements may provide for local contribution to other arms production programmes of the supplier or for the provision of technical support to the defence industry of the recipient. Indirect civil offsets are non-defence in nature. Indirect civil offsets can take a wide variety of forms, from support for industrial development to the marketing of agricultural products.

The principal attraction of the direct and indirect offsets provided for under arms imports often is their potential to contribute to local industrial development and economic progress. This potential has grown in concert with the increasing demand for advanced arms, particularly in emerging industrial states such as Brazil, Singapore, and South Korea, as this provides greater scope for high value-added industrial collaboration. Political authorities may approach arms imports principally in terms of civil- or defence-industrial development, or both. Where there is interest in exploiting the civil-industrial potential of offsets, this may focus on industrial development in its own right, industrial development as a means of generating employment, or both. The focus involved can have significant economic implications over the long term.

At their most basic level, offsets can provide a means of generating employment in defence or civil industries. In the case of the latter, this may involve activities far removed from the manufacture of any products associated with high-technology industry. Where offsets take the form of countertrade, this can involve decidedly low-technology activities such as food processing. Generally, far more attractive to political authorities is the capacity of offsets to promote employment and skills development in high-technology industrial sectors. Not only is it the case that employment in high-technology firms and enterprises tends to be higher paying and offers better long-term prospects than in low value-added resource extraction and processing industries, but this also strengthens the foundation for industrial development.

Interest in employing offsets to support defence-industrial development has been strong throughout the postwar period, with attention to offsets in the context of general industrial development growing for some time. Offsets offer particular advantages where they secure a commitment from the supplier to support capacity development in local industry beyond the life of the arms contract they are associated with. Technology transfer and workshare terms can be critical, if not decisive, factors in arms import decisions for this reason. This importance is recognized by arms producing firms and government officials responsible for arms exports. An Italian official asserted that where technology transfer was concerned, 'All countries ask for it and we are ready' to provide it.[46]

Political authorities in some states are satisfied with support for low-technology industrial sectors, while others seek to ensure that offsets support high-technology industrial development. The focus of offsets often reflects the state of development of the local industrial base and its perceived developmental requirements, with political authorities in many states recognizing the importance of providing a solid foundation for sustained industrial progress. Overly ambitious developmental aspirations can lead to demands for investment in what effectively are 'enclave' industries, however. These often prove commercially unviable and are difficult to sustain once the foreign investment provided for under the terms of an offset agreement ceases.

In order to support defence-industrial development, offsets may be structured to provide particular opportunities for defence firms and enterprises to expand their activities, or for civil-industrial firms to enter the defence field. States' expectations of how offsets should contribute to defence-industrial development vary greatly. This often reflects the state of industrial development, but in some states over-ambitious developmental strategies lead to efforts to employ offsets in a sub-optimal manner. Saudi Arabia provides an important example of this. Under its Vision 2030 strategic plan, the Saudi government aims to attain the position of spending no less than 50 per cent of its military expenditures locally, and to this end seeks to involve local industry in the production and support of the advanced as well as more basic types of arms it imports. Offsets provided for under arms import contracts are crucial to this effort. This represents a daunting challenge as the level of defence-industrial development in Saudi Arabia limits the capacity of local firms and enterprises to contribute meaningfully to the production of advanced arms.[47]

There was a marked increase in interest in exploiting the defence-industrial development potential of arms imports in the latter part of the Cold War which has endured. This reflects not only strengthened official interest in defence-industrial development in a growing number of developing and emerging industrial states, but the more competitive international arms market. In this environment arms producing firms and enterprises have been under great pressure to respond positively to customers' requests for direct and indirect military offsets, particularly where they are pursuing ambitious defence development programmes.

The case of South Korea is instructive in considering the role of arms imports in defence-industrial development. The South Korean government long has approached offsets as a crucial instrument of its defence-industrial strategy. Such is the importance attached to this that resistance to transferring advanced technologies has been sufficient to undermine the prospects of suppliers competing for South Korean arms contracts.[48] South Korea's approach has evolved in concert with its defence-industrial development. South Korean authorities initially focused on securing workshare for local industry as contributors to production programmes in established arms suppliers, gradually progressing to collaborative co-production arrangements and then to securing foreign support for the development of independent local arms production capabilities.[49] The maturation of the South Korean defence-industrial base has enabled a shift in emphasis to encouraging foreign investment in local defence firms and support for advanced indigenous arms development programmes, such as for the KF-21 Boramae fifth-generation fighter.[50] American industry features prominently in this strategy, but South Korea is engaging defence firms and enterprises from other states through arms imports as well.

Offsets often are approached as means of concurrent civil- and defence-industrial development. This is the case with Algeria, for example, where political authorities are intent on reducing their economic reliance on hydrocarbon exports as well as in producing a greater percentage of the arms required by its defence establishment.[51] The scope for states to accomplish this is determined in large part by the degree to which their civil- and defence-industrial sectors overlap. The extent of this in some states is such that there is considerable scope for cross-fertilization, with a strong basis for defence-related R&D and production to promote general industrial progress and for general industrial progress to contribute to the development of the national defence-industrial base. In many of the emerging industrial states this is the case with respect to both high- and low-technology industrial sectors.

It can be difficult to determine the primary objective of states' offsets strategies, but the focus may be stated explicitly or indicated by the nature of the arrangements involved. Even where provision is made for direct and indirect military offsets, the primary objective may not be the development of the national defence-industrial base. Provision for workshare arrangements or for collaboration which strengthens the foundation for sustained defence-industrial development by reinforcing ties with more advanced capability partners, or which establishes local R&D facilities with an obvious defence focus generally signifies a security focus, however.

Developed and emerging industrial states often approach the economic potential of arms imports in different terms from developing states. The economic benefits stemming from arms imports generally are more crucial to political authorities in developing states. Offset programmes widely are viewed in these states as providing important benefits in terms of fostering local industrial development.[52] This reflects their general level of economic development, which generates particular developmental requirements and objectives.

This testifies as well to the importance attached to progress in high-technology industrial sectors as a basis for economic development and to the expectation that they will be able to successfully exploit the opportunities provided by arms offsets. The offsets stemming from Saudi Arabia's purchase of American E-3 Sentry airborne early-warning aircraft were seen as a means of capability development in areas such as advanced manufacturing technologies and product support, for example.[53] While offsets may be applied to low-technology industrial sectors, a strong focus on provisions that support high-technology industrial development is common as a result.

The emerging industrial states are characterized by less of a focus on offsets as a means of economic development but have demonstrated the potential for offsets to concurrently support civil- and defence-industrial progress. Political authorities in states such as South Korea and Taiwan traditionally have regarded arms transfers as an important vehicle for industrial upgrading in both civil and defence terms.[54] Their emphasis shifted over time as offsets facilitated the sustained general industrial progress that led to these states reaching the developmental level of high-performing economies (HPEs). The success of this approach has been noted elsewhere, with political authorities in several East Asian states, including Indonesia, seeking to emulate their developmental strategies and success.[55]

Interest in the economic potential of arms imports is not limited to developing and emerging industrial states, but offsets generally are far less important, and the focus in developed industrial states differs significantly. These states have reached the point where offsets are no longer critical to their industrial development. Political authorities in many of these states still recognize and value the economic benefits of offsets, both in terms of industrial development and employment, however. Though this is a secondary consideration, political authorities in developed states still may seek to make the most of the potential offered by industrial offsets.[56] These states are notable for the defence-industrial focus of offsets in their arms imports. This is particularly important to developed states that are not at the forefront of arms development and production, and which can use arms imports to improve the capabilities of local defence firms and enterprises.

A further economic imperative is that which stems from interest in recovering an international debt. Purchasing arms may be seen as the only means by which a debt can be paid off. Such a situation can arise when an arms producing state has accumulated a substantial debt and proves unable to repay loans or pay for goods provided by another state other than through the supply of arms. This is not a common occurrence but does arise on occasion. Noteworthy examples of 'arms for debt' arrangements involved Russia, which incurred large international trade debts in the 1980s and 1990s which it proved unable to settle. Several states procured Russian arms as a result. South Korea accepted Russian aircraft and armoured vehicles, Hungary armoured vehicles, and China air defence systems in partial repayment for the sums they were owed.[57]

There is a final economic imperative for the import of arms. This involves the import of arms for the express purpose of resale. This may occur where political authorities are interested in providing arms which are more appropriate to the requirements of an intended recipient than those which national firms and enterprises are able to supply, as part of a programme of military assistance.[58] This requires the import of arms for retransfer to the recipient in question. Typically, the state transferring the arms imposes a surcharge, either to cover the cost involved in the transfer or to generate a profit. The resale of arms also can be a product of interest in exploiting the opportunity to serve as an intermediary to supply arms to a state that is engaged in a conflict. States in such a situation often are prepared to pay a premium for arms and domestic or international political considerations may deter some suppliers from providing arms directly. North Korea purchased and resold Chinese 'Silkworm' anti-ship missiles to Iran during its war with Iraq at 'a considerable profit'.[59]

## Arms Imports Between the Demands of Security and Economic Imperatives

The tension between security and economic imperatives generally is not as great in arms imports as that potentially confronting political authorities where arms exports are concerned. There is less prospect for a policy dilemma in arms import decision making as the economic and security imperatives of arms imports can overlap considerably.

Such tension as is evident largely stems from the terms under which arms are procured or the offsets that are involved. Where tension is present, this may reflect conflicting policy agendas. Policy actors may part company over the issue of whether economic or security requirements should be prioritized in deciding which arms to import; it might be the case that the equipment that best meets defence requirements offers less attractive economic benefits than a competing system. In Thailand, for example, such considerations pit the Ministry of Defence, which supports the use of offsets to promote defence-industrial development and self-sufficiency, against other government ministries that approach offsets as an opportunity to boost exports through countertrade.[60]

Tension arising from the dilemma of whether to import finished arms or to involve local industry through licensed production, co-production, or assembly is evident in many states. This 'buy versus build' dilemma often is generated by financial considerations. Procuring arms directly from the manufacturer generally is more cost-effective than some form of localized production. This reflects the lower unit costs resulting from larger production runs and the costs involved in establishing local production at whatever level this involves. Extensive upgrading of existing facilities or establishing entirely new facilities may be required if local production is to be undertaken. There are obvious advantages to this in terms of defence- and civil-industrial development, as noted above, but this has significant cost implications for states with limited resources. Developing states in particular may struggle to allocate the resources necessary for the localization of production. The high costs involved help to account for the familiar pattern where it proves impossible for a supplier to meet industrial offset requirements because of the industrial underdevelopment of the recipient or where a recipient fails to capitalize on offsets.

## Non-State Actors and Arms Imports

The imperatives driving arms importation by NSAGs essentially are those of security. This reflects the requirements of insurgent groups that are fighting either to secure some degree of local autonomy or the outright independence of the region or ethnic group that they represent, or to supplant the ruling regime. Arms are essential to these objectives, and few insurgent groups have access to arms production facilities. Where insurgent groups do produce arms, generally these are quite basic, such as SALWs, land mines, and improvised explosive devices.

Both the arms requirements and the arms import processes of NSAGs differ from those of state actors in important respects. Arms such as SALWs and man-portable SAMs that can be transported relatively easily constitute the focus of the acquisition efforts of most insurgent groups, at least until the point where they have reached sufficient strength to effect a transition to waging conventional warfare. Some insurgent movements operate armoured vehicles and small naval vessels, but arms such as these generally are obtained through battlefield capture.

The state-centric nature of the international arms transfer system and the international system in general severely limit the prospects for NSAGs to purchase arms through mainstream channels. NSAGs often are dependent on state support to some degree as a result. This may take the form of the active though covert supply of arms or acquiescing to efforts by a NSAG to circumvent arms export controls. Where state support is not forthcoming or does not satisfy the arms requirements of the NSAG and where it is unable to capture the arms it requires, a NSAG will have little alternative but to attempt to obtain arms on the black market.

The purchasing of arms by NSAGs is characterized by surreptitious processes. This includes purchasing dual-use items through 'front companies' to obscure the intended destination and use of the equipment and the theft of arms from state stocks. NSAGs also often resort to arms traffickers in an effort to meet their arms requirements. Once procured, arms often need to be transported along circuitous routes, with their supply into operational zones requiring exceptional measures. Palestinian insurgents have smuggled arms into Gaza using fishing boats to transfer them from 'mother ships' sailing from Lebanon,[61] while the LTTE operated a small fleet of merchant vessels outside of Sri Lankan territorial waters that served as 'floating armouries' for the supply of its forces.[62]

## Arms Imports and the Evolution of the International Arms Transfer System

Arms import trends are helping to define the post-Cold War international arms market, which features increasing demand for a growing range of products in an environment structured by an increasing number of suppliers. The impact of contemporary trends is unevenly distributed. States with greater need to import arms benefit most in the current environment of over-supply, but importers generally stand to benefit from increased supplier competition.

The demand for arms imports will remain strong despite sustained interest in defence-industrial development and determined efforts to promote arms self-sufficiency in developed, emerging industrial, and developing states alike. The difficulties inherent in developing and producing advanced arms are compounded by the accelerating pace of defence technological development, which renders the exercise of keeping pace with technological frontiers difficult. Political authorities in most states are forced to settle for semi-autonomous defence-industrial capabilities at best as a result. This being the case, states will have little recourse but to import arms.

Arms import requirements significantly influence the arms available in the international arms market. Defence capability development in many states is generating demand for increasingly advanced arms. While the defence capability gap with the developed states that are at the forefront of defence development trends remains substantial, growing numbers of developing states are procuring advanced arms such as intelligence, surveillance, and reconnaissance (ISR) aircraft, ballistic missiles, and surveillance radars. In the emerging arms producers the demand for more advanced arms is only partly addressed by their development of defence-industrial capabilities. Developing and producing a comprehensive range of arms long has represented a challenge even for most developed states and is proving more so as technological frontiers advance and the resource requirements and difficulty involved in developing and producing advanced arms spiral, as discussed in the next chapter. Only in exceptional cases has the expansion of arms production capabilities in developing and emerging industrial states freed states from the requirement to import complete systems. Continued reliance on arms imports has been a feature of states expanding their capacity to develop and produce arms since well before the Second Industrial Revolution in Europe.[63] This trend can be expected to continue as further states launch themselves on the path of the RMA, ensuring that import requirements will continue to influence the development and production of arms by defence firms and enterprises.

There has been a significant shift in arms import trends as defence industrialization in emerging industrial and developing states has progressed and as transnational defence production has become more widespread. This involves technical and material support for local defence-industrial programmes, with a growing trade in components, sub-components, and technologies. This is most readily apparent where the co-production of arms is involved, particularly in developing states which would be unable to produce arms without importing production inputs. This applies no less to established arms producers from the ranks of the developed industrial states, however. The supply chains of many of the arms produced in the major arms exporters now encompass offshore capability partners. Imports of production inputs are less critical to these states, however, as at the cost of some disruption to production they are in a strong position to develop local sources of supply should this prove necessary.

It is significant that arms, including components, sub-components, and technologies, increasingly are sourced from suppliers from among the ranks of the emerging industrial or even developing states. This involves both lateral transfers between emerging industrial and developing states and imports from these states by developed industrial states. The importance at the present time of Taiwan as a source of integrated circuits and South Korea and Turkey as sources of complete arms demonstrates the transformation of the global defence-industrial landscape engendered by transnational arms production processes. This transformation, which is the subject of the chapter that follows, is facilitating the emergence of new arms suppliers, underscoring the limitations of a hierarchical model of the global defence-industrial order based around 'tiers' of suppliers.

# 4 Transnational Industry and the International Arms Transfer System

The structural transformation of the basis for the development and production of arms has significant implications for the international arms transfer system. The structures of the international arms transfer and defence-industrial systems are co-evolving, with the transformation of the arms transfer system accelerating as transnational defence-industrial integration deepens. The hierarchical structures of the arms production and arms transfer systems are being eroded by transnational defence-industrial processes. Though transnational defence-industrial arrangements emerged well after their appearance in the civil-industrial sector and have developed far more gradually, interconnected civil- and defence-industrial processes ensure that trends arising in the civil-industrial sector will continue to diffuse to the defence-industrial sector.

The transformation of the defence-industrial landscape impacts on established and emerging arms suppliers in distinct ways, with the most significant effect on the latter. The substance of arms transfers is changing, with flows of production inputs assuming increasing importance. As well as generating increased horizontal and vertical flows of components, sub-components, and technologies, deepening transnational industrial integration is supporting the emergence of new arms exporters and the qualitative development of arms production capabilities in many states. This is contributing to the development of a far more complex international arms transfer system and facilitating the diffusion of advanced arms.

## The Emergence of a Transnational Arms Industry

The defence-industrial sector has general features that distinguish it from the civil-industrial sector. The domestic market which the defence-industrial sector serves usefully is conceptualized as a 'closed market' or a 'closed economy'.[1] Arms development and production traditionally have been structured on a national basis in the pursuit of defence-industrial autonomy. Security-driven interest in promoting autonomy through the support of 'strategic' industries generally remains strong, though the degree of success in developing self-sufficient defence-industrial capabilities varies considerably. Defence-industrial autonomy represents the ideal in many states but is more the exception than the rule. Another key area of difference concerns the nature of product demand. Arms often are produced to firm orders, rather than being supplied from rolling production lines. This reflects the specialized nature of arms. The third general difference is the impact of security considerations. The development and production of arms are highly securitized. This engenders distinct industrial processes.

The transformation of the defence-industrial landscape and the international arms transfer system owe more to chance than to design. Key to their transformation is the emergence and deepening of transnational defence-industrial processes deriving from industry-led trends that initially emerged and which are more fully developed in the civil-industrial sector. While established and emerging arms producers alike are subject to the trends involved to some extent and often seek to exploit the opportunities they offer, the emergence of a transnational defence industry was not the product of a deliberate strategy on the part of any state. The structural role of the state is such that official acceptance, if not support, is crucial to transnational defence-industrial integration, however.

The dynamics transforming the defence-industrial landscape are those of industrial globalization. Globalization, which has come to affect all but the most economically isolated of states as it has deepened, presents both opportunities and challenges. Globalization is problematic from a national security perspective due to its effect of increasing exposure to exogenous economic trends and developments. As well as their implications for the security of supply of arms, transnational defence-industrial ties potentially expose arms production processes to counterfeit and sub-standard components and sub-components supplied by offshore capability partners. Concern over this issue in the context of production inputs from non-Western states such as China has been growing in the United States and elsewhere for some time.[2]

The negative effects of globalization for defence industries are accompanied by potential benefits. Its capacity to undermine defence-industrial autonomy may be offset by some important advantages. These include its potential to facilitate access to technologies developed offshore, the prospect of reduced procurement costs through economies of scale in arms production, and its contribution to the competitiveness of defence firms and enterprises. Official perspectives on globalization vary greatly. These often reflect the strengths and weaknesses of states' defence-industrial bases as well as their respective security agendas. Concern over globalization generally is more pronounced in established arms producers than in states where defence-industrial capabilities are less developed. The defence-industrial benefits of globalization are appreciated even in major producers such as the United States which have the least to gain from the processes involved, however.[3]

The structural transformation of the global industrial landscape has developed gradually. The pace of industrial globalization has accelerated in recent decades but has roots that extend back over the course of the last century and a half. It is important to distinguish between the earlier stages of the process, which usefully are conceptualized as industrial internationalization, and the more fundamental transformation of fully developed globalization with its unparalleled influence on defence-industrial processes. The stage for this transformation was set by the Second Industrial Revolution which emerged in Western Europe in the nineteenth century. This ushered in profound changes in the organization of industrial operations in the states where it took hold, setting in train processes that led to the spatial redistribution of production and R&D on a regional and even global basis.

## *Industrial Internationalization*

The earlier stages of the transformation of the industrial landscape were groundbreaking but not nearly as radical as those that followed. The internationalization of industry was defined by the replication of functions traditionally restricted to the 'home' states of firms. This involved establishing offshore facilities to undertake local production of designs developed with the requirements of the home market in mind. These facilities generally took the form of wholly owned subsidiaries. This trend largely was driven by industrial requirements. Firms localized production as a means of more effectively serving export markets by reducing product costs and providing a means of overcoming local protectionist barriers.

Industrial internationalization represented no challenge to the established spatial hierarchy of industry. The scope of the offshore redistribution of industrial operations remained relatively limited and these remained highly centralized, with R&D remaining a function of facilities situated in the home states of parent firms and offshore production facilities remaining subordinate to and under the effective control of parent firms. Operational integration generally was limited to unidirectional transfers of some of the components or sub-components necessary for production and these production networks generally were highly regionalized.

The effects of industrial internationalization were mixed. The integration it engendered supported the development of production capabilities in states that possessed an industrial base already. More rarely, this facilitated the emergence of new centres of production. In the Netherlands East Indies, for example, General Motors established a truck assembly plant in the 1920s.[4] This effect was significant, however, and provided an important foundation for the development of what we now know as globalization. Industrial internationalization had a much more limited impact where technological diffusion was concerned. The extent to which knowledge transfer occurred through the redistribution of production was determined as much by local industrial capabilities as market requirements. Technological diffusion was greatest in states with mature economies that were already relatively highly industrialized.[5] States with more developed industrial bases were far better positioned to absorb and apply transferred technologies.

Industrial internationalization was most evident on the part of civil industry. The more limited development of internationalizing processes in the defence-industrial sector reflected limited market demand. Issues similar to those facing their civil counterparts confronted defence firms and enterprises as they pursued export opportunities, and a number of European defence firms established offshore subsidiaries.[6] These subsidiaries localized arms production as part of arms transfers, in some cases also engaging in the adaptation of arms to meet local requirements. More common was the establishment of subsidiaries producing what now are referred to as dual-use items. Ford, for instance, established a truck plant in the Soviet Union in the interwar period that supplied both the defence and civil markets.[7]

Such defence-industrial internationalization as occurred largely was industry-led, but there were cases in the interwar period where this was initiated or supported by states which struggled to produce and import arms. Germany, for example, sought thereby to circumvent the restrictions imposed by the Treaty of Versailles. To this end Germany collaborated with the Soviet Union to establish defence R&D and production facilities in that country that would benefit both states.[8] The pressing requirements generated by the Second World War strengthened state support for internationalization. That conflict saw the United Kingdom produce Fairmile gun boats from prefabricated component parts at twenty-six overseas sites as far afield as Jamaica, Dar-es-Salaam, and Auckland.[9]

Defence-industrial internationalization generally failed to elicit a strong state response. This reflected the limited impact of this trend and the fact that internationalization generally was restricted to states that were not the subject of particular security concern on the part of political authorities in the home states of firms internationalizing their operations. There was little evident concern even over industrial internationalization's potential contribution to defence-industrial development in those states that sought to exploit the advantages it offered. Security concerns had little impact on the diffusion of arms through defence-industrial internationalization as a result. Though limited in comparison to what was to come, defence-industrial internationalization did represent an important milestone and the most fundamental development in the emergence of a 'modern' defence industry since the advent of the production of arms on an industrial scale.

The limited extent to which internationalization developed in the defence-industrial sector and the dynamics of internationalization inform our understanding of the structural constraints on globalization and the distinct interests of state and sub-state actors where transnational industrial integration is concerned. The transnational integration that is central to globalization offers important advantages from the perspective of industry but from a state perspective this is not necessarily the case. Political authorities may regard transnational integration as necessary but recognize that this potentially benefits politico-military rivals. This suggests that transnational defence-industrial integration is likely to be led by industry in the absence of pressing security requirements and that integration is likely to be much more extensive in arms production than R&D.

### *Industrial Globalization*

While the genesis of industrial globalization can be found in industrial internationalization, globalization is more revolutionary than evolutionary in that it represents a much more fundamental restructuring of industrial processes. The scale of the transformation involved is significantly greater, with globalization increasingly defining R&D as well as production processes and producing relatively flexible interfirm arrangements. Industrial globalization is generating strong centrifugal tendencies and a global industrial landscape that is far less hierarchical than that produced by internationalization. Globalization corresponds in key respects to the more flexible, demand-driven post-Fordist industrial paradigm.

Industrial globalization has been led by industry. High-technology industry in particular has had to contend with rising developmental and production costs and the resulting need for economies of scale since the 1960s, the pressure from which has increased greatly in recent years.[10] This pressure stems from the demands of heightened competition in an environment of accelerating technological progress. The accelerating pace of technological progress is manifest in much more protracted developmental cycles and shortened product life cycles, with diminishing intervals between the introduction of new design generations as technological frontiers advance.[11] Technological trends suggest that the pressure stemming from the demands of competitiveness will continue to increase.

Many firms and enterprises are carefully considering their R&D and production strategies and are restructuring their operations in innovative ways with a view to developing more efficient and cost-effective approaches. Significantly, globalizing trends are not limited to established multinational enterprises (MNEs); many firms and enterprises which previously had not structured their operations internationally have developed functional arrangements with offshore capability partners. Global production networks (GPNs) increasingly are the norm, even in high-technology product sectors. The changed industrial dynamics are reshaping the global industrial landscape in important respects.

Transformed functional relationships are intrinsic to the spatial reorganization that characterizes industrial globalization. Industrial globalization is based on a distinct division of labour featuring close interfirm arrangements and distributed functional networks. The geography of globalization is functionally rather than spatially defined. Patterns of interaction are changing as firms and enterprises focus more on their core strengths. There has been sweeping industrial reorganization, with many firms and enterprises consolidating their operations, merging where this will strengthen their core capabilities, and divesting themselves of functions that capability partners can undertake more efficiently and at lower cost. This represents a significant strengthening of the approach known as 'horizontal integration', which involves drawing extensively on other contributors as opposed to the system of systems approach referred to as 'vertical integration', under which goods largely are the product of ideas and material inputs from within a single firm or enterprise. This division of labour reflects sectoral specializations and strengths rather than a sharp distinction between the home states of firms and enterprises and the offshore sites of subsidiary operations.

Industrial globalization involves a fundamental revolution in the relationship between partner firms and enterprises. Industrial globalization is characterized by close interfirm collaboration. Many capability partners are far more than secondary contributors under what is more of a team approach. There is growing peer-to-peer collaboration, with what formerly would have been treated as sub-contractors now an integral part of R&D and production programmes, playing a far more proactive role with responsibility in their area of competence. Interfirm production and R&D arrangements can take a variety of forms, ranging from strategic alliances covering a broad range of activities and multiple programmes to project-specific collaborative ventures.[12]

A key feature distinguishing industrial globalization from internationalization is the extent to which R&D and production centres are complementary, with minimal replication of capabilities. Typically, there is an overall design authority and lead or prime contractor with collaborating firms and enterprises supplying crucial but non-core inputs to development and production as sole-source contributors. Capability partners often are risk-sharing equity partners that potentially are involved throughout the product cycle, with design responsibilities and a role in determining the final configuration of products. As one industry executive explained, 'we don't want to replicate research and technology investments. We want to make sure we have a common strategy across the group'.[13]

These expanded interfirm partnerships require extensive technological sharing, deepening industrial interdependence in the process. Interfirm collaboration tends to be relatively flexible in order to accommodate changing requirements, even within the frameworks provided by long-standing strategic alliances. Collaboration generally is not limited to a fixed set of partners. Firms and enterprises may engage multiple industry partners through various strategic alliances or project-specific arrangements. Drawing on different capability partners for their particular assets can enable firms and enterprise to meet specific industrial requirements but greatly complicates interfirm arrangements.

It is important to note that the impact of industrial globalization is not limited to production. Globalization increasingly extends to processes of technological development as firms and enterprises seek to offset the increasing costs involved. The spiralling cost of R&D, particularly in high-technology sectors such as aerospace and ICT, is driving firms and enterprises to undertake this collaboratively.[14] R&D increasingly is structured transnationally. Global innovation networks (GINs) emerged more recently and are less prominent than GPNs, but pursuing technological development transnationally increasingly is the norm.

Collaborative R&D can take various forms. This can involve drawing on research undertaken independently abroad and partnering with offshore industry to co-develop products, as well as establishing offshore R&D centres as a means of exploiting local resources and cutting costs. Technological collaboration arrangements may overlap with those for production. This may reflect the strengths of particular capability partners in terms of both R&D and production, but generally is encouraged by high-technology developmental requirements. The requirement to maintain product effectiveness in an environment of rapid technological change drives qualitative upgrading through the application of technological advances throughout the production life of equipment. Development and production increasingly are conducted in parallel with a cross-feeding of results, rather than as entirely discrete phases. Firms based in developed industrial states are prominent in driving these trends, though collaboration is not reserved to these states.

The fragmentation of production and R&D produces a much more complex industrial landscape. Industry teams may incorporate capability partners from multiple states. Geographical proximity no longer offers great advantages, and capability partners may be situated within the same region or at much further remove. Such transnational industrial integration is producing a highly decentralized global industrial landscape. This features polycentric production and R&D, and far more fluid exchanges of components, sub-components, and technologies between firms and enterprises intra-nationally and internationally. Often this is organized to support just-in-time production. In this landscape the traditional distinction between the economic centre and periphery is eroding.[15] The concept of national industries remains valid, but this must be understood in the context of industrial globalization. For most states the boundaries delineating national industries are increasingly porous and their capacity to influence or control industry cannot be assumed.

Industrial globalization is very uneven in its scope and impact and the pace at which it is developing varies considerably. Industrial globalization is contributing to the emergence of new centres of production and, to a lesser extent, innovation, but the trends involved do not affect all states to the same extent, some being bypassed altogether. High-technology industry in the developed and emerging industrial states generally is deeply embedded in transnational industrial processes. There are important regional variations in the course of globalization. Some areas feature far more extensive embeddedness in transnational industrial processes than others as a consequence of long-established industrial trends. East Asia is one such region. The high-technology industries of many East Asian states, particularly the emerging industrial states that are considered HPEs, are highly integrated transnationally. Firms and enterprises in these states are well positioned to exploit the opportunities stemming from the transformation of the global industrial landscape. Transnational civil-industrial integration in a number of these states paved the way for integration into defence-related GPNs and GINs.

Industrial globalization holds considerable promise for developing states, but they generally are less well positioned to exploit its potential due to their more modest levels of industrialization. These states remain far less integrated transnationally than the developed and emerging industrial states, particularly where high-technology product sectors are concerned, but the attractiveness of the developmental model provided by the developed and emerging industrial states encourages political authorities to seek to emulate them in engaging transnational industrial processes. This is true even to some extent of North Korea.[16] This does not ensure that states in regions where industrial globalization is not as advanced will follow the path charted by North American, European, and East Asian states, however.

Industrial globalization presents political authorities with complex challenges. Political authorities generally recognize the importance of the processes involved in terms of development, industrial efficiency, and competitiveness. As a result, it typically is where processes of globalization impact negatively on national security that political authorities demonstrate conspicuous concern. This most commonly reflects recognition of the potential impact of industrial globalization on the availability of arms or to facilitate defence-related 'technology migration' to politico-military rivals. Establishing and maintaining an official position on industrial globalization is complicated by the fact that it can prove very difficult to differentiate between transnational industrial processes that have the potential to benefit industry and those that threaten national security interests. Even where industrial globalization has the potential to support defence-industrial development in rival states, for example, political authorities as well as industry may recognize the economic value of maintaining a local industrial footprint.

## Economic Imperatives and the Defence Industry

The defence-industrial sector has proven resistant to industrial globalization. While the beginnings of the trends that would in time produce a transnational arms industry can be identified in nineteenth-century Europe, its gestation has proven quite protracted.[17] The much more gradual pace of defence-related industrial globalization results from the requirements of national security and the scope for states to intervene in industrial processes in the pursuit of their security agendas. Political authorities generally place a high value on defence-industrial autonomy. While this proves quite elusive in practice, autonomy remains the ideal and political authorities in many states persevere in its pursuit. The importance attached to autonomy underlies incentives and restrictions which discourage or prevent industry from transferring key functions offshore or engaging offshore capability partners in ways that threaten the component and sub-component supplier bases of important arms programmes. Neo-mercantilism remains in vogue where defence industries are concerned, with many states strongly supporting firms and enterprises regarded as 'national champions'.[18]

The extent of civil-military industrial integration ensures that defence industries cannot remain entirely isolated from the trends which are restructuring the civil sector, though the impact has been limited by security considerations. Important industrial assets are common to the defence- and civil-industrial bases of many states. The production of arms, particularly advanced arms, requires contributions from a broad range of entities that do not exclusively serve the defence sector. Many shipbuilders constructing naval vessels produce commercial vessels as well, for example, and many producers of aerostructures do so for both civil and military aircraft. The importance of civil industry to the defence sector has been reinforced by the extent to which dual-use products feature in defence production. The transnational dynamics of defence-industrial development mirror those of the civil-industrial sector, though defence sector trends tend to follow well behind and may not develop as fully as those in the civil sector. These trends are undermining the autonomy of national defence-industrial bases, but far less than would be the case if national security concerns did not apply.

The structural transformation of the defence-industrial landscape reflects economic and political factors. National security concerns have mitigated the impact of globalizing pressures and the defence-industrial landscape remains more hierarchically structured than the civil-industrial landscape, with R&D and high value-added production still largely confined to a relatively small though expanding nucleus of states. Industrial globalization offers important defence-industrial benefits, however, in terms of the sustainability of defence firms and enterprises and their capacity to develop and produce advanced arms. These considerations have gone some way to offsetting concern in many states over globalization's effect of undermining the national basis of the defence-industrial base.

The changed post-Cold War security environment generated powerful incentives for defence firms and enterprises to restructure their operations. The precipitous decline in arms orders and arms related R&D expenditures that accompanied the end of the Cold War resulted in significant defence-industrial over-capacity in many established arms producers. This produced the large-scale industrial contraction manifest in the marked decline in the number of defence contractors in states such as the United States.[19] Increased pressure for efficiency and competitiveness encouraged many defence firms and enterprises to follow the path blazed by their civil counterparts in restructuring their operations. The defence-industrial sectors of many arms producing states experienced rationalization and consolidation as this trend developed.[20]

This industrial upheaval came at a point when defence firms and enterprises were facing unprecedented resource pressures. The cost of developing and producing advanced arms has been rising for some time.[21] Drawing on civil industry for commercial off-the-shelf (COTS) technologies could not wholly offset rising costs.[22] The developmental programmes of advanced arms also were proving more protracted. While combat aircraft were developed and entered production in as little as nine months in the early 1940s, by the late 1980s it was common for this process to take at least a decade.[23] The cost of developing and producing advanced arms and the time frame involved likely will continue to increase as technological frontiers advance and as operators demand incremental qualitative enhancements throughout the service life of arms. The practice of upgrading in-service arms through technology insertions to maintain their operational effectiveness increasingly is the norm.

By the 1980s, the spiralling cost of developing and producing advanced arms was driving closer interfirm collaboration in many arms producers. In exceptional cases, this led firms to collaborate on one project while competing on another.[24] As one researcher has noted, 'firms can be competitors and partners'.[25] In other cases this drove firms to investigate the possibilities of obtaining developmental funding from prospective export customers, as British Aerospace did when it was exploring the development of the new fighter aircraft which ultimately entered production as the Typhoon.[26]

The end of the Cold War marked a watershed in the course of defence-industrial globalization in another important respect. The changed international security environment provided greater space for political authorities to focus less on self-sufficiency in responding to industrial globalization. A general decrease in the prioritization of defence-industrial autonomy was evident in many states following the Cold War. This was supplanted to some extent by concern about the economic viability of the firms and enterprises forming the defence-industrial base in the post-Cold War procurement environment.

Political authorities in some states sought to direct defence firms and enterprises along paths that they expected would enable them to survive the shock of the defence retrenchment that accompanied the end of the Cold War. The American Department of Defense began to strongly encourage consolidation in the defence industry in the early 1990s.[27] At what has come to be known as the 'Last Supper', in 1993 American Secretary of Defense Les Aspin informed the senior representatives of a dozen major defence firms that the American government was prepared to allow some of them to go out of business as it considered that there were now twice as many defence firms as were required.[28] The American effort to persuade industry of the need for consolidation was mirrored by the governments of France, Germany, and the United Kingdom later in the decade.[29]

The pressure stemming from the developmental and production requirements of advanced arms has encouraged official support for the efforts of industry to develop more efficient operational approaches. The promotion of consolidation was accompanied in many cases by defence market liberalization and support for collaboration with civil industry in the interest of more effectively drawing on its strengths and promoting effective cross-fertilization between civil and defence research. The American government approached this in international terms. In 1994 the United States launched an initiative designed to broaden collaboration in Western states through greater exploitation of dual-use technologies and products.[30]

Official initiatives designed to reduce production and developmental costs and timescales often have regularized what have become established practices in industry. This includes the 'agile manufacturing' and the spiral and concurrent development initiatives providing for overlapping R&D and production which emerged in the early 1990s in an effort to promote greater efficiency. National 'smart procurement' initiatives pursued under arms acquisition reform programmes have sought to promote more efficient and cost-effective arms development by fostering closer relations between state institutions and industry. These include public/private partnership agreements, integrated project teams (IPTs) and funding approaches such as private finance initiatives (PFIs).[31] Continuing support for initiatives such as these demonstrates the importance attached in many states to ensuring the viability of defence industries despite the strengthened security imperatives generated by heightened strategic competition.

State-sponsored defence-industrial collaboration traditionally has been programme-specific, with interstate arms programmes generally focusing on a specific project with a particular partner or set of partners. This is changing, however. There has been a steady growth in interstate framework agreements designed to facilitate long-term collaboration, some covering multiple project areas and others entire product sectors. These more open-ended defence-industrial collaboration frameworks also involve specific sets of states. Partners in collaborative defence R&D and production generally are drawn from the ranks of the developed and emerging industrial states, but significantly, this trend increasingly involves states that have not figured as collaborative partners in the past. The American–Indian Defense Technology and Trade Initiative (DTTI), which comprises a number of working groups, is a notable example of this.[32]

Despite the evident importance attached to collaboration and the narrow focus of most initiatives, the number of collaborative arms projects that ultimately have failed to meet their expectations is quite high. Often the rocks that defence-industrial collaboration has foundered on are not so much technical as political. The daunting challenge presented by the difficulties involved in finding sufficient political common ground to provide a basis for interstate collaboration is demonstrated by the experience of NATO. While it has had some notable successes, overall, its record of collaborative arms development and production has been disappointing.

The pressure generated by economic considerations can be significant even where the defence-industrial landscape is state dominated. Despite the relative unimportance of industrial profitability in such an environment, political authorities have been confronted by the requirement to develop more efficient means of developing and producing arms. The Russian defence industry has been subjected to several rounds of restructuring since the end of the Cold War in response to changed conditions, and recent years have seen extensive industrial restructuring of defence-oriented state-owned enterprises in China in the interest of greater efficiency.[33] This has seen enterprises such as the Aviation Industry Corporation of China (AVIC) dispense with non-essential and underperforming operations and in some cases transition to a mixed-ownership model.[34] This has been accompanied by civil-military integration, which has been emphasized as a means of modernizing the defence-industrial base in China since 2007.[35] The civil/defence-industrial distinction in China is eroding in the process.

The pressure generated by the accelerating pace of defence technological progress and the increasing cost of procuring advanced arms is manifest in the extent to which some states are prepared to collaborate in developing and producing arms. Determining how to best approach this often is far from straightforward, however. Globalizing trends have greatly complicated defence-industrial policy, with political authorities often torn between conflicting requirements. There is considerable tension in many states between the desire to maintain core national defence-industrial assets and the demands of industrial efficiency.[36] Striking a balance between these requirements can be difficult as a result. The implications of policy choices are not necessarily immediately apparent but can be brought into high relief in times of heightened international tension or conflict. During the Gulf War of 1990–91, for instance, American acquisition officials were forced to approach offshore manufacturers to secure the increased supply of components and spares for American-produced arms.[37] The Russo-Ukrainian War similarly is highlighting tensions between industrial efficiency and the requirements of national security.[38]

Arms importers are helping to drive transnational defence-industrial processes. Political authorities are contributing through their efforts to promote local defence-industrial development. Heightened competition for exports was evident long before the end of the Cold War and increased after that point as the demand for arms in many of the established exporters declined. This has encouraged localized production to serve export markets. The Israeli firm Rafael operates no less than eleven offshore production lines for its Spike anti-tank missile, for example.[39] This also has provided export customers with greater latitude to secure significant industrial offsets as part of purchase agreements. Arms importing states increasingly seek offsets arrangements that support defence-industrial development, in some cases to provide a basis for arms exports. There is strong demand for direct and indirect military offsets, including through establishing local subsidiaries or otherwise integrating local firms and enterprises into GPNs or GINs through joint ventures or other arrangements.

State interest in collaboration in arms development and production as a means of driving down spiralling arms development and arms production costs, particularly where advanced arms are concerned, is highly compatible with the industrial quest for competitive advantage. State interest in international collaboration in arms development and production was evident by the 1970s, but there was a striking increase in collaborative arms programmes after the mid-1980s that coincided with increasing interfirm collaboration. Since the end of the Cold War, formal interstate defence-industrial collaboration has expanded considerably. Increasing interest in international collaboration on the part of both state and industry has been mutually supporting in many cases.

## The Transnational Defence Industry

The globalized defence-industrial landscape is similar in many respects to that of the civil-industrial sector that emerged earlier. The key difference lies in the barriers to transnational collaboration erected by political authorities in the interest of national security. These barriers are far more substantial than those deriving from the commercial considerations which may impede civil-industrial collaboration.

The global defence industry is far more decentralized than formerly. The intricate network of defence-industrial ties that has emerged through the development of transnational R&D and production processes more closely resembles a mosaic, constellation, or a 'hub and spokes' with multiple hubs and overlapping spokes than a ladder or pyramid. This structure is highly fragmented, with polycentric arms development and production. Production and increasingly research networks integrate defence firms and enterprises based in different states through a dense network of ties. Interfirm linkages, including supply chains, can be quite complex and often are relatively flexible.

Transnational defence-industrial collaboration continues to deepen as firms and establishments strive to develop more efficient ways of developing and producing arms. In many cases industrial entities are restructuring their operations in a manner similar to their civil-industrial counterparts by focusing on core operations and relying on capability partners where this is more efficient and cost-effective. There has been a marked trend of portfolio rationalization, particularly on the part of defence firms in established arms producers. One senior industry representative rationalized the divestment of one of his firm's units as part of their strategy of fixing, closing, or selling any unit that was not first or second in terms of global market share.[40] Many of the capability partners being relied upon to provide the products and services that firms and enterprises formerly would have provided themselves are based offshore.

This level of collaboration requires close structural ties. This is manifest in mergers and acquisitions of industrial units as well as the level of operational integration. The extent of integration and the nature of interfirm arrangements varies greatly. In some cases, firms seek out offshore capability partners for specific projects. In others, engagement is at a much more fundamental level and is pursued as part of a long-term strategy. While design lead and overall project management are exercised by a single lead contractor or a select group of firms or enterprises, their partners have considerable freedom of action in their particular areas of responsibility.[41]

The development of polycentric processes has been most marked in arms production but increasingly is a feature of defence-related R&D. Significantly, these processes encompass states which have not been prominent as arms producers in the past or which remain emerging arms suppliers. New forms of commercial entities have emerged in response to the requirements of this industrial landscape. These include specialist consulting services and 'design houses' such as the Irish armoured vehicle firm Timoney and the British ship design firm Steller Systems.[42] The relative importance of firms and enterprises in the international arms transfer system is increasing due to their role in this new global defence-industrial order.

The emergence of a transnational defence industry offers significant advantages for defence-industrial development. The most obvious advantage stems from its effect of greatly expanding the opportunities for arms production in qualitative as well as quantitative terms. Transnational defence-industrial processes serve as an important means of technological upgrading through technology transfers and the redistribution of advanced R&D where lead contractors support offshore production or where they contribute directly to the development of local R&D capabilities. Even established arms producers stand to benefit from processes such as these but this potentially enables states with less developed defence-industrial bases to effect quantum capability leaps in relatively short order. The emergence of a transnational defence industry means that for many states, the defence-industrial base is not so much declining as extending. The key features of the transnational defence industry and the respects in which it differs from the established structure are set out in Table 4.1.

**Table 4.1: General Features of Nationally Based and Transnational Defence Industries**

| | Nationally Based Defence Industry | Transnational Defence Industry |
|---|---|---|
| International structure | Hierarchical | Interlocking mosaic |
| Nature of R&D and production | Centralized | Polycentric |
| Extent of transnational integration | Low | High |
| Ease of international technological diffusion | Low | High |
| General direction of arms input flows | Downwards | Downwards, laterally, and upwards |
| Degree of state control | High | Low |

### States and the Transnational Defence Industry

Political authorities in many states recognize the value and exploit the opportunities provided by transnational defence-industrial processes. This is demonstrated by widespread acceptance of the integration of local firms and enterprises into GPNs and GINs. Many states seek to capitalize on the opportunities that transnational industrial processes present by actively engaging these processes at the national and international levels. The transnational defence industry is characterized by much more extensive state intervention at the national level than in the civil-industrial sector. This is most marked in crucial high-technology sectors such as aerospace and ICT. There is strong interest in international collaboration on R&D and production in many states, despite the inherent complexity of such programmes and the more protracted time frame that this tends to require. Approaching arms development collaboratively often requires allowing more junior partners significant input into the developmental process. This can be an important incentive for them to enter into such arrangements.

Despite its manifest benefits, the transnational defence industry presents a policy challenge in many states. This can be attributed in part to the inherent conservatism of the policy community where security issues are concerned. Policy actors with direct responsibility for ensuring national security tend to focus on the negative implications of economic trends, particularly where these concern the defence industry. This has significant implications for how states approach transnational defence-industrial processes. The threat that such processes pose to the integrity of the national defence-industrial base can generate policy responses that complicate efforts to meet the materiel requirements of the defence establishment. Security concerns may drive strengthened efforts to develop and maintain technological advantages as a means of counteracting the levelling effects of globalizing processes, which tend to erode technological advantages, for example.[43] This can be counterproductive; these same globalizing processes can offer significant benefits even to states where there are grounds for concern over the potential for eroding technological advantages.

Political authorities in many states are confronted by the need to balance the benefits of transnational defence-industrial integration with the vulnerability that this generates. Policy responses vary greatly. Not only has defence-industrial globalization developed at dissimilar paces in different states, but the impact differs greatly; there is considerable variation in the extent and nature of integration into transnational industrial processes. Defence-industrial requirements can be crucial to determining how political authorities approach globalization. These vary considerably between states and can evolve considerably over time. Political authorities in some states pursue ambitious defence-industrial agendas while others are satisfied with more modest objectives. Levels of transnational integration and defence-industrial strategies both are influenced by the local level of defence-industrial development. This helps to set the stage for how political authorities approach transnational industrial processes that affect the development and production of arms in terms of engaging industry at the national level and managing industrial relations at the international level.

Political authorities in many states recognize both the opportunities and the threats of industrial globalization, and it is not uncommon for states to seek to exploit the one while minimizing the other. Often there is a clear policy emphasis, however. A general distinction can be made between those states where the focus is more on the defence-industrial opportunities offered by globalization and those where political authorities focus on the vulnerabilities involved. It is useful to consider this in terms of established arms producers, emerging arms producers, and those states whose arms production capabilities remain underdeveloped.

Transnational defence-industrial processes are less critical to established arms producers due to their state of industrial development, but often are important to their defence-industrial programmes nonetheless. Firms and enterprises in these states struggle with the requirements of competitively developing and producing advanced arms that meet the demands of their defence establishments. The pressures of developing and producing advanced arms while still enabling their procurement in the quantities required have been experienced for some time. This is a particular challenge in Western European states but this is an issue even in the United States. Development and production of the Joint Strike Fighter, for example, was structured from the outset as a collaborative programme for this reason, with varying levels of national participation based on national interests and capabilities and American willingness to provide access to sensitive technologies.[44] Transnational industrial processes offer an important means of reducing R&D and production costs.

In these states official acceptance of some degree of local industrial participation in transnational processes is the norm but the extent of active state support for this varies considerably. Political authorities may negotiate formal interstate agreements as a means of providing a framework for industrial collaboration in defence R&D and production programmes as well as for general industrial collaboration. It is noteworthy that such agreements increasingly feature emerging as well as other established producers. In recent years, for example, the United States has signed collaboration agreements with Brazil and South Korea, as well as India.[45] Collaboration only emerged as an important issue for Japan following the reversal of its self-imposed ban on arms exports and the need to overcome the negative effects of the defence-industrial isolation that this produced. The near-exclusive focus on meeting the requirements of the Japanese Self-Defense Forces produced a relatively uncompetitive and inefficient oligopolistic defence-industrial landscape where firms produce arms that are relatively expensive.[46] Developing defence-industrial ties with Southeast Asian states, as well as European states and the United States, now is regarded as important by the Japanese government.[47] The established arms exporters can be expected to feature prominently as leaders as well as participants in collaborative arms R&D and production programmes.

Security concerns often impede but do not prevent the development of transnational defence-industrial ties in these states. Transnational defence-industrial processes can generate serious official concern. The extent of concern and the point at which it emerged varies considerably. In the United States, concern over the erosion of the defence-industrial base, with its potential to produce a 'hollow industry' through the loss of local capabilities, emerged following the Cold War.[48] Increasing American concern over supply-chain security was exacerbated by the disruption resulting from the Coronavirus pandemic which erupted in 2020. In other states significant concern emerged much more recently and is not as acute.

National security concerns drive concerned authorities in several established arms producers to seek to minimize the negative effects of transnational defence-industrial integration. Security concerns may be strong enough to compel political authorities to prevent further transnational integration in particular cases or reverse that which has developed. Political authorities may be guarded in their approach to interfirm defence-industrial collaboration, particularly where R&D is concerned. Political authorities may strive to prevent the erosion of sovereign capabilities in terms both of the autonomy of their defence-industrial bases and operational sovereignty through assured access to critical technologies.[49] International collaborative arms programmes face daunting obstacles as a result, even where participation is limited to firms and enterprises based in allied and friendly states. Security concerns ensure that political authorities will continue to be careful in setting the boundaries of transnational defence-industrial collaboration, to the extent that they are able to do so. This is particularly true of those states for which collaboration is less crucial.

In some established arms producers state support for local industrial participation in transnational industrial processes is tempered by concern over the implications for the development of defence-industrial capabilities elsewhere. This stems from recognition of the potential of transnational defence-industrial ties to serve as a vehicle for technological diffusion and industrial upgrading. Concern is most marked where there is significant potential for the erosion of qualitative technological advantages over actual or potential politico-military rivals. Political authorities in such states may devote considerable attention to managing the terms in which local industry engages offshore capability partners. The example of the United States is instructive. While the American government generally has not opposed efforts by high-technology American firms to globalize production or even R&D, security concerns have impacted significantly on how industrial ties with specific states are perceived and managed. China figures prominently in American efforts to establish boundaries for transnational R&D and production at the present time.[50] China, for its part, long has imposed strict restrictions on industrial integration in high-technology fields with states such as the United States.[51]

Concern over the defence-industrial implications of transnational industrial processes can drive near- and long-term policy responses. Near-term responses often take the form of restrictions on the transfer of what are regarded as critical technologies. This may require careful management of transnational industrial processes. More longterm in nature are strategies designed to protect what are regarded as strategic industrial assets. Concerned authorities may seek to keep strategic industries under full national or sovereign control, as difficult as this is in an environment of globalization where key activities may be sited offshore and the subsidiaries of local firms and enterprises may be wholly or partially foreign-owned. Efforts to promote national security may focus on specific firms and enterprises or entire industrial sectors. Sovereign control can be exercised through maintaining 'golden shares' in enterprises that are partly state-owned, which grant the state greater voting rights than ordinary shareholders. Interest in maintaining sovereign control over entire industrial sectors is most common where the state traditionally has dominated the industrial landscape, such as in China and Russia.

The emerging arms producers have much in common with the established arms producers, but their position is much more straightforward. Political authorities in these states generally face less of a dilemma in gauging the effects of transnational defence-industrial integration. The processes involved generally are viewed in positive terms. Transnational defence-industrial integration represents an important means of reducing technological risk as these states pursue their ambitious arms development and production programmes. These states are characterized by strong interest in defence-industrial development and their level of industrial development generally positions them to effectively exploit the opportunities offered by transnational R&D and production processes. The ground for this was prepared by their exposure to globalization in the pursuit of economic development. Recognition of the potential contribution of transnational industrial processes to defence-industrial development is informed by successful civil-industrial development, which benefitted greatly from the integration of local firms and enterprises in industrial processes centred in developed industrial states.

Political authorities in these states generally strongly support engagement of transnational defence-industrial processes. Many emerging arms producers benefit from local R&D and production capabilities by firms based offshore, as discussed in the following chapter. Defence-industrial engagement often involves ties to established arms exporters, but increasingly takes the form of collaboration with other emerging producers.[52] The potential benefits of engagement are most readily apparent in the emerging industrial states of East Asia. Transnational defence-industrial integration has contributed significantly to defence-industrial development in states such as South Korea, helping to narrow the gap with the established arms producers.

Other states largely have been bypassed by the industrial globalization trend, but this holds considerable attraction as a vehicle for defence-industrial development. This is demonstrated by strong interest in engaging transnational industrial processes through direct and indirect military offsets, even where the relative underdevelopment of local industry renders it difficult to build on engagement. The established and emerging arms producers often provide the blueprint where their defence-industrial development is concerned. States that have yet to attain their level of development generally embrace transnational defence R&D and production processes to the extent they are able. The potential benefits of engagement far outweigh any national security risks for these states.

States generally are struggling to keep pace with the policy requirements generated by defence-industrial globalization. This continues to present political authorities with daunting policy challenges and is contributing to the perennial struggle for defence-industrial reform in many states. It is important to bear in mind that states' positions on transnational defence-industrial integration are subject to change as their industrial profiles and policy requirements evolve. This was demonstrated by China, where political authorities began to demonstrate greater concern over the security implications of industrial globalization as deepening integration into transnational processes began to produce greater interdependence in key industrial sectors.[53]

## *State and Industry in the Transnational Defence-Industrial Landscape*

Industrial globalization has significant implications for the state/industry relationship. The relative importance of industry is growing in an environment where firms and enterprises have increasing scope to act in ways that conflict with national interests. Firms and enterprises generally are demonstrating greater independence. Shortly after the end of the Cold War Jacques Gansler noted that 'firms, properly acting in their corporate interests, are frequently taking actions which are either independent of or contrary to the interests of individual nations'.[54] This is the subject of considerable concern on the part of political authorities in many states, where defence firms often are treated as strategic state assets. The result is a generally more complex state/industry relationship.

The state/industry relationship is complicated by common interests alongside areas of difference. There is a clear convergence of interests in respect to the viability and success of defence firms and enterprises which encourages state support for transnational industrial processes that are important to industry. Set against this is tension arising from the nature of interfirm engagement through transnational processes. Considerable tension can arise where firms and enterprises are intent on exporting components, sub-components, and technologies required by transnational R&D and production but which political authorities regard as compromising national security. The capability partners engaged by defence firms and enterprises also can be a source of tension with the state. Political authorities prefer transnational collaboration with industry from states that are trusted partners, particularly where this involves advanced arms, and are interested in developing long-term collaborative relationships with trusted partners. Industry, on the other hand, tends to focus on the capabilities offered in developing collaboration. Conflicting state/industry interests can greatly complicate efforts to prevent transnational industrial ties from facilitating the development of defence-industrial capabilities in politico-military rivals.

State/industry tension over intellectual property also is growing as transnational industrial integration deepens. The fault lines on this issue are far less well defined than those of industrial engagement. Intellectual property issues arise in the context of transnational interfirm collaboration but are distinct and particularly complex. Collaborative R&D can complicate technology control efforts by generating intellectual property that belongs to foreign as well as local firms and enterprises. Security concerns often underlie the difficulties experienced in addressing intellectual property rights in collaborative arms programmes. This is demonstrated by the American-led Joint Strike Fighter programme.[55] The need to safeguard critical intellectual property can generate conflict with industry that threatens interfirm collaboration. In addition, interfirm intellectual property disagreements may compel political authorities to intervene in contractual disputes involving local industry.

States generally are in a strong position to influence the extent to which firms and enterprises structure their operations to the detriment of national interests or otherwise engage in activities that threaten national security. Even where states do not dominate the industrial landscape as operators of defence-industrial enterprises, they often possess considerable structural capacity to shape the landscape in the interest of security. This includes through their regulatory role and their role as providers of crucial infrastructure. In the United States, for example, the Committee on Foreign Investment in the United States (CFIUS) can review and prevent mergers and acquisitions of

American firms.[56] States also may intervene through interstate collaboration programmes. In practice, however, the application of state controls often is tempered by the need to ensure the long-term viability of firms and enterprises. This may require allowing them to structure their operations and operate in ways that are problematic in national security terms. Recognition of the importance of transnational processes to the development, if not survival, of industry in most states serves to discourage the imposition of such strict controls that firms and enterprises are rendered uncompetitive. The notable exception is provided by those states where the economy traditionally has been dominated by the state.

Where political authorities are intent on ensuring that transnational defence-industrial ties do not undermine national security, industrial oversight and management, particularly of defence firms and enterprises, assume greater importance. Effective industrial surveillance is complex in an environment of defence-industrial globalization. It is difficult for concerned authorities to monitor intra- and interfirm transfers of components, sub-components, and technologies. Transfers of concern may become apparent only long after their occurrence. Many of the arms export control violations dealt with by American authorities in recent years involve internal transfers with or between internationally distributed subsidiaries. It generally is the case that the more deeply firms and enterprises are embedded in transnational R&D and production processes the greater the scope for transfers of potential concern and the greater the difficulty in monitoring transfers.

The challenge of managing industry often is no less daunting. The independence of industry in most cases renders it resistant to state efforts to control its activities, particularly where this renders commercial programmes uneconomic. This is true even to some extent of states such as China, where the defence-industrial landscape is dominated by state-owned enterprises.[57] The transnational structure of many defence firms and enterprises reinforces their independence. Not only is it the case that they often structure R&D and production internationally, but the development of a transnational arms industry raises difficult policy issues through its effect of eroding the identity of defence firms. This is reflected in many cases in a significant shift in perspective. Thales, for instance, describes its strategy of R&D and production as 'multi-domestic', while QinetiQ identifies multiple 'home' markets and the chairman of Matra described his firm as 'American in the United States and

European in Europe'.[58] Many firms and enterprises are sensitive to the issue of national identity and recognize the negative consequences of being considered 'foreign'. This drives them to strive to offset potential concern over their foreignness by developing a strong local identity. IBM, for example, sought to maintain distinct identities in the major markets where it had a presence through local staffing.[59]

The state/industry relationship can be quite strained or even antagonistic at times and will continue to be characterized by considerable complexity as heightened strategic competition ensures that security and economic imperatives remain in fundamental tension. Despite this, cooperation between state and industry, which remains quite close in some cases, will continue to be important.

## Transnational Defence-Industrial Ties and the Arms Transfer System

The emergence and progressive development of a transnational defence industry has profound consequences for the international arms transfer system. The international arms transfer system is experiencing its most fundamental transformation since the nineteenth century as deepening transnational defence-industrial integration is transforming its structure in terms of actors, processes, and the substance of arms transfers. This transformation is contributing to the development of arms producers and to their emergence and development as arms exporters. These effects are most marked in states that traditionally have not been prominent as arms exporters but have had an increasing impact on established arms suppliers as well. This transformation raises important and complex policy issues. While presenting important opportunities, transnational industrial collaboration complicates arms exports and exacerbates concern over the security implications of arms transfers. Established explanatory frameworks fail to appreciate the implications of the transformation of the global defence-industrial landscape.

Transnational defence R&D and production processes are contributing to a much more complex international arms transfer system. Transnational arms production is contingent on far more extensive transfers of components, subcomponents, and technologies than were required in the past. While the volume and value of production inputs, as opposed to complete systems, is difficult to quantify, these clearly account for a significant and increasing share of the international arms trade. In 2017, for example, 'parts for military-type goods' comprised 30.5 per cent of American defence exports.[60] Significantly, the trade in production inputs involves a far broader range of suppliers than in the past. This is the case with production processes centred in both established and emerging arms producers. North Korea, for instance, has emerged as a major supplier of ballistic missile-related components and materials, none of which are to established producers.[61] Not all of the suppliers involved in the contemporary arms trade would be considered arms exporters if consideration was limited to the transfer of complete systems alone.

The transformation of the global defence-industrial landscape is facilitating the emergence and development of new arms suppliers. Some of these states, such as certain emerging East Asian suppliers, have developed into important suppliers of complete systems, while others are important through their contribution to arms production processes based in established suppliers. The importance of the established arms suppliers is not being undermined in the process; while emerging arms suppliers are supplanting established suppliers in some markets, more generally they are supplementing them.

The traditional hierarchical model of the international arms trade fails to capture the less clearly defined position of states in the contemporary arms transfer system. There remain important differences between arms suppliers, with some demonstrating far greater capabilities to develop and produce arms. Some states occupy specific niches in the arms market, and some remain far more prominent exporters than others. Interstate differences often are less distinct due to transnational defence-industrial integration, however. The contemporary arms transfer system features more extensive overlapping movements of components, sub-components, and technologies laterally and 'upwards' to more capable arms producers as well as 'downwards' to less capable producers. Arms transfer relationships are highly asymmetric, even between established exporters. This reflects local sectoral strengths and interfirm and interstate relationships that have developed over time.

Many states both import and export arms, but the impact of the transformation of the defence-industrial landscape varies considerably. The emergence of a transnational defence industry raises distinct concerns for arms imports and exports. Issues concerning the impact on arms imports are particularly salient in those states with more modest defence-industrial capabilities that are more reliant on imports, while the impact on arms exports is of particular concern in states which are established arms producers. Though transnational production networks facilitate the development and production of arms, this does not necessarily reduce states' dependency on arms imports. For many states, advances in arms production capabilities have the effect of generating increased imports of production inputs such as components and sub-components and requirements for ongoing technical support. This applies even to some extent to established arms producers which possess comprehensive defence-industrial capabilities. Arms production in many of these states is dependent to some degree on inputs from offshore industry.

The increased export prospects deriving from the transnational structure of the defence industry encourage efforts to exploit these opportunities. This applies to established and emerging arms exporters alike but is particularly noteworthy for its potential to encourage the entry of new suppliers into the international arms market. There are many states that have not traditionally exported arms and which still are not in a position to supply complete systems but are able to supply arms related components and sub-components. The transformation of the global defence-industrial landscape is expanding the ranks of the arms producing and exporting states.

The more complex arms transfer patterns resulting from increased transfers of production inputs in support of transnational production greatly complicates the task of managing the arms trade. Increasing flows of components, sub-components, and technologies raise significant industrial oversight and governance issues. This is even more the case where the development of industrial ties embeds local industry in processes that are centred offshore. Political authorities in many states remain protective of defence-industrial assets and must consider the potential implications for local firms and enterprises as well as the geopolitical implications in arms transfer decision making.

Arms export control generally represents a much more complex and difficult exercise in the current defence-industrial environment. This is addressed in detail in Chapter 7, but it should be noted here that the importance of transnational industrial processes to defence firms and enterprises often is such that political authorities must carefully consider the potential impact of restrictions and tailor them to ensure that they do not unduly harm the national defence-industrial base. The emergence and development of a transnational defence industry involves many more states in the production and export of arms, eroding the capacity of individual states to control arms flows. Governance of arms exports generally is weaker due to the extent to which firms and enterprises are transferring components, sub-components, and technologies to offshore subsidiaries and capability partners. This raises issues far more complex than those associated with the transfer of dual-use items, the control of which has proven problematic even for Western states with comprehensive arms export control regimes.

The transformation engendered by defence-industrial globalization generates requirements for much closer interstate engagement. This is necessary both to ensure the availability of the production inputs and manage the international arms trade. Technology transfer and sharing, workshare, intellectual property, and arms control issues are complex in this environment and may prove contentious as political authorities seek to pursue their diverse and often conflicting security and economic agendas.

This complexity is demonstrated by the requirement for engagement where arms exports draw on components, sub-components, and technologies sourced offshore. States may differ over whether particular arms should be exported or should be supplied to particular states. Issues such as these have complicated efforts to supply arms to Ukraine in the Russo-Ukrainian War, as noted earlier in this volume. Overcoming such differences may require significant compromise on the part of political authorities in one or more suppliers. General recognition of the difficulties involved in exporting arms in an environment of transnational defence-industrial integration has led some arms producers to go to considerable lengths to ensure that their products are not subject to foreign export restrictions.

The evidence at this point suggests that the process of defence-industrial globalization will endure, despite heightened international strategic competition. This will deepen the transformation of the international arms transfer system, encompassing further states as they develop industrially and are progressively drawn into transnational R&D and production networks.

# 5 The Emerging Arms Supplier States

The emerging suppliers are states that previously did not export or were relatively minor exporters and which now are demonstrating a capacity to fulfil substantial roles in the international arms transfer system on a sustained basis. Some of these suppliers now occupy important niches in the arms transfer system and are known for specific products or services, while others contribute to many facets of the arms trade. Despite their varied nature, emerging supplier states represent an objective category; these states are noteworthy for their potential to develop into established arms suppliers, as has been demonstrated by a select group of states in the postwar period. The developmental paths followed by emerging suppliers are not necessarily linear, however, and the process is difficult; many states fail to make the transition from production to meet local demand to production for export.

There has been historical transformation in the relative position of arms suppliers, with significant changes in the capabilities of established suppliers and the emergence of new supplier states. The new arms suppliers that rose to prominence from late in the Cold War are following a path that is distinct from that charted by preceded generations of suppliers in important respects, however. The emerging supplier states are both products and agents of structural transformation in the international arms transfer system. These states are notable for the nature of their development, production, and supply of arms and are affecting arms supply patterns. The role of the emerging supplier states is more complex than generally is appreciated due to their integration into transnational defence-industrial processes. This calls into question the conventional—though problematic—tendency to categorize arms exporters based on their capacity to produce complete systems.

## The Issue of New Arms Supplier States

The emergence of new arms suppliers can generate considerable concern. This derives in some cases from the potential of new suppliers to supplement or supplant established arms suppliers in particular markets. In other cases, concern stems from their perceived capacity to proliferate advanced arms with little forewarning.[1] New arms suppliers are regarded by some as generally destabilizing through their capacity to contribute to local and regional arms races.[2]

Concern often reflects the perspective that new arms suppliers differ fundamentally from established suppliers in a key respect. Some regard emerging suppliers as less inclined to observe established international arms transfer norms, including in terms of supplying arms to states and NSAGs in conflict zones, thereby contributing to the intensity and duration of conflicts in the developing world. While this perspective is subjective, some emerging suppliers appear particularly inclined to disregard established arms transfer norms. North Korea is a prominent example of an arms supplier that pays no heed to international arms transfer norms, indiscriminately providing arms to states and NSAGs in conflict situations and serving as a 'supplier of last resort' to states such as Zimbabwe.[3] Other emerging supplier states such as India and South Korea, by contrast, demonstrate strong support for international arms transfer norms.

Emerging supplier states have been the subject of increasing attention as their capacity to export arms and role in the international arms transfer system have grown. The contribution of emerging suppliers such as Iran and North Korea in meeting the materiel requirements of Russia since the outbreak of the Russo-Ukrainian War in 2022, including through the supply of UAVs and ballistic missiles, demonstrates their growing importance and is generating increasing official concern in Western states.[4]

## The Emergence of New Arms Suppliers

New arms suppliers emerge as defence-industrial capabilities develop and arms production expands in states where this was not well established or through a shift from an exclusive focus on meeting national requirements. The production of arms for national and export markets is not necessarily mutually exclusive, but this may require significant changes in the focus of developmental efforts, equipment standards, or programme time frames. Arms production for national and export markets can prove mutually supporting, with national requirements providing a basis for production for export customers and export orders effectively subsidizing the arms production base. The need to meet the exacting demands of export customers and to succeed in highly competitive international markets also may prompt product development or industrial upgrading. It is only to be expected that arms exporters would emerge from the ranks of states with a strong foundation of domestic production.

The emergence of new supplier states is not a recent phenomenon but took on greater importance in the nineteenth century as uneven industrial development in Europe widened the gap between those states which could produce comparatively advanced arms and those which could not. This gap widened as technological progress in the leading industrialized states accelerated. Demand from states which had no recourse but to import arms provided the basis for a relatively small group of industrialized states to export arms in quantity on a commercial basis. The ranks of this select group experienced little change and the structure of the international arms transfer system remained stable.

This state of affairs began to change following the Second World War as colonial entities attained independence and the Cold War prompted an unprecedented global drive to develop defence capabilities. Interest in defence-industrial development was general as states aspired to import the European—and American—arsenal as well as army. As one analyst noted late in the Cold War, 'In the 1960s, every Third World country wanted a steel plant; today every quasi-industrial power wants [to produce] a jet fighter.'[5] Despite the determination with which defence industrialization was pursued, the development of comprehensive defence-industrial capabilities proved an elusive goal for many states. Much of the demand for arms could only be met through imports, most of which came from established arms suppliers. The ranks of the arms exporting states gradually expanded to meet this demand.

It is important to situate this shift in the context of general industrial trends. The emergence of new arms supplier states has been strongly associated with the state of the global defence-industrial landscape. The trend of deepening industrial globalization has significant implications for defence R&D and production capabilities. This structural transformation is facilitating the emergence and development of new arms producers and suppliers by providing the means to overcome industrial resource limitations and technical challenges in production and R&D. The transformative effect of industrial globalization is greatest in the developing and emerging industrial states.

The importance of industrial globalization stems in no small part from its capacity to expand the channels for industrial engagement, including by promoting long-term interfirm relationships. Sub-state actors long have been crucial to the development, production, and export of arms, but the contribution of firms and enterprises is changing, as noted in the previous chapter. Their scope to operate independently of political authorities is increasing as industrial globalization deepens and transnational R&D and production become more the norm. The potential of these actors to support defence R&D and production will grow as industrial development in emerging industrial states progresses. The defence industries of emerging arms suppliers such as Brazil and South Korea are highly globalized, for example.

As well as facilitating defence-industrial development in emerging supplier states, the greater freedom of action and relative independence of sub-state actors is strengthening the capacity of states to circumvent international arms sanctions and generally complicates general efforts to manage the international diffusion of arms. Firms and enterprises have increasing scope to undermine supply-side national, multinational, and multilateral arms control measures by supporting states' efforts to develop their production bases and achieve higher levels of defence-industrial self-sufficiency. The defence-industrial progress registered by embargoed states such as South Africa was due in no small part to the assistance provided by offshore industry.

The relationship between defence- and civil-industrial development can be critical to the development of new supplier states. Success in sustaining processes of defence-industrial development often is due in no small part to the foundation provided by successful civil-industrial development. The contribution of high-technology firms and enterprises is critical to defence-industrial development due to their capacity to absorb and apply new technologies, including those transferred under offset arrangements, and to facilitate the integration of COTS components and sub-components in defence production programmes. Firms that are successful in meeting the needs of the civil market also generally are in a better position to undertake defence production and R&D where this does not immediately generate high returns. Limited domestic demand for arms in many emerging suppliers means that they are more likely to procure arms in small batches, with little opportunity to exploit the advantages of economies of scale. The importance of civil-industrial development is suggested by Taiwan's apparent interest in exploiting the potential of export-led economic development as a means of 'fundraising' to support independent defence production.[6]

Economic development is strengthening the potential for the civil-industrial sector to support defence-industrial development in emerging supplier states. The developmental trajectories of a number of these states follow the path charted by the developed industrial states. This is not entirely coincidental. This enables states to more effectively exploit the potential provided by transnational industrial ties. The developmental strategies of several states are informed by defence-industrial requirements. This is most readily apparent on the part of the East Asian HPEs that are emerging arms suppliers. Defence industrialization in states such as South Korea have been embedded in general industrial development and their impressive defence-industrial progress has provided a basis for significant arms export profiles.[7]

Strategies that draw upon the assets of the civil-industrial sector are not incompatible with what are for emerging suppliers more traditional approaches. Interest in exploiting the potential of arms imports to secure defence-industrial support from established arms producers remains strong across the ranks of the emerging suppliers. Direct and indirect military offsets often serve as a key instrument for the development of states as arms exporters as well as arms producers. Production of components and sub-components for an established supplier or the localization of production through the transfer of complete 'turnkey' production lines has considerable potential to facilitate entry to the international arms market. Political authorities in many of the East Asian emerging suppliers long have sought to build on offsets.[8] South Korea's T-50 Golden Eagle trainer/light strike aircraft programme drew upon technical support that Lockheed Martin provided as an offset requirement of South Korea's purchase of F-16 fighters, for example.[9] Offsets supporting local defence-industrial development are recognized as contributing to the emergence of new competitors, but observers have noted that there is little alternative to offering offsets in the highly competitive international arms market.[10] The increased competitiveness of the arms market following the Cold War has reinforced the importance of offsets.

Not all states are in a position to exploit the opportunities provided by industrial globalization or offsets. These states are compelled to contract for defence-industrial support on a commercial basis or secure this through military assistance. The provision of defence-industrial support as a form of military assistance is less common than in the past. This reflects the post-Cold War international security environment, in which political authorities generally have had less incentive to provide military assistance, but also the high political costs that can be incurred in providing such support. One notable emerging arms supplier, North Korea, largely has relied on its own resources and on illicit offshore procurement of components, sub-components, and technologies in developing and producing arms.

The transition from arms importer to arms producer can prove protracted and difficult. It can take some time to establish and develop local arms production capabilities, even with foreign assistance. Multi-stage production programmes with phased increases in local content often serve as an important vehicle for the development of defence-industrial capabilities. A progressively increasing proportion of locally produced content can be pursued in concert with the qualitative development of local industrial capabilities. In many emerging suppliers the development of arms is based on imported systems. Only a select group of suppliers have succeeded at this point in successfully undertaking independent advanced arms programmes. It can prove even more difficult to develop the capacity to export advanced arms, with export customers often being more demanding than home governments with respect to equipment standards, cost, post-delivery support, and delivery schedules.

Despite the costs and difficulties involved and the mixed record of defence-industrial development, political authorities often demonstrate considerable faith in its prospects and pursue this with considerable determination. Their focus typically is on attaining the objectives involved, whether this is providing arms for the defence establishment, promoting industrial development, enhancing national prestige, or generating exports, rather than on the obstacles involved. India, for example, persevered with its Tejas strike aircraft programme despite a protracted and difficult development programme. The Tejas programme was launched in 1983 with what in hindsight has proven to be a highly over-optimistic six-year development phase.[11] This aircraft, which was intended to feature a very high degree of national content, was envisioned as a replacement for fighter aircraft such as the MiG-21. The Tejas has faced significant cost increases and production has yet to reach planned levels, with the result that the MiG-21 remains in Indian service. Advancing the project has required significant compromise of developmental goals, particularly that of autonomy in both development and production. India has had to accept extensive foreign assistance, including for the development of the Kaveri engine which was intended to power the Tejas.[12]

## Policy Imperatives and Defence Industrialization in Emerging Arms Suppliers

The defence industrialization that provides the basis for new arms supplier states may be motivated by imperatives of security, economic development, or some combination of the two. As noted earlier in this study, security and economic imperatives are not necessarily mutually exclusive but can generate distinct industrial requirements. The development and production of arms to meet the materiel requirements of the national defence establishment may be pursued regardless of its economic viability, for example, while meeting the needs of export customers may require production that does not contribute to the development of industrial expertise.

There is a strong relationship between the requirements of national security and the emergence of new supplier states. Security requirements represent the most fundamental objective driving political authorities to initiate and support defence industrialization. Self-reliance in the production, if not the development, of arms is commonly cited as the objective of defence-industrial development.[13] The importance attached to this often is demonstrated by the level of state support, which can be crucial given that domestic arms production generally is less cost-effective than importing arms. For many emerging suppliers, defence industrialization represents a form of import-substitution industrialization, albeit one that is driven by security of supply considerations. This occurs where defence industrialization is intended to supplant imports with locally produced arms in order to provide a greater measure of independence than that offered by relying on offshore suppliers. A focus on security imperatives may require significant comprises, however. The importance attached to responding to the perceived threat posed by neighbouring states has undermined India's search for defence-industrial autonomy, as demonstrated by the Tejas programme, for example.

In many emerging suppliers, the capacity to export arms derives from national production capabilities developed in response to past difficulties in procuring arms and interest in ensuring that this will not recur. A notable example is provided by South Africa, which in 1977 was subject to a global arms embargo by the United Nations.[14] Even being blocked from obtaining a single critical system can prompt political authorities to pursue defence industrialization. Restrictions on arms transfers to Turkey, including components for Turkish arms production programmes, are reinforcing its drive to develop an autonomous national defence-industrial base, but the American decision to bar it from participation in the Joint Strike Fighter programme has been decisive.[15] The Russo-Ukrainian War is having the general effect of encouraging self-sufficiency, as Russia's reduced capacity to export arms removes a major source of supply for many states.[16]

Interest in defence-industrial development is by no means limited to states which have experienced difficulties in importing arms. Increasing general concern over national security can drive defence-industrial development. In South Korea, for example, the disquiet prompted by President Jimmy Carter's March 1977 announcement that the United States would withdraw its combat forces from the Republic by 1981 or 1982 drove an increased emphasis on defence-industrial development and self-reliance.[17] Developing a national capacity to develop and produce arms also has been approached as a means of insulating states from political pressure from supplier states in general. In some states, this is viewed as a sovereignty issue. In South Africa this is expressed in in terms of 'embedded autonomy'.[18] Developing autonomous defence-industrial capabilities has the added advantage of providing greater freedom of action to export arms.

Security imperatives often generate particular interest in developing and producing advanced arms. This is most readily apparent on the part of emerging suppliers that have reached an intermediate or better stage of defence-industrial development. This reflects several factors. These include the more limited number of potential suppliers of advanced arms, which results in greater security of supply uncertainties and increases the potential for suppliers to exploit the coercive potential of arms transfer restrictions. No less important are the difficulties involved in producing advanced arms on relatively short notice in times of heightened international tension or conflict, including in terms of 'surging' production to meet increased demand. Their complexity and the requirement for long-lead time production inputs renders this a particularly difficult exercise for advanced arms. Establishing an indigenous production capability in the event this is required provides a degree of security. It is noteworthy that even in Taiwan it appears to be more important to ensure that a production capacity for advanced arms exists than relying on local production as long as it is possible to import a comparable system.[19]

Economic imperatives are prominent in defence industrialization. There often is an expectation that local production, even where this requires the purchase of licences and production inputs, will cost less than importing complete arms and will save foreign exchange.[20] The fact that this often proves not to be the case has not dampened interest in attempting to realize such savings. This does not represent the principal interest of political authorities in many cases, however. Only in exceptional cases does the defence-industrial sector constitute a pillar of the national economy, but political authorities in many states demonstrate strong interest in exploiting the economic potential of defence industrialization.

There is considerable attention to defence industrialization as a developmental instrument. Defence industrialization can be regarded as a catalyst for general industrial, and thus economic, development through its capacity for industrial upgrading.[21] The president of Nigeria pronounced that the local construction of a patrol vessel 'heralded a technological transformation' for the country, for example.[22] Official interest in exploiting the developmental potential of defence industrialization is reflected in provision for indirect offsets and in projects of a dual-use nature.

Political authorities in some states regard economic development and national security as inseparable and pursue defence industrialization with both objectives in mind.[23] General industrial and defence-industrial strategies often are closely related. An integrated approach to defence-industrial development is readily apparent on the part of some emerging industrial states, particularly in East Asia. Malaysia approaches defence and civil industrialization in an integrated manner,[24] while Singapore's developmental strategy, which from the mid-1970s focused on high-technology capital-intensive industrial development, encompasses the development of a national defence industry.[25] Defence-industrial development in both South Korea and Indonesia similarly is being pursued in close association with industrial development.[26] Even where this is not a deliberate strategy, the trend in some sustained programmes of defence industrialization is for increasing mutually supporting civil/defence-industrial integration. This is the case with India.[27] It is unsurprising that qualitative defence-industrial progress has accompanied economic development in the emerging industrial states, as they are in a strong position to devote resources to defence-industrial base development and to direct and support firms and enterprises to this end.

It has been claimed that 'The pattern of third-world arms production has generally been determined by domestic industrialization strategies',[28] but the evidence does not always support this. As important as general industrialization has been in many cases, the numerous examples of 'enclave' defence industries structured independently of civil-industrial processes and the focus on defence-related offsets demonstrate that defence industrialization often is far from incidental.

Where economic imperatives play a significant role in driving defence-industrial development, this may come at some cost in terms of national security. This potentially occurs where economic objectives drive deepening transnational industrial integration, rendering the development of defence-industrial autonomy a much more complex and difficult exercise. Political authorities may consider this an acceptable compromise, however, at least in the short term, with a stronger emphasis on defence-industrial autonomy to follow the attainment of a certain level of industrial development. Concern over the implications for defence-industrial autonomy may be mitigated by recognition that this approach potentially provides a strong foundation for close and sustained engagement of offshore defence firms and enterprises. Security and economic imperatives will continue to engender the emergence of new arms suppliers.

## Processes and Patterns of Defence-Industrial Development

Processes and patterns of defence-industrial development vary considerably. While some states have registered steady development, progress in others has been sporadic, with periods of intensive defence-oriented industrialization interspersed with periods of relative stagnation. National security considerations help to account for uneven defence-industrial progress. Long-standing concern over an established security threat can drive sustained support for defence-industrial development while the emergence of a pressing security threat may prompt an effort to develop critical defence-industrial capabilities in an accelerated time frame.

Processes of defence-industrial development commonly are assumed to be linear, but this often is not the case. As is to be expected given the range of factors that potentially impact on the circumstances, resources, and objectives of states pursuing defence industrialization, progress has been very uneven. While some emerging arms suppliers have registered steady progress, others have not. Support for defence-industrial development may wane over time or arms programmes may face insurmountable developmental obstacles. Official support can be difficult to sustain where arms programmes fail to provide the desired results in the expected time frame, and it may prove difficult to continue to devote the resources necessary when the need to do so appears less critical.

Progress often is uneven within states, with important sectoral differences and generally far greater autonomy in the production than the development of arms. This may reflect defence-industrial strengths as much as defence-industrial priorities. In many states the developmental pace differs between low- and high-technology product sectors and between different high-technology product sectors due to the technical demands and resource requirements involved. Of the numerous aircraft-production programmes initiated by emerging arms suppliers, for example, few involve the development or even production of their powerplants.

The case of South Korea is instructive. Autonomy remains an important yet elusive objective even for this state, despite its solid foundation for production and R&D. Successive South Korean governments have pursued defence industrialization for over four decades and autonomy remains the cornerstone of its defence-industrial programme. Despite this, the drive for greater 'localised development and production of imported components' is tempered by interest in strengthening defence-industrial collaboration with other states, as demonstrated by the recent decision to redesignate its offset policy as 'industrial co-operation'.[29] This is an issue that confronts political authorities in many states as they reach a certain threshold as arms producers, where they require close assistance if they are to advance further. In the case of South Korea, this means not only that its success in developing and producing advanced arms has not delivered defence-industrial autonomy, but the level of autonomy has reached a plateau beyond which it is difficult to progress.

Patterns of defence-industrial development can suggest the objectives involved. Distinguishing objectives is not necessarily straightforward, however, due to the general tendency to pursue programmes for the production, if not the development, of different types of arms simultaneously. The importance attached to developing as well as producing arms and the extent of the local contribution may help to indicate whether a process of defence industrialization is driven by security or economic considerations. Where the production of arms is initiated on relatively short notice, with no apparent consideration of sustainability or its long-term industrial impact, this suggests a focus on addressing pressing security threats, for example. An emphasis on contributing to offshore production lines or on the production of arms for which there is no local demand suggests an economic focus. The form of any offsets also can be instructive. Offset demands that support specific arms programmes or the development of capabilities specific to defence requirements, rather than on general industrial upgrading, may suggest a focus on security requirements. The structure of defence industries similarly can be highly revealing. State efforts to develop protected national defence industries generally indicate strong concern over national security.

While there is considerable variation between cases and over time, there are some general features of processes of defence industrialization. One key feature in most cases is the role of external support, despite the frequently avowed intention of independent arms production. Rarely has defence industrialization proceeded in the absence of foreign technical assistance provided on a commercial or military assistance basis. China represents an important exception to this; following its political break with the Soviet Union in 1960, the Chinese government embarked upon a programme of accelerated defence-industrial development. China's effective isolation from states that could offset the loss of Soviet defence-industrial support left it with no alternative other than to proceed based on its own, relatively limited, resources. China developed comprehensive independent defence-industrial capabilities though many of the arms it developed and produced were derived from foreign designs that were obsolescent if not obsolete.[30] As shown in Table 5.1, firms based in established producers play a crucial role in arms development and production programmes.

Defence-industrial support in its various forms may be obtained from a variety of sources. This includes from industry on a commercial basis, from

**Table 5.1: Principal External Sources of General Design Assistance in Aircraft-Development Programmes in Emerging Arms Suppliers**

| Emerging Supplier | Aircraft Programme | Aircraft Type | Source of Support |
|---|---|---|---|
| Argentina | IA-63 Pampa | Trainer | Dornier (Germany) |
| Brazil | C-390 Millennium | Transport | Boeing (United States) |
| Chile | Pillan | Trainer | Piper (United States) |
| India | Dhruv | Transport/utility helicopter | Messerschmidt-Bölkow-Blohm (Germany) |
| India | Tejas | Strike aircraft | Dassault-Breguet (France) |
| South Korea | KUH-1 Surion | Transport/utility Helicopter | Airbus Helicopters (France/Germany) |
| South Korea | T/A-50 Golden Eagle | Trainer/light strike aircraft | Lockheed Martin (United States) |
| South Korea | Light Armed Helicopter | Attack helicopter | Airbus Helicopters (France/Germany) |
| South Korea | KF-21 Boramae | Fighter | Lockheed Martin (United States) |
| Taiwan | AT-TC-3 Tzu Chung | Trainer/light strike aircraft | Northrop (United States) |
| Taiwan | F-CK-1 Ching Kuo | Fighter | General Dynamics (United States) |
| Turkey | Kaan | Fighter | British Aerospace (United Kingdom) |

states on an official basis, from individuals recruited for their specific expertise, or some combination of these. This may involve interfirm arrangements for project-specific joint ventures or longer-term strategic alliances, or formal interstate programmes. Established arms producers traditionally have figured prominently in the provision of support, regardless of whether this has been provided on a commercial basis or as a form of military assistance.

Individual 'technological mercenaries' can play a significant role in providing support. Many of the more ambitious arms development and production programmes in what can be regarded as the first generation of new arms producers to emerge following the Second World War relied on the expertise of such actors. Several states obtained the services of scientists and designers that had contributed to German arms programmes during the Second World War. They played a key role in programmes such as Egypt's Al-Zafer and Al-Qaher ballistic missile programmes and India's HF-24 Marut fighter programme.[31] More recently, retired engineers from several countries were recruited to support the development of Taiwan's first locally constructed submarine.[32]

Significantly, support for defence-industrial development increasingly comes from other emerging arms producers. The potential for this was demonstrated by the emergence in the 1980s of collaborative clandestine missile development programmes such as the Condor project of Argentina, Egypt, and Iraq.[33] The progressive development of defence-industrial capabilities in new supplier states positions them to support other emerging suppliers as well as both contributing to and building on arms production and R&D programmes based in established arms exporters. Defence-industrial collaboration with other emerging arms producers may be pursued as a means of overcoming technological hurdles and sharing resource burdens. The former can be a crucial consideration where the nature of the programme is such that assistance is critical but unlikely to be forthcoming from established arms producers. Collaboration may be programme-specific or long term and comprehensive in scope.

While collaboration can contribute greatly to arms R&D and production in emerging suppliers, this can greatly complicate arms programmes by limiting the freedom of action of these states. Efforts by the Arab Organization for Industrialization (AOI), which was established in 1975 by Egypt, Qatar, Saudi Arabia, and the United Arab Emirates to collaboratively produce arms, were impeded by difficulties in resolving differences over administrative and decision-making roles, for instance.[34] This helps to account for the commercial basis of much of the defence-industrial collaboration among emerging supplier states.

Emerging suppliers are most prominent as providers of defence-industrial support to other emerging suppliers. Their growing prominence in this role is to be expected given the contribution of exports to the sustainability of defence-industrial development in many of these states and widespread interest in reaping the economic benefits of arms exports. This is very important to North Korea, for example, where international sanctions have limited its access to revenue streams from legitimate economic activities for some time. As a result, North Korea has emerged as a major provider of defence-industrial support to states which are themselves subject to sanctions or which otherwise experience difficulties in securing such support.[35] The importance of emerging suppliers as sources of support can be expected to grow as their defence-industrial development progresses and their capacity to provide support grows.

Regardless of the source of support and whether this is provided on a commercial basis or as military assistance, the transnational processes discussed in the previous chapter facilitate its provision. Transnational production and R&D, even where industrial integration has not developed through the pursuit of defence requirements, often provide the basis for offshore support for the defence-industrial programmes of emerging arms suppliers. Many of the emerging arms producers that have registered the most impressive progress are East Asian HPEs which have been able to exploit transnational industrial processes to the full. As noted above, this does impose particular strictures on defence-industrial autonomy, but political authorities may consider this acceptable or see little alternative.

The importance of offshore defence-industrial support is widely recognized at the official and industry levels in emerging supplier states. This has encouraged interfirm collaboration and official support for deepening integration into transnational industrial processes, despite its negative national security implications. State recognition of the importance of ties to established arms producers is manifest in measures such as the negotiation of interstate agreements facilitating long-term defence-industrial collaboration and the organization of forums for interindustry discussions. This also drives efforts to exploit offsets as a means of supporting defence-industrial development. China, for example, used its order for Russian Su-27 'Flanker' fighters to master production of the airframe and to develop a capacity to integrate weapons and systems of its own design onto this platform.[36]

The contribution of defence-industrial support varies. This reflects their capabilities, recipients' level of industrial development, and the requirements of arms programmes. States that have reached a more advanced stage of defence-industrial development are more likely to draw on offshore sources for project-specific support, such as technical expertise to overcome a particular developmental obstacle or for the supply of critical technologies, components, or sub-components. Foreign firms and enterprises may feature as subcontractors to arms programmes where this is the case. States with less developed capabilities may require support that is far more extensive and of a more fundamental nature. This may include managerial advice or assistance in the industrial upgrading of underperforming firms and enterprises. Arms development and production programmes in these states may be pursued under the supervision, if not the direction, of foreign firms or enterprises, either on a commercial or state-to-state basis. The potential of suppliers to support defence-industrial development can have a significant influence on arms import decisions, as discussed in Chapter 3.

The many and varied paths of defence-industrial development do not necessarily follow a consistent pattern. This renders problematic the efforts to outline a common path manifest in what are sometimes referred to as 'ladders of production' and 'tiers' of producers. Defence-industrial development in emerging arms producers commonly is conceptualized as a process of linear qualitative improvement marked by progress through sequential stages of development.[37] In practice, however, capability development generally is episodic and sporadic rather than corresponding to the 'classical' model deriving from the experience of the established arms producers. The questionable applicability of this model is most marked where defence R&D is concerned. The assumed interest in developing a foundation for more comprehensive and advanced defence-industrial capabilities that informs thinking on 'ladders of production' is general, but the conventional wisdom is flawed in presuming continuity or that there necessarily is any progress at all. The development of states' defence-industrial capabilities may in fact stagnate or regress.

Common to states pursuing defence-industrial development is interest in replicating to some degree the success of the established arms producers. This contributes to the tendency to view defence industrialization through the lens provided by the developmental successes of established arms suppliers. The states which have developed comprehensive defence industries and which are established arms exporters provide the model for emerging arms suppliers as they do for developing states in general in terms of providing overall developmental benchmarks. Interest in following the example of these states does not mean that emerging suppliers necessarily approach defence industrialization in a similar manner or aspire to similar technical standards for arms, however.

Patterns of defence-industrial development can be complex. Development generally is initiated at a relatively rudimentary level. This does not necessarily involve the licensed production of arms or even the production of components or sub-components but may take the form of the provision of MRO services for arms operated by the national defence establishment or by another state. This was the pattern with the aerospace industries of South Korea and Taiwan.[38] Alternatively, the production of components and sub-components in support of production processes centred offshore may constitute the initial step in developing an indigenous arms production capability. When emerging arms producers commence the production of complete systems, this generally does not involve production of the entire article concerned. This may take the form of assembly from semi-knocked-down (SKD) or completely-knocked-down (CKD) kits, or co-production, under which key components still are imported. The distinction between co-production and complete production is important but contemporary production even in established arms producers generally involves components and sub-components sourced offshore. The nature and scale of the foreign contribution is telling; with co-production this is far more crucial.

Local production capabilities may develop over time, with progressively increasing local content and the supply of production inputs by OEMs on a reducing scale.[39] Progress is not necessarily incremental, however, and many states have failed to manage the transition from assembly to relatively independent production capabilities, still less the production of indigenously developed arms. Using licensed arms production as a basis for developing OEM capabilities poses a particular challenge where advanced arms are concerned.

Patterns of defence-industrial development in emerging arms producers are determined in part by the objectives involved. Political authorities may be motivated by economic motivations such as supporting industrial development or generating employment, in which case far more challenging and costly independent production is less important. Where defence industrialization is driven by security imperatives, efforts to develop and sustain momentum in defence-industrial development often are pursued with greater determination. Political authorities in these states are more likely to initiate ambitious development programmes for arms that are relatively advanced or which possess high symbolic value and can serve as objects of national pride.

Arms development and production programmes in emerging supplier states often fall short of expectations. The record of indigenous advanced arms development programmes is replete with failed initiatives, arms that fail to meet their intended technical specifications, and development schedules that prove far more protracted than planned. Arms development and production programmes may result in what are effectively technology demonstrators, rather than operational production-configuration examples of equipment. Even where operational systems result, qualitative shortcomings may result in production being scaled back. Nonetheless, even arms programmes that fail to mature may still deliver important industrial, political, and military benefits.

The prospects for defence-industrial autonomy over the long term are not necessarily encouraging, but this in part reflects contemporary industrial processes. Deepening industrial globalization has meant that equipment that is wholly local in content remains the exception rather than the rule even for established arms producers, as noted above. Continuing reliance on offshore developmental and production inputs if not formal partnering with other states has important implications for the drive for defence-industrial autonomy in emerging arms producers. The new norm for both the development and production of arms, particularly where advanced types are concerned, is that they are pursued through processes that are to some extent transnational. Nonetheless, even relatively modest indigenous capabilities may provide states with a measure of self-sufficiency.

Defence industrialization will remain important to emerging arms suppliers despite the difficulties and expense involved and mixed record to date. The determination with which political authorities in many states pursue defence industrialization in the face of daunting financial and developmental obstacles is telling. The importance attached to indigenous defence industries in many cases is such that political authorities are unwilling to allow them to fail. Defence firms and enterprises typically are approached as strategic assets and supported through subsidization and protectionism. The Indonesian government, for example, provided cash injections to save the three largest state-owned defence enterprises from bankruptcy during the Asian Financial Crisis of 1997–99, arguing that it was 'important to the country's future' to do so.[40]

## Issues in the Emergence of New Supplier States

There are several factors that can affect the form, pace, and sustainability of the defence-industrial development underlying the emergence of new arms suppliers. These issues potentially limit the scope for the development of new arms supplier states and help to determine their contributions to the international arms transfer system.

The general trajectory of defence industrialization in emerging arms producers is wholly conventional even if it does not necessarily parallel the pattern of the established arms producers. Defence industrialization in emerging producers reflects national requirements and the difficulties involved in developing defence-industrial capabilities. The general model involves a progression from less- to more-advanced arms programmes. Progress may involve incremental refinement rather than pronounced qualitative leaps. Emerging producers are confronted by challenges similar to those faced by established producers but generally have fewer resources with which to overcome developmental obstacles. This is changing, with their defence-industrial development now facilitated in many cases by the structural transformation of the global defence-industrial landscape, though at the cost of rendering defence-industrial development far more vulnerable to exogenous influences.

Generally, it is only where processes of defence industrialization are well advanced that this involves arms of indigenous conception other than for unsophisticated equipment types. The early production generations of arms in emerging suppliers generally owe their origin to designs developed elsewhere. These often are heavily derivative; they are either produced under licence without modification, are unlicensed copies, are versions of the original, or otherwise bear a close configurational resemblance to the original. The 'localization' of arms designs may be quite limited in scope, with relatively minor changes necessary to adapt them to specific local requirements or production capabilities rather than substantial redesign. As development progresses, designs of foreign origin are more likely to be substantially improved upon, including through the integration of new technologies.

Emerging suppliers are closely associated with the production of arms that fall short of international standards appertaining at the time and which are less advanced than those produced by established suppliers. Arms produced by emerging suppliers often do not represent the state of the art and may be obsolescent or even obsolete in nature. This may reflect interest in producing proven designs and in using proven components wherever possible as much as the state of local defence-industrial capabilities. Such an approach minimizes developmental risk and generally is more cost-effective, and the requirements of expediency or affordability may dictate such an approach. It generally is some time before emerging suppliers develop R&D capabilities that position them to undertake significant innovation. Relatively few arms producers ultimately reach this point. Despite often-determined efforts, many emerging suppliers find it difficult to keep pace with technological advances, let alone close the gap with established arms producers.

Another factor that must be considered is the scale of production. The arms programmes of emerging suppliers often result in low-tempo series production of arms in modest or even token numbers. This particularly is the case where production is geared to national requirements and the producer fails to secure export orders. As a result, what is considered quantity production in emerging arms producers may effectively represent what would be regarded as small-scale or even boutique production elsewhere. Where limited national requirements preclude substantial orders the production tempo may be intentionally kept low as a means of extending a production run, as states may struggle to keep a production line open otherwise. This can be important to sustaining production facilities, particularly in the case of 'enclave' industries, and provides a basis for production on a larger scale should this be required.

The pace of defence-industrial development in emerging arms producers often is relatively slow. The processes involved generally prove particularly protracted where states follow paths that do not seek to build on the assembly, co-production, or production of foreign arms. Several factors contribute to this state of affairs. The greatest challenge stems from the requirement to acquire and master new technologies. This helps to account for the strong focus on low-technology categories of arms in emerging supplier states, at least initially. Economic constraints also play a crucial role. As a rule, local arms production is disproportionately expensive due to the need to establish production facilities and the relatively small scale of production involved.

The failure of defence industrialization to progress as rapidly as intended can be cause for concern as this may undermine national security and compels states to continue to import arms and to continue to draw on substantial offshore defence-industrial support. This also has significant economic implications where defence industrialization is approached as a means of industrial development. Concerns over drawing on offshore support remain despite the obvious advantages offered by the greater technological access that derives from integration into transnational industrial processes. The gestation period of defence-industrial development can prove quite protracted, compounding the difficulties inherent in narrowing the technological gap with the established arms producers and serving as a pacing factor in the development of export capabilities. This means that relatively few emerging producers develop into major producers in the short term, limiting the emergence of major new arms suppliers.

Where defence-industrial development proceeds at a comparatively rapid pace, this may come at a high cost in terms of sustainability. Security requirements, including those deriving from regime security, can drive political authorities to initiate ambitious high-prestige arms programmes which are impractical given the state of the local defence-industrial base. Not only are such programmes difficult to see through to fruition, but they are less likely to provide a basis for the development of further projects of a similar nature. High-profile flagship programmes that have not been realized and which did not contribute to the long-term development of local defence-industrial capabilities include Argentina's Namcu and Pulqui and Egypt's HA-300 fighter projects. These projects failed despite the fact that they embodied mature technologies and failed to provide a basis for the development of new combat aircraft.

Sustainability represents a fundamental issue in the emergence of new arms suppliers. Political authorities in many of these states pursue defence industrialization with long-term defence-industrial base development in mind. Individual programmes often are undertaken with the dual objective of addressing a specific materiel requirement and developing capacity that will provide a basis for meeting more demanding future requirements. Sustaining a process of defence-industrial development is difficult, however, and it often is the case that regardless of the success of an arms development or production programme, it fails to provide the intended industrial foundation. States might not even be able to maintain the capacity demonstrated by a particular arms programme, still less produce or develop subsequent generations of arms, without external assistance. Many emerging arms producers only manage to register defence-industrial progress in absolute rather than relative terms.

Those emerging arms suppliers where defence industrialization rests on a strong civil-industrial foundation have far better prospects for sustained progress in defence R&D and production. Several of these states have made impressive strides and have successfully kept abreast of developmental trends in specific industrial sectors. Most of the emerging arms producers that have registered significant progress and developed into major exporters are states where the defence industry is embedded in the civil-industrial sector. As China and North Korea have demonstrated, it is possible to sustain defence-industrial progress in the absence of extensive civil/defence-industrial integration, but at the expense of efficiency and at considerable cost in terms of resource allocation.

There are a number of factors that help to explain why defence industrialization represents such a difficult exercise. Fundamental in many cases is the requirement for ongoing state support. In many emerging arms suppliers the role of the state is crucial due to the relative underdevelopment of the industrial base and the uncertainty of commercial success in highly competitive international markets. Firms and enterprises may be dependent on domestic orders, for which they may receive preferential consideration, or rely on direct state support. Political authorities often underestimate the difficulties involved in sustaining defence industrialization and the burden involved may prove unsustainable. The difficulties involved in this are compounded by political considerations. Sustaining the focus necessary to support defence-industrial development over time can be difficult due to competing policy objectives and changes in government. Finally, crucial foreign assistance may not be forthcoming over the long term. This is vulnerable to changing political relationships and policy priorities on the part of supporting states. This was the experience of China, which suffered an abrupt loss of crucial support for its missile programmes when its relationship with the Soviet Union deteriorated in 1960.[41]

Sustaining defence industrialization is complicated by the structure of the defence industry in many emerging arms producers. The protectionist perspective informing the industrial strategies of many of these states and the essentially captive nature of the domestic defence market means that there generally is less incentive for industries to be technically efficient and to innovate. Firms and enterprises may be less competent to take on technological challenges and to respond to emerging demands than would be the case if they did not receive preferential treatment and their primary market was less certain. Also, since their primary focus is on serving a restricted market, economies of scale often are unobtainable. Firms and enterprises often occupy monopolistic positions in their respective fields. This can provide greater scope for inconsistent production standards as well as encouraging low-risk design approaches. Defence industries in many emerging arms producers are relatively uncompetitive.

In such an environment state support, and often guidance, are all the more crucial. Emerging supplier states are characterized by extensive state involvement in the development and production of arms. This is consistent with the more interventionist role of developmental states in civil-industrial processes. The state role can range from support for marketing to a direct role in R&D and production, with facilities wholly or partly government owned. In some emerging arms producers, defence R&D and production are the responsibility of military services. The importance of direct financial support for industry in the form of loans or grants has declined in the more successful emerging suppliers, but generally continues to distinguish emerging from established arms suppliers. The role of the state often renders defence firms and enterprises in emerging suppliers less sensitive to changing market conditions. This has significant implications for arms exports. Defence firms and enterprises have needed to become more competitive and efficient where exports have grown in importance.

## New Supplier States and the International Arms Transfer System

The emergence of new arms suppliers is not a recent phenomenon, but their impact on the international arms transfer system is greater than in the past. Formerly, this merely introduced new suppliers to the system. This had the effect of increasing the options available for states needing to import arms without fundamentally altering the system. While there was change in terms of which states were capable of exporting arms as new suppliers emerged and supplemented or even in some cases supplanted established suppliers, such change largely was gradual and structural change was limited and infrequent. The ranks of the arms exporting states remained relatively thin where more advanced categories of arms were concerned and often the position of established arms exporters was not undermined as many emerging suppliers did not develop the capacity to produce the full range of arms.[42]

Interest in exporting is strong across the emerging arms producers. The importance of exports is due in part to the fact that arms production often is uneconomic otherwise. In many emerging producers domestic demand is insufficient to render production economically viable. The case of Brazil is instructive in this regard. Defence industrialization was promoted by the state in the interest of both national security and national development and by the mid-1980s key firms such as Avibrás, Embraer, and Engesa were focusing on exports.[43] These firms achieved notable successes as exporters, particularly in Latin America, the Middle East and Sub-Saharan Africa, and they expanded their production capacity and developed new designs to satisfy export demands. As was the case elsewhere, Brazil's defence-industrial sector was severely affected by the post-Cold War contraction of the international arms market. Engesa, which in its heyday had been a key supplier of armoured vehicles to developing states, did not long survive the end of the Cold War. Many emerging suppliers now have little recourse but to export if the state is not to have to underwrite arms production.

The contemporary example of South Korea is indicative of the potential of emerging arms suppliers. It has demonstrated both the importance attached to arms exports and a successful transition to a major arms exporter to developed as well as developing states. Other emerging arms producers are focused more on domestic requirements or are demonstrating more nascent capabilities at this point, but even in Taiwan, where domestic defence requirements loom large due to the existential threat posed by China, it is considered important to export arms.[44]

There are several characteristic features of emerging arms suppliers. The primary focus of defence firms and establishments on meeting domestic requirements can affect their arms export prospects. Arms that are optimized for local requirements and operational conditions may be ill-suited to the needs of export customers, and firms and enterprises may have little capacity to adapt designs to meet the distinct requirements of export customers. This effect is compounded in some cases by the structure of the domestic defence market. As noted above, its relatively closed nature means that competitive bidding for contracts is less the norm, thereby removing an important incentive for the efficient development and production of arms. This results in the comparatively high unit cost that often characterizes arms production, including licensed production, in these states, potentially rendering the products of emerging suppliers uncompetitive. One final feature reflects the recent emergence of some of the new arms producers as arms exporters. These states are relatively poorly positioned as arms exporters, lacking the experience, export infrastructure, and export networks that can play such an important role in facilitating exports.

The defence-industrial development of several emerging arms producers has provided the basis for meeting the needs of particular sections of the international arms market. Defence-industrial specialization means that some of these suppliers are niche producers. North Korea, for example, is prominent in supplying states that experience difficulties obtaining arms from other suppliers. The emerging arms suppliers are most notable as sources of less-advanced arms but several have developed to the point where they are able to supply advanced arms. In this they are treading the path blazed by previous generations of new entrants to the international arms market. The daunting obstacles to defence industrialization in many states, which include dependence on offshore production inputs and on foreign designs for which they do not have access to proprietary data or hold export licences, will continue to limit the number of states developing to this point, however.

The contemporary emergence of new suppliers has far-reaching consequences for the international arms transfer system. These suppliers are having more than a local or passing effect. Lateral transfers feature prominently in the arms exports of the emerging suppliers. The nature of arms production in most emerging suppliers renders their wares of principal interest to customers from among the ranks of the developing and emerging industrial states. The expanding ranks of the emerging arms producers is generating increasing competition for this segment of the international arms market. One of the effects of this trend is some loss of market share by established producers which cannot compete effectively against producers that are able to offer the more cost-effective arms that meet the needs of the developing states. The contribution of the emerging suppliers to the international arms transfer system is by no means negligible, as their emergence is expanding the options for the procurement of arms, particularly for developing and emerging industrial states. The wider options resulting from the expanded ranks of arms exporting states also provides arms buyers with greater leverage in dealing with established arms suppliers.

The developed state market is the traditional preserve of the established arms producers, which are developed industrial states, but this gradually is changing. There is a significant shift deriving from the qualitative transformation of the capabilities of a select group of emerging suppliers, which is enhancing their competitiveness in an expanding range of markets and product sectors. The East Asian emerging suppliers in particular are registering impressive qualitative development. As well as enabling them to progressively meet more of their own arms requirements, this is providing a strong basis for arms exports to states with demanding requirements. By the 1980s, defence-industrial producers from the developing world were supplying components and complete systems to developed industrial states such as France, New Zealand, and the United States.[45] This trend has strengthened. Some measure of the success of suppliers such as Singapore and South Korea can be gauged by their exports of arms to European members of NATO in recent years.

The developmental trajectory of emerging suppliers is important in view of the strengthening norm against the supply of arms to states in conflict situations and the potential of these states to fulfil such a role. Iran and North Korea have played a crucial role in replenishing Russia's depleted ammunition stocks and providing combat UAVs and other arms following its invasion of Ukraine, for instance.[46] Most of the emerging supplier states appear intent on entering the mainstream of the arms transfer system, however, and are supplementing rather than supplanting the established suppliers. Singapore and South Korea, for example, imposed sanctions on Russia following its invasion of Ukraine in 2022.[47]

More significant over the long term is the role of emerging arms producers in supporting defence-industrial development in other emerging suppliers. In this the role of emerging suppliers is most distinct from that of the established suppliers. Emerging suppliers can support defence industrialization through industrial offsets and sub-contracted production, and their arms transfers can serve as a design catalyst in recipient states.[48] Emerging suppliers fulfil a significant role in providing direct support for the development, production, and modification of arms. The support of emerging supplier states has been crucial to the development of defence-industrial capabilities in other states, contributing to their emergence and development as arms suppliers. An indication of the defence-industrial support provided by emerging suppliers is provided in Table 5.2.

Emerging arms suppliers fill a crucial niche in supporting the defence-industrial programmes of states that are unable to secure assistance from established suppliers. This is particularly important for states intent on

Table 5.2: Emerging State Supplier Assistance for Arms Development and Production Programmes

| Supplier | Area of Support | Recipients |
|---|---|---|
| Brazil | Aircraft, missile systems | Egypt, Saudi Arabia, United Arab Emirates |
| Egypt | Missile systems | Argentina, North Korea |
| India | Naval vessels | Myanmar |
| Iran | Electronics, missile systems, UAVs | Indonesia, Russia, Yemen |
| Iraq | Missile systems | Argentina |
| North Korea | Electronics, missile systems | Iran, Myanmar, Pakistan, Sudan, Syria |
| Singapore | Armoured vehicles, artillery | Saudi Arabia, Thailand, Turkey |
| South Africa | Armoured vehicles | Azerbaijan, India, Jordan, Kazakhstan, Nigeria, Sri Lanka |
| South Korea | Aircraft, armoured vehicles, artillery, naval vessels | India, Indonesia, Paraguay, Saudi Arabia, Thailand, Turkey |
| Turkey | Aircraft, armoured vehicles, naval vessels, UAVs | India, Indonesia, Malaysia, Pakistan, United Arab Emirates, Uzbekistan |
| United Arab Emirates | UAVs | Algeria |

developing and producing advanced arms, including WMD-capable delivery systems such as cruise and ballistic missiles. Emerging arms producers which have developed a capacity in these areas have played a crucial role in supporting capacity development in other emerging industrial states through the transfer of technologies and production inputs.[49] North Korean developmental assistance in the form of technology and components has been crucial to Iranian, Pakistani, and Syrian ballistic missile programmes, for example.[50] It is noteworthy that North Korea initially was assisted in the development of such weapons by Egypt, and that over time North Korea evolved from a supplier of complete ballistic missiles to a supplier of components, materials, and manufacturing equipment.[51] Iran has in turn emerged as an important source not only of ballistic missiles, but of relevant developmental assistance. It has assisted Syrian efforts to develop a ballistic missile production capacity.[52]

## *Emerging Suppliers and the Structure of the International Arms Transfer System*

Debate over the impact of the emergence of new suppliers on the international arms transfer system is vigorous and of long standing. Examining the structural impact of defence-industrial development in emerging suppliers is complicated by its mixed record to date and by the nature of the contemporary arms transfer system. As noted earlier in this study, there is no clear hierarchy of arms producers and suppliers.

The fact that few emerging arms producers have attained the level of the established arms producers demonstrates at a minimum that any structural change at this point has been quite limited. The few new entrants to the international arms market that have succeeded in achieving an arms transfer profile in the postwar period sufficient to qualify them as established arms suppliers include China and Israel. There are a number of emerging arms producers at the present time that are quite prominent suppliers, demonstrating significant capacity as niche suppliers or in multiple fields. This select group of states includes Brazil, South Korea, North Korea, and Turkey. These states have developed advanced defence-industrial capabilities and their importance as arms exporters extends to providing technical assistance for the development and production of arms. Even these states, however, are limited in their defence-industrial capabilities and thus their export potential. None of them are in a position to develop and produce the full range of arms that they require without extensive assistance. North Korea, for example, produces a comprehensive range of arms, but still makes extensive use of imported components and sub-components and its R&D capabilities in most areas appear limited to developing derivatives of foreign designs, with relatively few designs that are completely new.[53] While such an approach has much to commend it while developing the defence-industrial base or as an economy measure, this demonstrates that these states have yet to develop defence-industrial capabilities comparable to those of the established suppliers. The emerging suppliers remain secondary to the established suppliers for the present.

In some cases, resource limitations and the nature of domestic arms requirements limit the prospects for emerging suppliers to develop into leading arms exporters but as South Korea has proven, there is considerable scope for states to be able to develop relatively comprehensive arms development and production capabilities. This is demonstrated by its Boramae fifth-generation fighter programme. While this is being undertaken with the support of firms such as Lockheed Martin and the assistance of Indonesia as a subordinate partner, South Korea is one of a handful of states, only three of which are outside of Europe and North America, to lead such a programme. Brazil has demonstrated considerable potential as well with its aerospace industry, several of the designs of which have been quite successful in export markets. Its track record in other product areas has been less impressive, however. Brazil's history noted above illustrates its difficulty in sustaining arms capabilities.

The extent to which arms production in emerging suppliers continues to rely on inputs from established arms suppliers suggests that emerging suppliers are not transforming the structure of the arms transfer system in another important respect. It appears that many emerging suppliers have succeeded only in exchanging one form of dependency for another, substituting dependency on arms related components, sub-components, and technologies for dependency on complete systems.[54] While many emerging suppliers expend considerable effort on developing secure access to arms, in most cases this results in quasi-autonomy at best, with nominally independent R&D and production programmes. Aircraft programmes in these states typically involve fitting indigenous airframes with imported powerplants, avionics, and other critical systems, for instance. Dependency at this level is in some respects much deeper, as the requirement for external defence-industrial support of this sort closely ties states to specific suppliers. While political authorities can choose—or be compelled—to seek out new sources of support, the costs of doing so can be very prohibitive. The costs involved in substituting suppliers of complete systems can be relatively low by comparison.

It is important when considering the issue of structural change, however, to bear in mind that this generally occurs over an extended period. The impact of important structural trends may not be apparent until the process has been underway for some time. Where states have succeeded in establishing themselves as important suppliers in the past, this has taken considerable time. The United States, for example, first emerged as an arms exporter following the conclusion of the Civil War in 1865 but its role as a supplier was quite modest at that point and it only rose to prominence with the Second World War. This demonstrates the difficulties of analysing the 'rise' of new arms suppliers in a restricted time frame.

It also is important to consider whether the evident failure of the emerging producers to transform the structure of the international arms transfer system more in terms of supplanting established suppliers reflects structural change of a more fundamental nature. The international arms transfer system is becoming less clearly defined in terms of the relative position of states. Several emerging arms suppliers can be considered to have made substantial progress toward becoming established in terms similar to those of states that generally are considered established arms suppliers. These suppliers effectively have entered the mainstream of the international arms transfer system due to the manner in which they are engaging other states in the development and production of arms. The role of some emerging arms suppliers in providing defence-industrial assistance in the form of components, sub-components, technologies, and other forms of technical assistance to other emerging suppliers, as noted above, anticipates their potential as their defence industries mature. Other emerging supplier states are notable for their growing potential as sources of technology. Many of the emerging producers that show the greatest promise in these terms are East Asian HPEs, but this trend is by no means limited to this group of states.

The international arms transfer system is being transformed by the emergence of new supplier states through the changing substance of arms transfers. While the trade in complete systems remains important, this is being supplemented by a growing trade in production inputs. This trend provides considerable scope for emerging arms producers to contribute to the international arms market as suppliers long before they are in a position to produce complete systems other than under the direction of or with the assistance of established producers. In contributing to arms development and production programmes in other emerging arms producers and increasingly to production programmes in established producers, in important respects the emergence of new supplier states is helping to determine international arms transfer patterns, which is the subject of the next chapter.

# 6 International Arms Transfer Patterns

Long-term transfer patterns are a conspicuous feature of the international arms transfer system. Arms transfer patterns reflect the tendencies of states to source arms from specific suppliers. The existence of a pattern can be established where arms transfers display a degree of continuity over time that suggests the importance of underlying factors. This may be manifest in repeat orders for additional quantities of arms or the procurement of successive generations of arms from specific producers, though this does not necessarily involve an exclusive reliance on a single source. States may have preferred suppliers for all or some of their arms requirements. India, for example, has well-established arms transfer relationships with both Russia and the United Kingdom, with the former providing some 65 per cent of the arms in Indian service in recent years.[1] Russia has been notable as a supplier of armoured vehicles, air defence systems, aircraft, and naval vessels to India, while the United Kingdom has featured as an important supplier of aircraft. Arms transfer patterns should be understood as reflecting preferences rather than in a deterministic sense of ensuring what arms will be procured.

The basis of arms transfer patterns often is complex. These may reflect the strengths of arms suppliers, the requirements of arms importers, historical ties, or structural factors in the form of the changing dynamics of the arms transfer system, alone or in combination. Arms transfer relationships are not necessarily static; there is scope for new arms suppliers to emerge and supplant established suppliers. Arms transfer patterns can be very uneven because of differences in the supply environment for different types of arms; international transfer patterns for SALW often differ significantly from those for combat aircraft, for example. This reflects the greater availability of SALW and the relative ease of substituting suppliers compared to a category of advanced arms such as combat aircraft.

It is constructive to consider arms transfer patterns in the context of individual states and patterns that are applicable across particular groups of states. Understanding arms transfer patterns is important in two respects: consideration of their basis can help to explain arms export and -import decision making in individual cases, and the trends involved are highly instructive in terms of the evolution of the international arms transfer system. An understanding of arms transfer patterns can help to account for the apparent irrationality of arms transfers in particular cases and can demonstrate the influence of factors such as the technical features of arms. As well as explaining present trends and developments, an understanding of international arms transfer patterns facilitates analysis of future arms transfer trends and developments.

The issue of arms transfer patterns is not as straightforward as it may appear at first sight. What might be considered the 'classic' pattern of the supply of arms from states with comprehensive defence-industrial capabilities to those that lack such capabilities is in fact much more complex. As well as between states, arms transfer patterns may differ between regions and with respect to different categories of arms, as noted above. The extent to which national arms transfer patterns reflect sectoral or regional patterns varies. This is due to local requirements and circumstances and the dissimilar impact of structural factors. It is important to examine the arms transfer patterns in terms of local circumstances as well as in the context of general trends as a result. Arms transfer patterns can shift significantly over time as circumstances and requirements change.

Analysis of international arms transfer patterns is complicated by the fact that these may only become apparent with the passing of considerable time. Intervals between national arms orders make it essential to analyse arms transfers in an extended time frame. It can be quite difficult to identify emerging patterns from the mass of individual arms transfers. Particular care must be taken in characterizing arms transfer patterns on the basis of examples provided by states that are in conflict or immediate post-conflict situations, though as noted below, conflict situations can mark important watersheds for arms transfer patterns. The requirements generated by conflicts, particularly where these are protracted, can help to overcome the innate conservatism of defence establishments where materiel requirements are concerned. Conflicts generally generate substantial arms procurements and may prompt reconsideration of equipment choices. Where states are seeking to reconstitute their forces following a conflict or address pressing operational requirements in responding to emerging threats, this often drives less carefully considered arms procurement decisions, however. Such 'stopgap', 'emergency', or 'urgent operational requirement' purchases may prove an interim solution where arms are incompatible with doctrinal requirements or equipment in service, with the result that they themselves require replacement by more suitable arms when finances and circumstances permit.

The deepening structural transformation of the global defence-industrial landscape has important implications for arms transfer patterns. The emergence of a transnational defence industry with highly distributed arms production and an increasing number of arms exporting states generates new requirements while providing unprecedented opportunities, both of which manifest in arms transfer patterns. There is considerable scope for the emergence of new arms transfer patterns involving emerging arms suppliers in this far less hierarchical arms transfer landscape. Arms flows are far less unidirectional in this environment, with greater horizontal transfer of complete systems and increasing transfers of production inputs such as components, sub-components, and technologies. There is growing scope for the emergence of arms transfer patterns based on defence-industrial requirements rather than the supply of complete systems. This scope will increase as transnational arms production becomes more the norm and the ranks of the arms producing states expand.

## National Arms Transfer Patterns

There are distinct patterns of arms transfers at the level of individual states. These patterns generally are more readily apparent on the part of arms recipients than suppliers. Arms import decision making tends to be highly pragmatic, with equipment selected on the basis of its capabilities or economic considerations, though political considerations also may play an important role. This reflects general interest in acquiring arms that best satisfy operational requirements on the most favourable terms possible, though some compromise in terms of either aspect may be necessary. Notwithstanding the advantages of selecting arms which meet these criteria regardless of their origin, there can be a high degree of continuity in arms transfers that suggests that far more than the capabilities of equipment or the terms on which they are available is involved. Suppliers feature particular attributes and there are many that fill important niches in the international arms transfer system. There are many legacy customers of individual arms suppliers. Some arms transfer relationships have developed over the course of decades, proving resilient in the face of supplier and recipient regime changes, the development of new generations of arms, and the emergence of competing suppliers.

Technical and political factors play key roles in establishing and sustaining arms transfer relationships. Even in the environment of expanded and much more rapid technological diffusion produced by processes of industrial globalization, substantial differences remain between the arms developed and produced by different states. The levelling effect of transnational defence-industrial integration is offset to a considerable extent by security-driven political barriers. As well as contributing to the enduring character of defence-industrial traits in many states, political considerations strongly influence arms transfer relationships. International arms transfers are highly politicized.

The technical features of arms can promote long-term arms transfer relationships. This particularly is the case where advanced arms are concerned. Continuing procurement of arms from an established supplier is encouraged by the distinct features of arms that result from the design philosophies of their developers. Arms often manifest design paradigms that are particular to a certain national industry and which limit compatibility with the products of other suppliers. Distinct design features might be limited to a specific firm or enterprise or might apply to an industrial sector in general. There were important general differences between the features and support requirements of arms designed in the United States and the Soviet Union, for example.[2]

The impact of technical features extends to transitioning to new generations of arms. Drawing on an established supplier potentially is far more straightforward than switching to designs offered by other suppliers. This is encouraged by incremental design approaches, which contribute to continuity between successive generations of arms in important respects. It generally is considerably less difficult to induct arms that are the products of traditional suppliers because they are likely to be to some extent compatible in operational and maintenance terms with arms that are in service already. The continued procurement of arms from a particular source may be more cost-effective as well as easier to introduce into service. This consideration contributes to India's enduring preference for Russian arms.[3] Operators of particular models of arms often order improved variants despite the availability of superior designs from other suppliers. This helps to account for the continued export success of Russia's ubiquitous Mi-8 'Hip' family of helicopters despite their obsolescence, having entered production in the Soviet Union in the 1960s.

The importance of this factor is demonstrated by the difficulties confronting defence establishments where support from traditional arms suppliers ceases.[4] The importance of post-transfer support from original arms suppliers is such that support arrangements are standard features of arms contracts. The importance of support from original arms suppliers can be particularly crucial where arms have only recently entered service or represent a qualitative advance on those previously operated. States may be unable to continue to operate arms in the absence of this support. Post-transfer support requirements generally are strongest with respect to advanced arms such as aircraft and naval vessels but their importance is determined in part by the capabilities of the operator; military establishments which are less experienced will require greater post-transfer support.

The experience of states denied such support is instructive. It is not uncommon for operators to experience marked declines in equipment serviceability levels following the loss of the support provided by arms suppliers. This was the case with Iran following the revolution of 1979 and the resulting loss of American support, and with Egypt following the deterioration of its relationship with the Soviet Union in the mid-1970s. The end of Soviet support for Egypt's air force resulted in a precipitous decline in levels of aircraft serviceability, leading President Anwar Sadat to lament that the lack of spares would soon result in its equipment being 'nothing but scrap' and to a desperate search for alternative sources of spares.[5] Interest in restoring access to spares for American-produced arms was sufficient to encourage Iranian officials to engage their American counterparts soon after the revolution, though political developments in Iran soon put an end to this.[6]

While this is to some extent a political issue, as this often results from deliberate intervention on the part of authorities in arms suppliers concerned to prevent the provision of support in the interest of national security or for some other reason, some states have a better reputation for post-transfer support for arms than others. This can contribute to the development of arms transfer relationships, potentially at the expense of relationships with states where post-transfer support falls short of a recipient's expectations. This consideration has a negative effect in the case of the United States, as the American government has a recognized track record of denying post-sales support for arms of American origin or which incorporate American components and sub-components in the pursuit of its policy agenda.[7] China also has a poor reputation for post-transfer support, but this stems from the shortcomings of Chinese high-technology industry.[8]

The potential for states to offset the loss of support from traditional suppliers may be quite limited. Other suppliers may find it difficult or impossible to provide crucial MRO services and to supply the replacement parts formerly available from the manufacturer. There is some scope from states where similar arms are produced under licence, but arms production licences may prohibit providing spares and support without the express approval of the OEM, if not the government of the state concerned. Rather greater potential lies in those states where arms reflect similar design influences. This may be the result of the licenced production of arms at one point or the design parentage of their arms. In the case of arms of Russian origin, China and the former Eastern European members of the WTO have some capacity to compensate for the loss of support. It was to China, India, and Yugoslavia, all of which operated Soviet arms of similar vintage and produced Soviet-designed arms, that the government of Egypt turned for support in maintaining its substantial inventory of Soviet arms in the 1970s, for example.[9] More recently, Pakistan turned to Russia as a source of components for the JF-17 Thunder fighter it co-produces with China.[10]

The difficulties involved in obtaining post-transfer arms support from alternate suppliers generally are far greater where advanced arms are concerned due to their technical specifications. Technical standards, including software standards, differ across states and firms and enterprises may design equipment to proprietary technical standards. This is manifest in compatibility issues between systems from different producers and the effort required to integrate components from different suppliers on platforms such as aircraft and naval vessels. Arms producers often strive to protect crucial technical details of their products from competitors. Firms and enterprises may be unwilling to release technical data that would enable other firms and enterprises to develop compatible systems. In this they may be supported by political authorities which seek to safeguard critical technologies in the interest of national security. This issue arose when Turkey announced its intention of purchasing SAMs of Russian or Chinese origin, as their integration with equipment of Western origin would require revealing key technical details of the latter.[11] Access to technical details is even more problematic where ownership of the intellectual property is held not by an arms supplier, but by a third party that is based in another state.[12] Deepening transnational R&D and production means that this is increasingly common. The complexity of this issue is demonstrated by the friction over access to intellectual property between the states that are collaboratively developing and producing the Joint Strike Fighter.[13]

The impact of technical factors is reinforced by technological trends. Diminishing intervals between the advent of successive generations of arms and the rising costs of defence-related R&D mean that even major military powers are retaining arms in service longer than previously was the norm. This generates significant obsolescence issues as states which seek to retain a qualitative military advantage are driven to modernize arms to keep them viable, in lieu of replacement. The capacity to perform 'mid-life' arms upgrades is not necessarily a monopoly of the original producer, but they have an inherent advantage in integrating new technologies into their designs. Technical specifications can render upgrading arms or replacing unsupportable components a difficult and expensive proposition where this is pursued without the support of the OEM. Modernization programmes often are pursued by or at least in collaboration with original arms suppliers as a result. This complicates efforts to compensate for a loss of support by turning to alternate suppliers, reinforcing ties with traditional arms suppliers.

The tendency to sustain distinct design approaches over time reinforces the impact of technical factors on arms transfer patterns. Design continuity is reinforced by states' operational requirements. National design predilections reflect doctrinal and organizational factors deriving from operational requirements, which themselves may reflect particular operational environments. China, for instance, has designed and produced tanks that are comparatively lighter than equivalent designs available from other suppliers. Models such as the Type 62 and its apparent successor, the Type 15, are optimized for service in regions of China where the terrain is unsuitable for tanks of conventional size and weight.[14] States' operational requirements may evolve over time but often they demonstrate considerable continuity.

The defence-industrial strengths of arms suppliers help to determine their export profiles. The focus of defence firms and enterprises in some states on meeting the particular requirements of a national defence establishment positions them to meet the demands of export customers with similar requirements. States which have demanding arms requirements are well positioned to meet the needs of other states with demanding requirements which are unable to produce arms to the standard required and yet possess to the means to afford such arms, for example. The example of China is instructive. Chinese arms designs offer reasonably advanced capabilities combined with robustness and are less demanding in their maintenance requirements. Chinese arms costs also are competitive compared to the offerings of many suppliers. The cost advantages of Chinese arms are reinforced by the willingness of the government to provide credit and flexible terms to export customers.[15] These features render Chinese arms particularly attractive to states with quantitative and qualitative requirements that cannot readily be met by other arms suppliers due to their resource constraints.

Some suppliers occupy distinct niches in the international arms transfer system by virtue of their defence-industrial strengths. Their positions might derive from 'niche technologies' which particular firms or enterprises are uniquely equipped to supply. This might enable states to effectively meet the needs of particular sections of the arms market, providing a basis for sustained arms transfer relationships. As well as that of China noted above, examples include Russia, whose recognized expertise in ground-based air defence systems has positioned it as a supplier of successive generations of SAMs and other air defence systems to states across the globe, Denmark, which is prominent in the field of airborne countermeasures systems, and Germany, which effectively has dominated the post-Cold War international market for conventional submarines through direct sales and licensed production in states such as Indonesia and South Korea. North Korea is another important example. In addition to its role as a supplier to states which traditionally have operated arms of Soviet design, it now occupies an important niche as a supplier of ballistic missiles.[16]

The position of a supplier may reflect a general sectoral strength or may be based on the reputation of its industry. Particular firms and enterprises are well respected for their signature products and have established themselves as suppliers over an extended period of time to a large customer base. The superiority of Mauser's rifle design in the late-nineteenth to mid-twentieth century was such that at some point more than half of all states were equipped with Mauser rifles, with an estimated total of 100 million produced worldwide.[17] Many states purchased successive models of Mauser rifles. To the extent to which the dominance of an individual firm, enterprise, or national industry endures, this can provide the basis for follow-on orders.

The role of defence-industrial support considerations in defining arms transfer patterns has increased with the expansion of arms development and production in emerging arms producers. As noted in the previous chapter, support in the form of components, sub-components, and technologies generally is crucial to defence-industrial programmes in these states. This generally strengthens arms transfer patterns deriving from other considerations. The capacity and willingness to support defence-industrial programmes reinforces the importance of suppliers which are able to supply arms that meet a state's requirements; only occasionally does this represent the principal consideration in procurement decision making. This can be a deciding factor in choosing between rival bids which otherwise are quite strong.

Some suppliers are stronger in this respect than others. This reflects established attitudes toward the provision of defence-industrial support and the depth of security concern over technological diffusion as much as their defence-industrial capabilities. Russia has demonstrated little interest in providing defence-industrial support other than where key allies and customers are concerned. India stands out as the most notable recipient of Russian defence-industrial support following the Cold War. Defence-industrial ties with the United States, for its part, are appealing due to the capacity of American industry to provide support, but security-driven American technology controls can limit the scope for this. The capacity to provide defence-industrial support tends to reinforce arms transfer relationships with Western European arms suppliers. Industry in these states generally is both highly competent and relatively open to providing support on a sustained basis, though important differences between states remain. The relative ease of manufacture of Chinese arms has much to recommend China as a source of defence-industrial support, but Chinese industry has been slow to develop this potential and enduring quality control issues in Chinese high-technology industry undermine its attractiveness in this role.

The competitive climate of the international arms market has a major influence on the impact of supplier strengths on arms transfer patterns. Some sections of the arms market are comparatively saturated, providing importers with greater freedom of choice, while other product areas are far less competitive, strengthening the position of national industries or individual firms and enterprises that have developed relevant expertise. Maintaining a market position that sustains arms transfer relationships can be quite difficult but is particularly so in environments where the presence of many competitors produces forces suppliers to go to great lengths to meet the requirements of prospective customers. Technological frontiers may advance at a rapid pace in such an environment, complicating efforts by leading firms and enterprises to maintain their market position. The extent to which suppliers can dominate particular sections of the international arms market does not necessarily endure indefinitely.

Supplier states also may occupy a particular position in the international arms transfer system by virtue of their general attributes. This includes their official approach to arms transfers. The official position on arms transfers can provide a foundation for continuing arms transfer relationships and thus arms transfer patterns. Political authorities in some states are far more proactive in their pursuit of economic or security objectives through arms exports than others. This may extend to openness to offering expedited delivery of arms as an incentive to prospective customers. Such a capability may stem from industrial over-capacity, the capacity of the state to direct industry to meet particular export requirements, or willingness to relinquish delivery positions for arms that are on order. The capacity to meet short delivery timescales renders such suppliers attractive to states which have pressing requirements. This is an important attribute to states in regions characterized by heightened tension such as the Middle East. Even where pressing requirements are not a factor driving arms procurements, this can reinforce established supplier/recipient relationships.

Flexibility in payment terms also can influence arms transfer patterns. Some suppliers are prepared to offer financial incentives such as extended or otherwise highly advantageous credit terms to secure export customers. Other suppliers are more open to countertrade as a basis for supplying arms. Flexibility helps to account for Russia's continuing importance as an arms supplier to states which following the end of the Cold War have had access to arms supplies from Western sources. Indeed, Russia established arms transfer relationships with new customers, many of which are states of the Global South, on the strength of this feature. Such suppliers are better positioned to meet the requirements of developing states, which generally face greater difficulties in affording imports of advanced arms.

Another important supplier attribute is that of discretion. Avoiding publicizing the quantities of arms supplied, delivery timetables, or the fact that they are being supplied at all can be important to recipients for reasons of national security or to avoid aggravating relations with neighbouring states. This often is particularly important in times of conflict, but some states seek to obscure their defence development programmes as a matter of course. It is possible for customers to insist on non-disclosure clauses in arms contracts, but this is not always effective. Some suppliers have a reputation for discretion. Israeli firms and enterprises, for example, often do not publicly identify their customers. Some suppliers are not in a position to meet customer expectations for discretion due to the level of transparency inherent in their arms export processes. The oversight role of Congress in the United States, which requires notifying it of proposed exports over a certain threshold, makes it difficult for the American government to meet the expectations of some states in this respect.

Also important is the extent to which internal arms transfer norms influence export decision making. As is discussed in much greater detail in Chapter 7, this varies greatly. Some suppliers are distinguished by their more discriminating approach to arms exports. They are more inclined to consider issues such as the human rights records and what they determine to be the legitimate requirements of prospective customers in reaching export decisions. As well as resulting in fewer arms exports by the Western liberal democracies than otherwise would be the case, this often serves to reinforce the tendency to export to states with which Western states enjoy relatively close political relations. Closely associated with this is the issue of political conditionality. Western states are more inclined to impose conditions on the supply of arms. This might involve where arms are deployed and how they are operated.

Other suppliers are far less inclined to allow considerations of the uses to which arms are likely to be put or prospective customers' human rights records to preclude arms transfers, or to abide by international arms embargoes. Coincidentally, several states where arms export decision making is relatively unencumbered by expectations of recipient behaviour or international arms transfer norms, and which are less concerned with the impact of arms exports, are also quite flexible in terms of payment options. This can serve to reinforce arms transfer relationships with states that find it difficult to obtain arms from other suppliers. The absence of conditionality is contributing to the success of emerging arms suppliers such as North Korea, just as it was for China at an earlier point in time.

There is a particular sub-set of these arms suppliers that is important to note. These states are the 'suppliers of last resort'. These are distinguished by their apparently apolitical—if not amoral—approach to the supply of arms. These suppliers are the subject of considerable concern and notoriety as a result of their perceived role in fuelling intra- and interstate conflict and their capacity to enable states which are the subject of arms embargoes to receive arms regardless of such restrictions. This is a role that often has been filled by 'pariah states', which are less bound by prevailing norms and themselves have limited access to the international arms market. Germany, for example, provided crucial arms support for fellow international pariah the Soviet Union during the interwar period.[18] Other states have filled this role in the postwar period. For some time, China had a reputation as an indiscriminate supplier of arms. It occupied a unique niche as a supplier to authoritarian regimes that were unable to obtain arms elsewhere.[19] States such as North Korea and Iran feature as suppliers of last resort at the present time. Both play prominent roles in exporting arms to pariah states and to NSAGs, particularly in the Middle East.[20] Both also are supplying arms to Russia following its invasion of Ukraine. In a curious reversal of roles, Russia reportedly has sought to pay for North Korean arms through countertrade arrangements.[21]

It is difficult to generalize as states' defence-industrial profiles can be quite complex and national capabilities can vary greatly between categories of arms, but some illustrative examples of the contribution of supplier attributes to arms transfer relationships are provided in Table 6.1.

The effects of technical features and the general attributes of arms suppliers are reinforced by historical ties between suppliers and customers. There are a number of long-standing arms supply relationships which have seen particular arms producers assume an important role in equipping particular states. The established role of a supplier in meeting the needs of a state reflects satisfaction with the performance of the arms provided and the terms under which they are provided and suggests a high degree of confidence that this will remain the case. These relationships can be general in nature or can be specific

**Table 6.1: Supplier Attributes and Interstate Arms Transfer Relationships**

| Arms Exporter | Exporter's Attributes | Recipient |
|---|---|---|
| China | Reasonably advanced, moderately priced arms available for delivery on relatively short notice with no political conditionality | Pakistan |
| Russia | Advanced, robust, moderately priced arms with no political conditionality | India |
| United Kingdom | Advanced arms, with support for direct and indirect military offsets | Saudi Arabia |
| United States | Advanced arms, with the cost offset through military assistance | Israel |

to particular categories of arms. India, for example, has relied on the Soviet Union and Russia for armoured vehicle imports for decades while relying on Western, particularly European, suppliers for combat aircraft as well as the Soviet Union and Russia.

Where arms transfer relationships are between states that share a close security relationship, this often serves to reinforce the relationship. As well as the general security benefits deriving from supporting allied and friendly states, significant procurement, logistical, and operational advantages derive from operating similar models of arms. The extended production runs resulting from additional orders produce economies of scale offering cost benefits to both suppliers and recipients, the interoperability of arms facilitates the support of arms over their service life, and operational synergies facilitate joint operations. This potential is widely recognized by arms suppliers and recipients alike. Since the 1950s the American government has promoted production, procurement, and 'cooperative logistics' efficiencies through equipment standardization with allied states, for example.[22] The United States encourages key states, such as India, to sign Logistics Support Agreements (LSAs) which provide a basis for the cross-servicing of common types of arms.[23] Under the *Capacité Motorisée* agreement signed in 2018 the French and Belgian governments committed to equipping their armies with the same equipment and systems.[24] The benefits stemming from standardization also encourage procurement of successive generations of arms, contributing to the development of arms transfer patterns.

Arms supply relationships often are an important facet of patron/client relationships. As discussed in Chapter 2 of this study, security imperatives can lead states to provide arms on favourable terms to other states as part of military assistance programmes. While in some cases the provision of support is short term, intended to address specific pressing security threats, in others this is more long term in nature, with the supply of arms on a sustained basis. Such a level of commitment on the part of an arms supplier often reflects a close political relationship of long standing and the recognition of common interests, such as countering the threat posed by a particular rival. This helps to explain China's position as a supplier of arms to Pakistan since 1966.[25] Former colonial powers fulfil such a role in some cases. This is demonstrated by France's position as an arms supplier to its former Sub-Saharan African colonies. Not only did France provide these states with their initial fleets of aircraft upon independence, but often it continued to supply aircraft long afterwards. The provision of arms by sponsor states reached new heights during the Cold War. This practice was characteristic of major powers and their principal allies during this period. This was readily apparent in the Middle East, where states could anticipate rapid replacement of arms lost during conflicts as a result.[26] This also provided an opportunity for qualitative improvement as the arms supplied often were more advanced that those that had been lost in combat. Heightened strategic competition suggests that the importance of defence support relationships is likely to increase.

Close security ties increase the likelihood that states will be influenced by their suppliers as to how they organize and equip their defence establishments. This often extends to following their lead in matters of operational doctrine, including doctrinal innovations associated with technical advances. The defence establishments of supplier states often serve as developmental models, encouraging the adoption of similar types of arms. The defence establishments of recipient states often mirror those of their suppliers in important respects as a result. This effect can help to sustain arms transfer patterns even in the absence of ongoing military assistance.

Continued reliance on specific suppliers also is encouraged by the economic advantages conferred by security ties. The willingness of states to supply arms as a form of military assistance, at no or substantially reduced cost offers particular advantages to states which have limited means with which to procure arms. This can lead to states acquiring arms based on what suppliers are prepared to offer rather than those which best meet their operational requirements, however. This was demonstrated during the Cold War by the number of Soviet-supported developing states that procured air defence systems of limited utility given their security situations. More generally, this is manifest in the procurement of obsolescent or obsolete arms which the supplier is phasing out of service.

While there can be considerable continuity in arms supply relationships, arms transfer patterns can shift over time. Patterns, once established, are contingent upon a range of factors in both supplier and recipient states and can be influenced by developments in either. A key factor is continued interest on the part of political authorities. The importance of security interests in arms transfer relationships means that they are particularly sensitive to changes in the security environment and political shifts such as regime change in supplier or recipient states. This may encourage political authorities to reconsider drawing on traditional arms suppliers. This was the case with North Korea, which shifted from relying on the Soviet Union to China for arms in the late 1960s due to cooling relations with the former.[27]

Economic interests also can have this effect. Immediately following the Six-Day War in 1967, France ceased providing arms to Israel. This represented a major watershed for French policy as it previously had been Israel's principal arms supplier. It appears that France's decision was driven by economic considerations in the form of the prospect of more lucrative arms sales to Arab states.[28] The imposition of sanctions or the use of arms transfer relationships as a means of leverage also can prompt significant shifts in arms transfer patterns. France supplanted the United Kingdom as the principal arms supplier to South Africa after it imposed an arms embargo in 1963, for example.[29]

Shifts in arms transfer patterns may represent a form of political signalling. This may occur after political authorities have failed in their efforts to effect policy change in a supplier state by other means, for instance, or where they are intent on distancing themselves from the supplier. States may choose to demonstrate their independence from traditional suppliers by seeking out alternative sources of supply, as Saudi Arabia did from the United States in ordering ballistic missiles from China.[30] In some cases states diversify their arms suppliers as a means of avoiding over-reliance and vulnerability to a single supplier. This can affect the full range of arms transfers from a particular supplier or may be limited to a particular procurement, producing distinct arms transfer patterns for different equipment categories.

Arms import patterns also can be disrupted by conflict situations or pressing security threats that compel suppliers to prioritize their own needs over exports, forcing recipients to search out new sources of supply. This has been the experience of some established customers of Russia following the outbreak of the Russo-Ukrainian War.[31] Arms are at a premium during times of international conflict, particularly where conflict is protracted or widespread, limiting the options for states which depend on arms imports. Pressing operational requirements such as those stemming from the need to address unforeseen capability gaps may require the procurement of non-standard arms from non-traditional suppliers. The services of 'merchants of death' such as Zaharoff were in such high demand in part because of their capacity to meet the demands generated by conflict situations at short notice.

New arms transfer patterns also emerge through the loss of access to established sources of arms. States which are experiencing acute procurement difficulties have little recourse but to turn to alternate suppliers. This most often occurs where states are unable to access traditional sources of arms as a result of the imposition of formal or informal sanctions or embargoes by the broader international community. States' new sources of supply may lie outside of the mainstream of the international arms market and may be 'suppliers of last resort', as has been the case with some of the suppliers that Russia has turned to as a result of the industrial sanctions imposed in the wake of its invasion of Ukraine in 2022. This also may require the procurement of arms that otherwise would be considered unsuitable.

States also tend to be more open to considering the products of alternative suppliers where they are forced by circumstances such as unexpected peacetime attrition, the premature retirement of an equipment type from service, shortcomings in the arms procurement system, or setbacks in domestic arms programmes. Many states end up importing types of arms that they had unsuccessfully sought to develop and produce indigenously or which they need to replace on short notice. This can serve as a temporary expedient or can lay the foundation for new arms transfer patterns.

The demonstration of the effectiveness of arms under operational conditions also can produce a shift in arms transfer patterns. Conflicts serve as important proving grounds for arms, showcasing their capabilities to potential customers even more than operation under peacetime conditions. Mission-proven arms traditionally have been in high demand. This can be the case with a supplier's arms in general, a category of arms, or even a particular system. The Gulf War of 1990–91 provided several examples of this. The unexpected success of the American Patriot SAM against tactical ballistic missiles during that conflict paved the way for orders from a number of states, particularly in the Middle East, and the American use of Tomahawk cruise missiles in that conflict 'triggered global interest in obtaining cruise missiles'.[32] The 'Ukraine effect' stemming from the successful operation of arms by Ukraine in its war with Russia is informing arms requirements in Europe and beyond at the present time. There has been a spike in demand for combat UAVs such as the Turkish Bayraktar, rocket artillery such as the American High Mobility Artillery Rocket System (HIMARS), and ground-based air defence systems.[33] The poor performance of Russian arms in its war with Ukraine reportedly has led some established customers to reconsider purchases of Russian arms.[34]

While political authorities generally remain quite pragmatic in importing arms, the existence of an established arms transfer pattern does not necessarily preclude procurement outside of this pattern. State arsenals generally comprise arms from an eclectic list of suppliers. There is a crowded international marketplace for arms and arms related services that provides opportunities to draw on the offerings of numerous established and emerging suppliers; only exceptionally does a single arms producer dominate a particular category of arms to the extent that they constitute the only potential supplier. Some sections of the international arms market are more heavily competed than others, however. Some states are particularly flexible in the sense that they are willing to procure arms which are available simply because another customer was unable to take delivery. Such opportunistic exploitation was demonstrated by the number of states that reportedly expressed an interest in purchasing one or both of the Mistral-class amphibious assault ships that had been ordered from France by Russia, but which were blocked from sale in 2015.[35]

## General Arms Transfer Patterns

General patterns in the international supply of arms overlie national patterns. These are the product of broader trends and developments in the structure of the global defence-industrial landscape and in the international security environment. National and general trends have not developed in isolation from each other but the extent to which general arms transfer patterns affect individual states differs due to the varying influence of these trends and developments.

The international arms market is cyclical in the sense that periods of relative over-supply are followed by periods of relative under-supply. The state of the international security environment plays a key role in determining the general availability of arms through its effect of influencing both supply and demand. Periods of heightened international tension or major interstate conflict greatly increase the demand for arms. Where tension or conflict is protracted or widespread, this generally results in a contested arms market where there is significant competition for scarce arms supplies. In such an environment demand can far outstrip supply. This drives up the cost of arms and potentially forces states without access to arms supplies from state sponsors to accept arms that are ill-suited to their requirements, or which are obsolescent or obsolete, from whatever sources they can be obtained. This was demonstrated during the early stages of the Second World War, when many combatants were forced to accept arms of limited operational value, some of which dated from the First World War. Fortunately for the Allies the United States, which had not previously featured as a major arms supplier, was in a position to provide modern arms in quantity. Often states are forced to turn to new sources of arms. In this environment suppliers that are able to offer expedited delivery of arms have a particular advantage. This contrasts with the usual state of affairs where supply outstrips demand, producing an 'overheated' arms market where suppliers are forced to compete for export orders and customers can hope to negotiate more favourable terms.

The Russo-Ukrainian War has had an impact on arms transfer patterns that extends well beyond the combatants. This has produced a 'tight' arms market. This conflict is generating demand for arms in European and other states which are absorbing the lessons of the conflict and seeking to strengthen their military capabilities accordingly. This also is generating significant demand from states that have been donating arms to Ukraine. These states are backfilling their arms stockpiles, contributing to the 'sellers' market' where key categories of arms are concerned. This is reinforcing the importance of longstanding arms supply relationships with major suppliers such as the United States as states seek to replace the arms they have transferred.[36]

Where conflicts or heightened international tension involving major arms producers proves protracted, the arms supply situation may ease in time as production is stepped up to meet increased demand. That states will seek to increase production during wartime can be assumed. This was the case during the Second World War and marked the Cold War as well as the members of NATO, the WTO, and non-aligned states alike sought to meet heightened national and export demand for arms. The increase of production to the level necessary to satisfy demand ultimately results in a situation of over-supply following conclusion of the conflict or after international tensions have subsided.

The conflict-driven expansion of arms production often is achieved in part through establishing new production facilities which can have an impact on arms transfer patterns over the long term. During the Second World War the United States emerged as a key source of arms for Allied forces, including those of the United Kingdom and the Soviet Union, which themselves had greatly expanded production but were nonetheless unable to satisfy their arms requirements. The need to equip the expanding American defence establishment after the United States entered the conflict did not limit its capacity to supply arms to its allies in substantial quantities and the vastly expanded American production capacity provided the basis for its crucial postwar role as a supplier of arms on a commercial and state-to-state basis.

The international security environment also has a significant impact on arms transfer patterns through its capacity to generate competitive arms procurement in situations short of open conflict. This involves the phenomenon commonly referred to as an arms race. While there are some issues with the application of this concept, as discussed in Chapter 3, it does capture general procurement trends which have a significant impact on international arms transfer patterns. Arms races have a significant impact through their effect of generating heightened demand for arms. Central to many arms races is the drive to develop a military advantage in qualitative terms, though this is not invariably the case.[37] While heightened security concern often drives efforts to develop and produce more advanced arms, in many states the demand generated by the continuing quest for qualitative superiority can only be met through arms imports. Arms races have important consequences as well through their potential to generate or exacerbate local and regional instabilities, making interstate conflict more likely.[38] This can further increase international demand for arms.

The impact of arms racing on arms transfer patterns varies. The materiel requirements stemming from an arms race can reinforce established arms transfer patterns. This often proved the case with the Cold War due to the interest of major arms producing states in providing military assistance to allied and friendly states and the compatible interest of these states in reinforcing security relations with states in a position to provide defence support. There may be greater scope for the emergence of new arms transfer patterns where arms races are sustained, however, should this encourage increased defence production and the expansion of arms export capabilities. Where arms races arise as a result of specific events such as escalating tension over a territorial dispute, particularly where tension escalates rapidly, this also may be the effect. This is the case because political authorities may consider it necessary to procure arms on relatively short notice or in quantities beyond the capacity of established sources to supply, requiring them to turn to non-traditional suppliers.

The conclusion of an interstate conflict or a marked reduction in international tensions can produce an effect on the international arms market that is no less significant. The precipitous defence downsizing that generally accompanies the end of a major conflict produces an over-supply of arms. This often results from the release of substantial quantities of arms on the international market on short notice. The availability of large quantities of surplus arms which states are eager to dispose of as quickly as possible encourages making them available at modest cost or even for free on an 'as is, where is' basis. Arms might be transferred under military assistance programmes or released onto the open market. It is noteworthy that the emergence of the United States as a major international arms supplier was occasioned by the requirement to dispose of large quantities of surplus arms following the end of the Civil War in 1865.[39] The aftermath of the First and Second World Wars saw the transfer of huge quantities of surplus arms. It took the better part of a decade following the Second World War for the United States and the United Kingdom to give away most of their surplus arms.[40] More recently, the drawing down of American combat operations in Afghanistan after 2014 resulted in the transfer of some US$900 million in defence property.[41]

Post-conflict transitions can have a significant impact on the international diffusion of arms. The availability of significant quantities of surplus arms is very convenient for states engaged in post-conflict rearmament. States involved in a conflict may use the opportunity provided by its end to offset wartime losses, replace older equipment, and introduce new types of arms to fill capability gaps identified by the conflict. Many Western European states availed themselves of the opportunity to acquire modern American tanks in the years following the Second World War, for example. The attractiveness of the arms that are available following conflicts is not just a function of price and availability. Periods of conflict tend to generate accelerated defence technological progress. This particularly is the case with respect to more advanced arms categories such as combat aircraft. This may have the effect of rendering arms operated by states that were not parties to a conflict obsolescent or obsolete, providing a strong incentive to upgrade the local arsenal through the introduction of newer generations of equipment. In the wake of the First World War, for instance, the French government had to halt exports of the Renault FT tank, such was international demand for this groundbreaking vehicle.[42] This has contributed to the practice of 'cascading' discussed below and to the drive to acquire more advanced arms in many developing states following the Cold War.

This can affect arms transfer patterns in several respects. New arms transfer patterns can emerge from the efforts by states, some of which may not have previously figured as major arms exporters, to find customers for their surplus arms. Immediate post-conflict situations often are characterized by marked declines in arms production as a result of the ready availability of surplus arms.[43] This generates heightened competition for export sales as firms and enterprises seek to offset the loss of the wartime orders that they had developed the capacity to meet.

The defence-industrial trends accompanying the conclusion of a conflict can have a significant impact on arms transfer patterns in another important respect. The expansion of arms production resulting in the significant oversupply of arms noted above reduces the incentive for states to establish or maintain national defence-industrial capabilities in the aftermath of a conflict. This was the case with Argentina, for example, which decided not to proceed with a number of indigenous arms development and production programmes in the decade following the Second World War, including that for the Pulqui fighter, as this no longer made economic sense.[44] This can have the effect of reducing demand for components, sub-components, and technologies as well as creating conditions that discourage political authorities from pursuing courses of action that would contribute to the emergence of new arms exporters.

The example provided by the winding down and conclusion of the Cold War is instructive. This produced huge arms surpluses as the former NATO and WTO rivals reduced defence expenditures and their military establishments. Diminished tensions enabled these states to negotiate the Conventional Forces in Europe (CFE) Treaty in 1990, which resulted in the 'cascading' of arms within NATO as it used the requirement to reduce arms holdings as an opportunity to redistribute equipment to less well-equipped member states on highly favourable terms.[45] Such a trend did not materialize on the part of the states of the former WTO, however, though their disposal of arms accelerated following the collapse of the WTO. Severe reductions in defence establishments, reduced and cancelled arms orders, and defence-industrial over-capacity combined to release substantial quantities of arms onto the international market. The United States offered arms to many of its less-affluent NATO allies and other friendly states for free or at a nominal cost. While some of the arms released onto the international arms market by the members of NATO and the former members of the WTO were obsolescent or even obsolete, many were quite modern and represented a qualitative advance over those they replaced.

The post-Cold War 'buyer's market' produced by the glut of arms lasted until quite recently. This provided an opportunity for many states to replace older equipment types. This was as much the case with developed as well as developing states. This produced new arms transfer patterns in the process. The post-Cold War political realignment of states opened up new possibilities for some states as former arms transfer restrictions were relaxed or removed and states which previously were reluctant to procure arms from particular suppliers for political reasons now could do so with less concern. States with no previous or no recent history of importing arms from the Soviet Union ordered arms from Russia as it emerged as a serious competitor of Western firms in states that lay outside of its political orbit during the Cold War, for example. Despite this, many operators of Soviet arms continue to rely on Russia for arms and for the support of arms supplied during the Cold War. Significantly, several former members of the WTO which are now members of NATO remained reliant on Russian support of arms such as aircraft which they continued to operate. This demonstrates the strength of the arms transfer relationships generated by the support requirements of arms.

The impact of the end of the Cold War on arms transfer patterns where transfers of components, sub-components, and technologies are concerned generally was consistent with past precedent. There was less incentive to pursue costly and technically challenging defence R&D and production, and many ambitious arms programmes were abandoned. The emerging industrial states of East Asia constituted a notable exception to this trend. This reflected the strength of economic imperatives, which in many of these states continue to drive integrated programmes of defence- and civil-industrial development. East Asian states such as South Korea persisted with their efforts to develop their defence-industrial bases, supporting their development as arms suppliers.

The general effect of the end of the Cold War in reducing the incentives to pursue defence-industrial development, with its impact on arms transfers, has worn off. Recent years have seen a general upsurge in attention to defence-industrial development. This trend can be expected to continue as strategic competition between the United States and Russia and between the United States and China, not to mention other sets of international rivals, increases and as the general attractiveness of defence-industrial development grows. As well as generating increased arms imports in developed and emerging industrial states alike, this tension is undermining the consensus that has been crucial to efforts to strengthen the international arms transfer control regime. This issue is examined in the chapter that follows.

Intra-state conflicts also can result in the release of arms onto the international market, generating new international arms transfer patterns. This is the case where a conflict results in the loss of effective control over arms stocks by the state. The impact of this generally is distinct from that stemming from the deliberate post-conflict disposal of surplus arms stocks. The loss of state control often results in the uncontrolled diffusion of arms, which is most likely to be to the benefit of NSAGs and states that have limited access to arms on the mainstream market. The civil war in Libya which resulted in the collapse of the regime of Muammar Gaddafi in October 2011 released a flood of arms, including SALWs and man-portable SAMs, on to the illicit arms market. These have been trafficked throughout the Sahel region of Africa.[46] The conflict in former Yugoslavia in the 1990s similarly resulted in a sharp increase in weapons trafficking and there are concerns that this will be the case with Ukraine as well.[47]

Finally, it is important to bear in mind that there may be important regional arms transfer patterns. Not only can this suggest how arms transfers within the region in question may develop, but they can inform thinking about how arms transfers may develop in regions with similar environments. There can be significant regional variations in arms transfer patterns. Both regional security and defence-industrial trends can contribute to this. As noted above, arms races can be regional in scope, and the late- and post-Cold War 'cascading' of arms was specific to Western Europe. Some regions are characterized by distinct security dynamics and patterns of military modernization, generating distinct arms requirements. Arms transfer patterns are particularly complex in the Middle East, where the procurement or payment for arms by third parties is more prevalent than elsewhere. South America was characterized by a general pattern of defence modernization in the 1960s and 1970s that generated similar demands for combat aircraft that largely were met through the importation of Mirage fighters from France.[48]

Consideration of regional arms transfer patterns is instructive. The general pace of defence development in East Asia is accelerating, generating strong demand for advanced arms, including on the part of states whose defence establishments traditionally have been organized and equipped primarily for internal security roles. Several East Asian states are important arms producers, with the result that an increasing proportion of the demand for advanced arms is being met within the region, either indigenously or by other East Asian states. China now features as an important arms supplier for a number of Southeast Asian states, for example, while the importance of South Korea as an arms supplier is increasing. The development of arms production in East Asian states such as South Korea, Singapore, Indonesia, and Malaysia is generating growing demand for components, sub-components, and technologies, only some of which are being supplied from within the region. This contrasts with Sub-Saharan Africa, where military modernization also is accelerating but at a far slower pace and from a much lower starting point. While demand for advanced arms in this region is growing, modernization here is far less marked than in East Asia, and the significantly lower level of regional defence-industrial development results in substantially lower demand for components, sub-components, and technologies.[49] Little of the demand for arms in Sub-Saharan Africa can be met by regional producers. The arms requirements of African states largely are met by established arms suppliers.

## The Implications of Arms Transfer Patterns

Consideration of national and international arms transfer patterns can offer useful insights into national arms import decisions and regional trends, though they by no means are decisive with respect to either. While political authorities are quite pragmatic and there are a range of factors that can cause them to look beyond their traditional suppliers, arms transfers often are influenced by underlying factors. This helps to explain why some states procure arms from particular suppliers even when more effective or affordable alternatives are available or where they are dissatisfied with their performance as suppliers. The example of India is instructive. India long has relied heavily on the Soviet Union and now Russia for advanced arms such as combat aircraft, missile systems, and naval vessels. While India now is drawing more on the United States and other suppliers for advanced arms, these states have yet to supplant Russia despite the latter's poor post-Cold War record in terms of the serviceability and cost of the arms it has supplied to India.[50] India's dedication to Russia as a supplier is such that it has gone so far as to pay for the completion of the construction of naval vessels originally intended for the Russian navy so that it could then purchase or lease them from Russia.[51] Issues with the availability of Russian arms following its invasion of Ukraine and India's positive experience operating aircraft of American origin which it has procured in recent years may in time engender a shift in its reliance on Russia, however.

Arms transfer patterns can help to determine the prospects for new entrants to the international arms market. Established arms transfer patterns can limit the potential for new entrants, particularly where these are emerging suppliers without a strong reputation in their field. Emerging suppliers may need to outperform established suppliers in cost or qualitative terms or in their flexibility in meeting customer requirements if they are to secure export orders. The postwar record demonstrates the stability of established arms transfer patterns; there are relatively few examples of emerging suppliers displacing established suppliers on a sustained basis. Even Israel, which has attained considerable prominence in the international arms transfer system and now figures as an established supplier, largely focuses on the supply of particular categories of arms.

# 7 Managing the Conventional Arms Trade

Official attention to the issue of managing the international arms trade is of long standing. The security implications of the unrestrained diffusion of arms, particularly where this involves states that are regarded as potential or actual adversaries, and the potential advantages of controlling access to arms as a coercive instrument ensures that this will remain the case. Concern over the diffusion of categories of arms which are regarded as destabilizing, such as ballistic missiles and combat UAVs, contributes to this.[1] The level of official concern varies between states and can wax and wane over time, but the general importance of arms transfer control has increased over the course of the postwar period. Arms transfer control is episodic in the sense that initiatives often emerge in response to specific concerns. It can prove difficult to sustain arms transfer controls in the absence of a perceived threat as a result.

The nature of conventional arms transfer control has changed over time. Prior to the Second World War, controlling arms transfers was entirely the remit of individual states. States remain the basic unit of analysis for arms transfer control, but international collaboration is widespread and no longer limited to informal arrangements. Space does not permit even surveying the extensive network of overlapping multinational and multilateral initiatives that along with national initiatives constitute the global arms transfer control regime, but it is important to note that national and supranational measures are mutually supporting, and that the international regime for managing the arms trade has deepened over time.

There has been an important shift as well in the objective of arms transfer controls. Until relatively recently, arms transfer control was pursued with the intention of preventing altogether transfers of specific types of arms or transfers to particular states or NSAGs. While such efforts continue, particularly at the national level and through multinational arrangements, there now is strong emphasis on managing the diffusion of arms. This still commonly is framed in terms of arms control, however.

## Issues for Arms Transfer Control

Arms transfer control may be driven by interest in preventing or impeding defence capability development or as a means of exerting political leverage. It can involve a focus on arms transfers to or by a particular actor and on arms in general or on a particular category of arms. Both the requirements and prospects of transfer controls differ according to the objective and the subject of concern. Where the subject of arms transfer controls has established an indigenous capability to develop and produce arms, for example, it may be recognized as crucial to target the transfer of arms related components, sub-components, and technologies as well as complete systems.

The fact that concerned authorities in so many states struggle to control arms transfers testifies to the difficulty of the exercise. The difficulties inherent in effective arms transfer control are exacerbated by the often-fragmented nature of the policy landscape. In many states the substance of the items subject to control and the implications of export-control decisions encourage an interagency response involving bureaucratic actors with distinct, parochial interests. In the United States, this includes the Departments of State, Defense, and Commerce. American arms transfer controls are informed by multiple control lists, some of which are more restrictive than others. These include the United States Munitions List, the Militarily Critical Technologies List, and the Developing Science and Technologies List.[2] Restrictions on American arms exports may stem from bureaucratic, legislative, or executive actors. It was Congress, for example, that barred the American government from exporting the F-22 Raptor fighter.[3] The American government is required by law to inform Congress of any potential transfer of arms with a value of US$25 million or more, Congress having a review period of thirty days in which it can bar a proposed sale.[4] Congressional efforts to restrict exports may be motivated by national security concerns, economic concerns, or concern over the human rights records of prospective recipient states. In the United States, as elsewhere, there are interdepartmental arrangements for liaison and the coordination of arms export control efforts, but in practice policy coherence proves elusive.[5]

The pursuit of arms transfer control is complicated by the importance of arms transfers to suppliers and recipients alike. There is general international recognition of the right of states to export and import arms. The former was enshrined in the Convention Respecting the Laws and Customs of War on Land (commonly referred to as the Hague Convention of 1907), while in the interwar period the League of Nations affirmed the right of states to import arms.[6] Arms transfer controls may involve a trade-off between security and economic imperatives. In some states the same bureaucratic actors that are responsible for arms control also have a formal role in promoting arms exports. Tension between the economic and security demands of arms exports and the security demands driving arms transfer controls in many states is unlikely to abate.

Arms transfer control is complicated as well by deepening industrial globalization. This is having a significant impact on international flows of arms related components, sub-components, and technologies, as noted in this study. These items, particularly technologies, are relatively difficult to control. It is a challenge to maintain current technology control lists in an environment of rapid technological change and diffusion. This challenge is exacerbated by the extent to which the trade in production inputs is conducted on an intra-firm basis, rendering many transfers difficult to detect. The challenge posed by the scope for firms and enterprises to defy official policy in supplying arms and arms related production inputs is daunting. Effective oversight and regulation of transnational industrial processes is difficult, even where the state dominates the defence-industrial landscape. The Chinese government has struggled for some time to develop effective arms export controls, for example.

## Approaches to Arms Transfer Control

Arms transfer controls are by nature discriminatory. They reflect the unequal international distribution of defence-industrial resources and interest on the part of political authorities in states which are possessed of greater resources in limiting, if not counteracting, the levelling effect of arms transfers.

There are two general approaches to arms transfer control. Under the first, concerned authorities endeavour to impose controls on the proliferation of arms and arms related products under what David Cooper terms 'capability-denial'.[7] This approach can focus on arms control in qualitative or quantitative terms, or both, and can be applied to a category of arms in general or focus on transfers to a specific actor or group of actors. This approach is non-consensual in that it does not rely on the cooperation of potential recipients. Measures which are imposed by states that are in a position to supply arms, including through retransfer, are termed export or supply-side controls. Such an approach may reflect interest in employing arms transfer controls as an instrument of statecraft. During the Cold War, for example, Western states approached export controls as 'the economic arms of containment' against Eastern Bloc states.[8] The prospects for supply-side controls are greatest where the target has limited arms production capabilities and is not able to source arms from alternate suppliers.

The second approach to arms transfer control is consensual, with arms transfer control embraced by supplier and recipient states alike. This is characterized by arrangements under which states consent to abide by legally constructed norms regarding the supply and acquisition of particular categories of arms or against their possession altogether. This approach strives to be as comprehensive as possible in terms of participation. This approach is inequitable where it does not prevent states with the capability to develop and produce the arms in question from possessing them. It has been noted in developing states that even arms transfer controls that apply to developed industrial states discriminate in favour of these states as their extensive arms production capabilities leave them less dependent on arms imports.[9]

The norms which underpin arms transfer control regimes and which inform arms transfer narratives have evolved over time and are reinforced by application. Strengthening international norms are encouraging increased interstate collaboration on arms transfer controls. This is the case with respect to both general approaches outlined above. This trend is most readily apparent in terms of arms transfers to zones of conflict and to states where defence establishments serve as instruments of oppression. There is widespread recognition of the potential of arms transfers to exacerbate conflict situations and strengthening attention to the issue of limiting, if not preventing, the supply of arms to states which by virtue of their domestic or international behaviour are regarded as beyond the pale.[10] Particular concern is reserved for states that are sites of internal conflict. This trend is manifest in reluctance to supply arms to states engaged in conflict, with many states reluctant to provide 'offensive' arms to states at war, and some banning altogether the transfer of arms to combatants for the duration of a conflict. There is considerable elasticity in what are understood as 'conflict zones', however.

There is less international agreement over the control of arms transfers to what are referred to by some as 'rogue' states. These states have figured prominently in the arms transfer control efforts of some key suppliers in the post-Cold War period. This highlights the subjective nature of norms and their limitations as a basis for arms transfer control. The norms around the supply of arms to rogue states reflect perspectives that are by no means universal; they are contested by states that are not necessarily deeply committed to the cause of arms transfer control and by states which are situated outside of the arms control community altogether. The level of commitment long has been an issue for arms transfer controls. Some exporters are far more permissive than others and are prepared to disregard international norms concerning the supply of arms. This was the case with the UN arms embargo on South Africa, for example. While the French government publicly declared its support for the international arms embargo, South African production of French arms, with French assistance, continued without interruption.

The importance of interstate collaboration to arms transfer control is growing even while the adherence of some states which formally participate in multinational and multilateral arms control regimes remains problematic. Developing common ground where arms transfers are concerned remains an elusive objective. There are no comprehensive global or even regional standards on the arms trade, despite the UN Disarmament Commission adopting Guidelines for International Arms Transfers in 1996, and national perspectives on items that should be subject to control and to whom they should be controlled differ markedly.[11] Perspectives often are influenced by economic considerations, with states reluctant to jeopardize their arms exports. This tendency was strengthened by the precipitous decline in arms orders that accompanied the end of the Cold War. This greatly complicates the development of multilateral export-control lists.

Conventional arms transfer control benefits from the attention of civil society groups. Civil society has played a prominent role in promoting arms transfer controls in the postwar period. Civil society actors have helped to highlight the importance of arms transfer control, both in the context of specific states and more generally and have encouraged and supported national initiatives.[12] The non-governmental organizations (NGOs) active in this area may be driven by concern over human security or what they perceive as 'militarism'. Civil society actors are far more prominent and far more effective in some states than others, and it is important to note the existence of NGOs, as well as industry groups, that for various reasons oppose controls on the arms trade.[13] The potential for collaboration between political authorities and civil society groups on arms transfer control is greatest in those states that comprise the Global West. Civil society interest in arms transfer control generally increases in the wake of major international conflicts, as was the case following the Gulf War of 1990–91.

The global arms transfer control regime is highly fragmented, comprised of a patchwork of arrangements of varying scope. This is a product of the distinct requirements of the control of different types of arms and states' varying commitment to the control of transfers of different types of arms. National, multinational, and multilateral arms control regimes are highly complementary and between them address many facets of the international arms trade but remain works in progress as responsible authorities strive to manage arms transfer control in the complex environment produced by deepening transnational defence-industrial integration and the expanding ranks of the arms exporting states.

## National Arms Export Control Regimes

National arms export control regimes as these now are understood are a relatively recent phenomenon. It was only in 1933 that Belgium introduced the first comprehensive licensing requirement for arms exports, and even this did not apply to the retransfer of foreign-made arms.[14] Formal bans on the supply of particular types of arms or to particular states or regions, and rudimentary export-licensing regimes date back to at least the seventeenth century but were not notably effective.[15]

A general strengthening trend in national export controls has been evident for some time, but some states remain far more restrictive arms exporters than others. National arms export controls can address the types and standard of arms supplied, the quantities they are supplied in, and the states to which they are supplied. In some states, restrictive practices are the product of domestic political considerations, with political authorities influenced by public expectations about what types of arms should be made available to which states. The strongest set of self-imposed restrictions were those enshrined in the 'Three Principles' policy introduced by Japan in 1967, which effectively banned arms exports. These restrictions only began to be relaxed in 2011, although exceptions previously had been made on a case-by-case basis and restrictions had not been stringently applied where dual-use equipment was involved.[16]

The principal concern underlying export controls in most states is to ensure that arms exports do not undermine national security. States may impose restrictions in response to specific sets of circumstances or in the pursuit of particular security objectives. Restrictions, which may be intended to be temporary, are approached as a means of limiting or undermining the military capabilities or compelling policy change on the part of another state. This may be pursued to counter the threat posed by a politico-military rival or to encourage an end to a conflict, for instance. Restrictions also may be imposed on states engaged in internal or international conflicts which have resulted in significant civilian casualties. Many states have been sanctioned for this reason in the postwar period. Notable examples include the sanctions imposed on China by the United States and the EU following the Tiananmen Square Incident and those imposed as a result of concern over the civilian toll from the fighting in Yemen. Several European states have restricted or banned altogether arms transfers to Saudi Arabia and other Gulf states involved in this conflict, in some cases going so far as to suspend export licences and prohibit the delivery of arms which was underway.[17]

Though often approached as a short-term measure, arms transfer restrictions may be maintained for some time. Sanctions introduced in response to specific situations may be continued if the subject remains a source of concern, for example. American controls on the export of strategic goods to China, which were occasioned by its entry into the Korean War, lasted for decades, and were only gradually relaxed following the 'normalization' of Sino-American relations.[18] The arms embargoes imposed on Iran and North Korea by various states similarly have proven enduring.

National arms transfer controls may target the firms, enterprises, and even individuals involved in the supply of arms as well as states. This reflects recognition of the important role of sub-state actors and their relative independence, as well as interest in many cases in preserving important economic or political relationships. Targeted sanctions are an established feature of American arms transfer controls. The American government has applied targeted sanctions in an effort to limit Russia's arms production capacity following the outbreak of the Russo-Ukrainian War. More than 4,000 commercial entities and individuals, including a number of Iranian firms supplying UAVs to Russia, have been sanctioned by the United States since 2022.[19] Targeted arms transfer controls also are approached as a means of changing state behaviour. Chinese sanctions on American firms supplying arms to Taiwan supplement long-standing efforts to persuade the American government to ban arms exports to Taiwan.[20] China's importance as a market provides it with considerable leverage over offshore industry.

There are a number of characteristic features of national arms export controls. Arms export decision making in many states is informed by guidelines on which states may receive arms. When Japan formally abolished its ban on arms exports in April 2014, for example, it supplanted the original Three Principles with the Three Principles on Transfer of Defense Equipment and Technology.[21] Other states adopt more flexible approaches that facilitate satisfying policy requirements as they emerge. Determination of which states may receive arms often is informed by considerations of the security implications of their transfer. Arms exporters commonly discriminate to some extent between states which are allies or with which they otherwise enjoy close political and security relations and those with which they do not. The former may qualify for streamlined export approval processes while other states may be subject to quite stringent processes or be barred from receiving arms entirely.

Relevant authorities in many states develop lists of arms that are subject to control, as a means of informing export decisions and licensing requirements. Control lists may be quite detailed and encompass arms related technologies and services. Some states distinguish between 'lethal' and 'non-lethal' arms in making arms export decisions, with the latter subject to far less stringent controls. 'Non-lethal' arms might include equipment such as transport vehicles and cargo aircraft. This distinction facilitates export decision making, with non-lethal arms potentially available to a much broader range of customers with fewer restrictions. Typically, the regulation of arms exports includes a formal process for the review of export requests.

Controls on arms transfers may extend to ensuring that they are not retransferred without permission. There is significant concern over the transit-country trade with sanctioned states. The retransfer of arms without the permission of the original supplier represents a challenge for arms control. Many states require that prospective customers submit end-use certification to confirm that they are the ultimate operators of the arms which they seek to procure. Some suppliers take this a step further by imposing post-transfer controls. This can involve making the supply of arms conditional on the recipient committing to no onward retransfer without the prior approval of the supplier, including when the arms are phased out of service. Many of these suppliers are prepared to deny states permission to retransfer arms. The United States is prominent in endeavouring to ensure that recipients do not retransfer the arms it supplies without its permission. It traditionally has retained retransfer authority, with a veto on onward transfers of arms of American origin.

Some states reinforce their export controls by providing for verification measures to deter retransfers. The United States is noteworthy for this approach. The American government negotiates post-delivery monitoring where it has particular concerns. American efforts focus on advanced arms embodying sensitive technologies. As well as the comprehensive Golden Sentry end-use monitoring programme, the United States has more specialized arrangements.[22] It can make the transfer of arms conditional on signing an End-Use Monitoring Agreement (EUMA) or an End-Use Verification Agreement (EUVA), which permit post-delivery American checks on arms. The intrusiveness of these arrangements can serve as an impediment to arms sales. India only signed an EUMA covering the purchase of American aircraft following two years of negotiations, and only after the United States agreed to allow India to determine the time and location of American verification inspections.[23] The American government also may exercise third-party 'shutter control' on advanced technologies by requiring arms recipients to sign Technology Safeguard Agreements (TSAs), which prevent unauthorized access to protected technologies as well as their retransfer to third parties.[24]

Post-transfer monitoring also is pursued as a means of preventing the retransfer of arms by NSAGs. The American government has been notable for tracking arms supplied to states and NSAGs in conflict zones. Concerned about the implications of American-supplied arms being turned against a fellow member of NATO, it has sought to ensure that arms supplied to Syrian

Kurdish forces are not transferred to Kurdish groups fighting the Turkish government. It does this by maintaining a database of the arms its supplies and the Kurdish commanders to which they are being supplied.[25] American personnel have been inspecting stocks of arms supplied to Ukraine following the outbreak of the Russo-Ukrainian War, out of concern for the potential of captured arms to be retransferred by 'pro-Russian forces'.[26]

Effective arms transfer controls can entail a high cost. Restrictive transfer controls can have a negative impact on arms exports and arms production and development, including by severely limiting interfirm and interstate arms collaboration. Restrictions can lead to tensions with other producers, which may respond by ensuring that the arms they develop and produce do not contain components, sub-components, or technologies that are subject to restrictions. This drives a number of producers to develop product versions that are free of American input in order to ensure that they will be able to compete for export orders, for example.[27] As well as potentially costing the United States important export opportunities for complete arms, American determination to control the diffusion of its arms limits exports of components and sub-components. This also renders some foreign defence firms reluctant to collaborate with American industry. This has greatly complicated collaborative R&D on the Joint Strike Fighter, for instance.[28]

The integrity of national arms transfer controls is a subject of enduring concern. The efficacy of national arms control regimes varies. Political authorities in some states are less invested in arms transfer control than others and their application of export controls can be ineffective. Arms exports to conflict zones such as Bosnia in the early 1990s were facilitated by the weak export-control regimes of states such as Russia, for example.[29] In some states this is the product of ineffective oversight of the defence-industrial sector. State oversight capacity may be limited by the lack of accountability of private firms or even state-owned enterprises. In other cases, official inattention is to blame. The fact that attention to arms transfer control in many states is episodic, driven by concern over specific threats, means that export controls may be applied with less diligence where there is no clear threat. The effectiveness of arms transfer controls also may suffer as a result of the parochial interests of bureaucratic actors which have an interest in ensuring that arms are exported. These are crucial issues for arms transfer control as the implementation of controls primarily remains a national responsibility.

Export controls are not necessarily always applied consistently even in states where political authorities are deeply committed to arms transfer control. Arms transfer controls most often suffer where security or economic considerations encourage political authorities to relax restrictions. The pressure to export arms can be considerable, even in states which are not economically dependent on arms exports. Political authorities in some states respond to this pressure by disregarding their formal standard of arms export control on a selective basis. This can take the form of regulating industry less closely or rendering arms transfers deniable by sanctioning the supply of arms through third parties or offshore subsidiaries. The disparity between formal policy and actual practice can be quite marked at times, even in states that traditionally have strongly supported the rules-based international order.

The United States is conspicuous as the state where arms transfer control has been the subject of the greatest sustained attention in the postwar period. This is manifest in vigorous policy debate over export controls and in the development of a comprehensive arms export control framework. American authorities strive to ensure that sub-state actors adhere to export guidelines and generally act decisively where there are indications that a firm or an individual has not. The focus of American attention has shifted over time in concert with security requirements. During the Cold War, American authorities were particularly concerned about the 'technology trade' to the Eastern Bloc, including transfers of components and sub-components and arms transfers to states such as China. The post-Cold War focus has been less clearly defined. There is increasing concern over China, to the point where this now represents the principal target of American arms transfer control efforts. There is strong concern at this time as well over Iran, North Korea, and Russia, demonstrated by determined American efforts to encourage other states to implement or strengthen arms transfer controls. The Russo-Ukrainian War has prompted close attention to the sophisticated Russian procurement networks which are supplying it with crucial production inputs and technologies, and on Iranian firms producing UAVs for Russia.[30]

Arms transfer control efforts face daunting challenges as a result of the transformation of the defence-industrial landscape. Transnational defence-industrial ties have considerable potential to render national arms export control regimes highly porous. Interfirm collaboration in arms R&D and production of arms generally entails the transfer of sensitive technical data as well as components and sub-components to capability partners, including any that are based offshore. Firms and enterprises may transfer items of concern without regard for national export guidelines. The requirement to address concerns arising from transnational industrial ties was prefigured by late Cold War developments, when the American government was compelled to sanction the Japanese firm Toshiba and the Norwegian firm Kongsberg for transferring advanced arms production equipment to the Soviet Union, in what became known as the 'Toshiba Affair'.[31]

Political authorities in many states, including the United States, seek to address their concerns over interfirm collaboration in a manner which is sensitive to the needs of domestic industry. This approach, which requires dealing with collaboration on a case-by-case basis, reflects recognition of the importance of transnational collaboration to firms and enterprises; there is concern over the potential impact of arms transfer controls on their competitiveness. Individual firms engaged in breaching sanctions are disciplined, but rather than imposing heavy fines and custodial sentences, the emphasis often is on moderate penalties and ensuring that firms take remedial action to ensure future compliance.[32] This often contrasts with the approach taken where foreign firms and enterprises are concerned. The American approach in such cases often is quite robust, for example, as demonstrated by the targeted sanctions on Chinese firms and enterprises supplying critical items to countries of concern.[33]

Interstate collaboration on arms transfer control has become more crucial and more complex as industrial globalization has deepened. Collaboration is important to effective industrial oversight and governance in an environment of transnational industrial integration. Transnational industrial processes by definition involve participants in more than one state and intra-firm activities in particular are difficult to identify and manage. Collaboration is complicated by potential conflicts of interest. States may be reluctant to limit their arms export prospects by cooperating with the arms control initiatives of other states, particularly where the recipient is not regarded as posing a significant threat to its interests. American authorities long have encouraged their counterparts to exercise arms transfer restraint in cases of particular concern, with varying success. In 1985, the United States reportedly prevailed on Israel to not supply A-4 Skyhawk strike aircraft to Argentina at the request of the British government.[34] In the wake of the outbreak of the Russo-Ukrainian

War, the United States has sought to discourage China from supplying arms to Russia.[35]

The United States is in a strong position to influence states to exercise restraint in supplying arms due to its willingness to exploit the leverage provided by the importance of production inputs of American origin and the importance of American arms programmes. In 2004 the United States suspended Israel's participation in the development programme for the Joint Strike Fighter in response to its use of American-supplied technology to upgrade UAVs Israel had previously supplied to China. In 2005, following the crisis in relations with the United States resulting from its arms exports to China, Israel agreed to consult with the United States where exports of 'sensitive' arms were involved.[36] The strength of American opposition to arms sales to China led Israel, which is dependent on the United States for advanced arms, to refuse Chinese requests to purchase arms after that point.[37]

The importance of arms transfer control as an instrument of statecraft is growing. American authorities, for example, are exploiting the potential of arms transfer control as a means of undermining the capacity of other arms suppliers to profit from arms exports. A notable example is the Countering America's Adversaries Through Sanctions Act (CAATSA) that was introduced in 2017. This initiative, which targets Russia, Iran, and North Korea, provides for punitive sanctions on states that procure arms from these suppliers and on financial institutions which facilitate their arms exports. The strong focus on Russian arms exports that is evident at this point likely reflects the more limited scope for sanctioning states that are procuring arms from Iran and North Korea. Though it has had some successes, the impact of the Act has been less than intended. In part this is because Russia and customer states such as China and India have developed means of payment that avoid banking institutions that are subject to American sanctions, and in part because of the granting of waivers by the United States.[38]

The difficulties experienced by concerned authorities in controlling arms transfers, even with formal and informal cooperation with like-minded states and the exercise of arms transfer control remotely through the extraterritorial application of some transfer controls, demonstrate the limitations of national arms transfer controls. This has helped to drive efforts to strengthen institutional norms and institutionalized arrangements that formalize and legitimate arms transfer control by securing some degree of commitment on the part of states parties.

## Multinational Arms Transfer Control

Multinational arms control mechanisms represent a rational step for political authorities which recognize the limitations of national arms transfer controls. While multilateral arms control, which is discussed in the following section, offers greater potential as a solution to the problem posed by the limited capacity of individual states to control developments and processes that are situated entirely or in part in other states, multilateral arms control mechanisms generally prove much more difficult to establish and sustain. Multinational arms control represents acceptance of the need to extend the scope of arms control and recognition of the more limited prospects for developing multilateral mechanisms.

Multinational regimes offer the prospect of strengthening controls on arms transfers where securing broad international agreement is likely to prove elusive, either in terms of the target of controls or the intended approach. Multinational arms transfer control initiatives typically are developed to address concerns arising in the context of specific cases and arising out of specific sets of conditions. Multinational initiatives often emerge in response to international conflicts but may be prompted by internal conflicts. Examples include the Arms Embargo Agreement on transfers to China agreed by a number of states in 1919 in response to the civil war there and the embargo on arms transfers to Bolivia and Paraguay imposed in 1934 after evidence emerged of atrocities committed in the fighting over the disputed Gran Chaco territory.[39] Multinational initiatives can be formal or informal in nature, but informal regimes are far more common than is the case with multilateral initiatives. Where arrangements are informal, generally this involves measures that are more robust than bilateral coordination. Like their multilateral counterparts, multinational regimes serve as key means of strengthening norms and setting codes of conduct.

Multinational arms control regimes are distinguished from multilateral regimes by the scope of their membership. Multinational regimes reflect the interests of a relatively limited group of states. These 'coalitions of the willing' are comprised of states that have common cause in thwarting efforts by particular states or NSAGs to acquire arms, to prevent the proliferation of a particular category of arms, or to relieve an international conflict by denying arms to the combatants. The nature of the case is such that it may be difficult to secure broad international support and there may be only limited interest in extending the circle of participants. The Proliferation Security Initiative (PSI), for instance, was launched by the United States in 2003 as means of interdicting transfers of WMDs and delivery systems such as ballistic missiles. The PSI's focus on the interdiction of arms shipments restricted its membership base. International support for the Initiative expanded over time in concert with increasing recognition of the need for such an instrument, however.

Collaboration can prove a daunting exercise even where there is common ground as to the arms to be controlled and the states to which controls should be applied. In 1951, for example, France, the United Kingdom, and the United States signed the Tripartite Declaration Regarding Security in the Near East restricting arms transfers in an effort to prevent an arms race between Israel and its Arab neighbours, but by 1953 this had been violated.[40]

## Multilateral Arms Transfer Control

As is the case with multinational arms control, multilateral arms control is a relatively recent phenomenon. The early focus was on restricting the trade in firearms to native groups in Africa. The Brussels Treaty of 1890 banned the sale of more advanced breechloading firearms in a large section of the continent while permitting the sale of less effective smoothbore muskets.[41] This initiative represented a major advance on previous understandings to control arms transfers to native groups in Africa and the Americas, which did not require formal commitments and lacked broad international support.[42]

Multilateral arms control mechanisms are distinguished from multinational mechanisms by their broader, more inclusive, and equitable membership basis. Multilateral arms transfer controls may be influenced but are not dominated by a single state. Multilateralism offers considerable promise in controlling arms transfers to particular target states as well as more generally. This is demonstrated by the UN's role in imposing mandatory arms embargoes, which command considerable authority in the international system and encourage the strengthening of national arms transfer controls. The frameworks provided by multilateral arrangements greatly strengthen efforts to control arms transfers over the long term. See Table 7.1 for a list of mandatory UN state arms embargoes.

Table 7.1: Mandatory United Nations State Arms Embargoes[43]

| State | Date Implemented | Date Suspended, Lifted, or Refocused on Non-Governmental Forces |
|---|---|---|
| Afghanistan | 2000 | 2002 |
| Cote d'Ivoire | 2004 | 2016 |
| Eritrea | 2000 | 2001 |
| Eritrea | 2009 | 2018 |
| Ethiopia | 2000 | 2001 |
| Haiti | 1993 | 1994 |
| Haiti | 2022 | Still in force |
| Iran | 2006 | Still in force |
| Iraq | 1990 | 2004 |
| Liberia | 1992 | 2009 |
| Libya | 1992 | 1999 |
| North Korea | 2006 | Still in force |
| Rwanda | 1994 | 1995 |
| Sierra Leone | 1997 | 1998 |
| Somalia | 1992 | Still in force |
| South Africa | 1977 | 1994 |
| South Sudan | 2018 | Still in force |
| Southern Rhodesia | 1966 | 1979 |
| Sudan | 2004 | Still in force |
| Yugoslavia | 1991 | 1996 |
| Yugoslavia | 1998 | 2001 |

Numerous multilateral arms transfer control initiatives have been launched in the postwar period. For the most part, these are export-control regimes with binding contractual arrangements that set out the obligations of states parties. States parties generally are required to follow a particular code of conduct and abide by export guidelines that are informed by lists of items which are subject to control, which are maintained by the multilateral body concerned. Multilateral arrangements also facilitate information sharing, in some cases through formal mechanisms established for this purpose, and can serve an important confidence-building role.

Multilateral arms control initiatives have been developed to respond to the proliferation of specific types of arms or to prevent transfers to particular states or groups of states over the long term. The comprehensiveness of multilateral initiatives potentially renders them far more effective than the aggregate national arms transfer controls of individual states. In codifying and promoting common standards of conduct on the export of items of concern, multilateral arrangements reduce the scope for states to source arms from alternative suppliers, and by facilitating the exchange of information between states parties they help to impede illicit arms transfers. Multilateral regimes often are complementary, contributing in their own fields to the global arms transfer control regime.

Multilateral arms transfer control regimes reflect and legitimize particular sets of norms. The regimes that are structuring the international arms transfer control landscape at the present time reflect and reinforce Western values and norms encouraging arms transfer restraint. The United States plays a critical role in extending and encouraging support for these norms, though its support for multilateralism has proven inconsistent. The importance of arms control multilateralism in the United States waxed and waned following the Cold War. While individual American presidents stand out as unsupportive of multilateral arms transfer controls, this is more an issue of the degree to which a particular president regards multilateralism as more of an impediment than an asset.[44] The United States continues to play a key role in promoting arms transfer standards reflecting its national and human security perspectives that underpin multilateral arms transfer controls.[45]

Developing multilateral arms transfer controls presents daunting challenges. In general, the more comprehensive the scope and the more stringent the controls of the proposed regime, the more difficult the exercise of obtaining sufficient consensus to operationalize the regime. Establishing a broad consensus can prove elusive due to the heterogeneous collection of states that generally it is important to engage. Initiatives may be difficult to sustain in the face of their conflicting political and economic interests. The United Kingdom endeavoured to establish a multilateral embargo on the supply of arms to both sides in the Nigerian Civil War, but this effort collapsed with the British decision to support the Nigerian government, for example.[46] This helps to explain why some multilateral mechanisms involve more binding arrangements than others; developing sufficient common ground for an initiative to proceed may require compromising on the robustness of its measures. Multilateral processes often pit advocates of strict controls against those supporting greater flexibility. Finding common cause is all the more difficult where there are concerns that arms transfer control efforts are motivated at least in part by economic considerations, such as preserving a competitor's market position. Multilateral arms transfer control regimes often are comprised of uneasy partnerships of states whose interests coincide only in part.

The difficulties involved in securing the international consensus necessary for multilateral arms transfer control are demonstrated by the experience of the EU. There are many established European arms exporters and efforts to develop a common approach to arms exports have had to contend with differing political interests and export cultures.[47] It was only in 1995 that the EU was able to agree on a common policy on the export of dual-use items, after years of negotiations.[48] Difficulties in harmonizing export rules have resurfaced, despite the EU's Common Position (2008/944/CFSP—8 December 2008), which sets out general guidelines on arms exports. This document is subject to varying interpretations, complicating efforts to implement a common approach. Extensive defence-industrial integration and differing national positions on the export of arms combine to produce considerable friction. Germany's unwillingness to supply arms to Saudi Arabia because of its human rights record and its military intervention in Yemen impacted French and British exports, for example. This prompted British Foreign Secretary Jeremy Hunt to write to his German counterpart in February 2019 to request that Germany adopt a more lenient approach.[49]

Most multilateral arms transfer control initiatives focus on the issue in a particular context. Notable examples include the Coordinating Committee for Multilateral Export Controls (COCOM), which was established in 1949, and its successor from 1996, the Wassenaar Arrangement on Export Controls for Conventional Arms and Dual-Use Goods (WA). The WA represents a major advance on COCOM, with its more comprehensive scope reflecting the changed international security environment resulting from the end of the Cold War. The Missile Technology Control Regime (MTCR), which was established in 1987, saw its membership expand following the Cold War, with former adversaries of the Western states that founded it joining its ranks. The belated expansion of the membership bases of the WA and the MTCR demonstrate the difficulties inherent in developing a common approach, even where there is common cause.[50]

Progress toward developing an overarching regulatory framework for the international arms trade has been slow. There were a number of initiatives between the interwar period and the end of the Cold War, but these either proved abortive or had little practical effect.[51] Discussions on a conventional arms transfers (CAT) treaty, which began in 1977 and initially were limited to the United States and the Soviet Union, ultimately foundered on the rocks of states' security and economic interests.[52] It was only following the Cold War that it proved possible to realize significant progress on a CAT treaty. Increasing attention to this issue was manifest in the promotion of export guidelines by the EU and the Organization for Security and Co-operation in Europe (OSCE) and in various treaties banning the transfer of particular categories of arms, such as the Convention on Cluster Munitions and the Convention on the Prohibition of the Use, Stockpiling, Production and Transfer of Antipersonnel Mines (commonly referred to as the Ottawa Treaty) of 1997.[53]

The UN Register of Conventional Arms (UNROCA) represented an important step toward the general regulation of international arms transfers. The Register, which was established in 1991 as a confidence-building measure, is universal in scope and non-discriminatory in the sense that its measures apply to all participating states equally. The Register is intended to prevent states from accumulating excessive and destabilizing arsenals of arms and to this end provides for voluntary annual reporting on specified categories of arms. Its focus on major weapons means that other categories of arms of concern, such as land mines, are excluded.[54]

The UNROCA prepared the way for the development of a multilateral regulatory framework for conventional arms transfers. This now exists in the Arms Trade Treaty (ATT). Negotiation of the ATT began in 2006 and it was adopted by the UN on 2 April 2013 and entered into force on 24 December 2014. The Treaty neither seeks to ban the international transfer of any category of weapon nor to supplant the existing national regulations on arms exports of any state, but to enhance transparency and promote higher standards of regulatory practice. The ATT does expect states parties to refrain from exporting to states which are likely to employ arms in a manner that would breach international humanitarian law and is intended as a means of addressing the illicit arms trade.[55]

## Challenges to Arms Transfer Control

There are a number of political and technical challenges to arms transfer control. The most fundamental of these is the general tension between the economic and security imperatives of arms exports and the security imperatives of arms transfer control. The concurrent pursuit of arms exports and arms transfer control in many states compels political authorities to compromise on export controls. The incentive to do can be very strong even in the states that traditionally have provided international leadership on arms transfer control. The pressure to factor economic considerations into export-control decisions generally increased following the Cold War, as noted earlier in this study.

Political authorities in many states struggle with arms transfer controls. This is demonstrated by the seemingly perpetual exercise of arms export control reform in the United States. The American debate surrounding this issue is quite complex, involving as it does considerations of economic competitiveness, industrial growth, the sustainability of the defence-industrial base, the need to support allied and friendly states, and the desire to limit the proliferation of advanced arms.[56] Policy consistency is difficult when the division of powers between the executive and legislative branches provides scope for the latter to exercise considerable initiative in arms export and control issues. Congress has on occasion sponsored strong sanctions that have clashed with administration efforts to manage the arms embargo against China.[57] Congress also has hindered efforts to develop a defence trade community with allied states through its efforts to support American defence firms. The protectionist and parochial 'Buy American' purchase restrictions periodically advanced by Congress complicate efforts to negotiate the necessary agreements and Congressional opposition delayed the implementation of defence trade treaties with Australia and the United Kingdom.[58] This has significant implications for arms transfer control, as discussed below.

The discretionary nature of state involvement represents another major challenge for arms transfer controls. The integrity of controls is undermined by states which remain outside transfer-control arrangements, or which comply in a manner that falls short of the spirit of the arrangement concerned. As China has demonstrated, informal adherence is a weak substitute for formal participation. The guarded view of multilateralism demonstrated by China's approach reflects a weak fundamental commitment to the objective of arms transfer control. China was a relative latecomer to this exercise and only gradually developed the regulatory mechanisms required to effectively meet its informal arms control commitments. This remains the case, with ongoing international concern over the integrity of Chinese export controls, though China now is a party to the ATT.[59]

Even multilateral arms transfer control mechanisms may provide considerable scope for interpretation which can be exploited by states parties. The effect of this is compounded by the importance of national arms transfer controls, which are crucial to the meeting of multilateral and multinational transfer-control obligations. The effectiveness of arms transfer controls can suffer where there is weak industrial governance, and lax or indifferent enforcement of arms transfer controls. This was a factor in the 'Toshiba Affair' discussed earlier.[60] This may result from capability shortcomings or a lack of concern on the part of political authorities.

The challenge of arms transfer controls stems in part from the nature of arms transfers. Some types of arms are particularly difficult to control. This has proven the case with SALW and man-portable SAMs due to their extensive diffusion, compact size, and in the case of the former, ease of production. As far back as 1971 no less than 111 states were producing small arms and small arms ammunition.[61] Production is far more widely distributed now, with more than 600 firms producing SALW by 2001.[62] There also is thriving pre-industrial 'handicraft' SALW production in a number of areas, including by some NSAGs.[63] The difficulty that can attend efforts to determine the origin and means of supply of arms greatly complicates arms transfer controls. Where the illicit trade in SALW is concerned, the quantities involved in individual transfers can be quite modest, rendering detection difficult. The UNROCA does not even attempt to address holdings and transfers of small arms.[64] The challenges of controlling man-portable SAMs drove a clandestine American programme to buy back some of the in excess of two thousand Stinger launchers that had been supplied to Afghan guerrillas fighting the Soviet-supported regime during the 1980s.[65] More recently, the American government has been compelled to investigate reports that Javelin anti-tank missiles had been retransferred to combatants in Libya, with a State Department official declaring that 'We take all allegations of mis-use of US-origin defence articles very seriously'.[66]

Other categories of arms also present challenges for arms transfer control. Dual-use equipment is difficult to control due to the scope for procurement through unregulated commercial channels. There is the potential for commercial vehicles and even aircraft such as helicopters which can be adapted for military service with relative ease to be transferred without export clearance. The intangible nature of arms related technologies represents an even greater challenge for arms transfer control, the importance of which has been heightened by the advent of cyber warfare instruments.[67] It can be difficult to determine the uses to which technologies and dual-use items will be put and no less difficult to detect their diversion from legitimate civil applications.

Interstate tensions over export controls are exacerbated by transnational production, as the positions adopted by states impact on their industrial partners. Firms and enterprises are subject to such restrictions as are placed on them by political authorities in the states where they are based and in which they operate. Arms transfer control expectations and standards vary considerably, as does the extent to which political authorities enforce them. An export-control decision on the part of a state whose industry supplies components, sub-components, or technologies that are incorporated in arms produced in another state may prevent it from accepting or fulfilling an export order, for example. This is a long-standing issue where arms including American production inputs are concerned, as the American government's approach to arms transfers is far more restrictive than that of many states and it has been prepared to exercise arms control at this level, as noted above.

Particular difficulties attend arms transfer control where sub-state actors are concerned. It is difficult to regulate transnational industrial processes and transactions given the complicated and often opaque nature of intra- and interfirm functional relationships. The not inconsiderable capacity of sub-state actors to operate beyond the confines of state control is increasing in concert with deepening industrial globalization. Transnational industrial structures provide considerable scope for firms and enterprises to circumvent arms export controls by producing arms in subsidiaries based in states with weaker export controls. During the First Gulf War, for example, the German firm Messerschmidt-Bölkow-Blohm supplied helicopters to Iraq from a production line in Spain.[68] This issue is exacerbated by the globalization of supply chains, which obscures the provenance of components and sub-components.

Arms transfers to NSAGs also pose a challenge to transfer-control efforts. Transferring arms to NSAGs is improper under generally accepted international norms, but occurs on a considerable scale nonetheless. Even states that generally feature as supporters of strong controls on arms transfers have engaged in this practice in the postwar period. The status of arms transfers to NSAGs has meant that there is no formal framework for dealing with this issue, and the security imperatives driving the practice limit the possibilities for developing such a framework. Some effort to strengthen international norms on this has been made, however. The most notable of these have been conducted under the auspices of UN efforts to address the illicit trade in arms, but there remains little international support for restraint.[69]

## The Shifting Boundaries of Arms Transfer Control

There has been no point in the modern era when arms transfer control has not represented a challenge at some level. Concerned authorities are endeavouring to overcome the limitations of arms transfer controls by strengthening established approaches and supplementing existing transfer-control mechanisms.

Determined efforts are being made to encourage arms suppliers which remain outside arms transfer control regimes to formally accede or at least informally adhere to their export guidelines. Often such efforts are led by the most dedicated regime members and pursued through bilateral engagement. While the United States has provided international leadership on sanctions targeting China, it long engaged China in an effort to secure its adherence to regimes such as the MTCR as well as encouraging the development and strengthening of its national arms export controls. The further socialization of China in the common pursuit of arms transfer control is likely to present a challenge given heightened Sino-American strategic competition.

International norms represent another important focus of efforts to strengthen arms transfer controls. Political authorities generally are sensitive to how their states are regarded in the international community and a desire to be seen as meeting international expectations can play an important role in encouraging them to abide by generally accepted international norms. This contributed to China's 1991 announcement that it would abide by the export guidelines of the MTCR.[70] The Chinese government declared its intention of further strengthening export controls when allegations surfaced in 2011 that Chinese state-owned enterprises had discussed arms sales with Libya.[71] International criticism similarly encouraged an important shift in Chinese arms export policy towards Sudan.[72] The engagement of states such as China, however informal this may be, helps to reinforce international arms transfer norms. There is considerable scope for this as some multinational and multilateral arms transfer control regimes provide for varying levels of participation and informal as well as formal adherence in the interest of extending export controls. This was the case with COCOM, for example, which the United States effectively extended to Taiwan, and which it developed special arrangements to apply to China under the 'China Green Line'.[73]

Concerned authorities in some states are seeking to address their arms transfer control concerns by developing closed groups of selected trusted industrial partners. These 'approved communities' may be formal or informal and may be comprised of states or firms and enterprises, but where the latter is the case their home state is a crucial factor. Approved communities tend to reflect security relationships of long standing. This is one of the functions of the trilateral Australia, United Kingdom, United States (AUKUS) grouping, for instance.[74] They function by harmonizing to some extent national regimes for the control of arms or the components, sub-components, and technologies incorporated in arms.[75] The higher level of assurance this provides reduces the risk of diversion to states of concern and facilitates eased restrictions on arms transfers within the community. Membership generally qualifies firms and enterprises for preferential treatment and states for streamlined access to arms and arms related production inputs, particularly those involving advanced technologies. In some cases, community members are eligible to exchange goods and services without an export licence and firms and enterprises are pre-approved for exports. The preferential treatment accorded such 'trusted suppliers' can represent an important incentive to adopt more restrictive export practices.

The United States makes extensive use of this approach. Its best-established arms trade community is with Canada, but it has developed separate communities with other states, including the United Kingdom, with which it long has enjoyed a 'special relationship'. Canada has aligned its export controls with those of the United States, while the United States has signed several bilateral agreements providing access to sensitive technologies on the condition that the British government strictly control the technologies involved.[76] American interest in this approach strengthened following the Cold War. The Defense Trade Security Initiative (DTSI) launched in May 2000 with the objective of streamlining the export-licensing process was structured on this basis. The DTSI facilitated expedited transfers of arms, including technologies and arms related services, to the members of NATO, Australia, Japan, and Sweden. This included exemption from licensing requirements for approved firms 'that demonstrate export and licensing policies and procedures comparable to those of the United States'.[77] More recently, the United States has worked to develop a closer defence trade relationship with India and has negotiated formal bilateral defence trade treaties with 'major defense partners' such as Australia and the United Kingdom.[78]

## *Arms Transfer Control Through Counter-Proliferation*

The perceived limitations of conventional arms transfer controls have led political authorities in some states to adopt strategies of counter-proliferation. Counter-proliferation focuses on disrupting the flow of arms by interdicting arms transfers as they occur, rather than ensuring that orders are not placed or promoting restraint on the part of arms suppliers or recipients. This can take the form of seizing or destroying shipments or stocks of arms.

Interdiction of arms transfers typically is practised where the requirement is perceived as pressing and there is little prospect for preventing the transfer otherwise. France sought to interdict the flow of arms to the *Front de libération nationale* (FLN) which was fighting for the independence of Algeria. Between 1957 and 1962 the French navy stopped more than eighteen vessels carrying arms for the FLN and sank at least three others.[79] The Soviet Union sought to interdict supply lines from Pakistan bringing arms to the *mujahedeen* in Afghanistan.[80] There has been increasing resort to counter-proliferation since the Cold War. Since 2013, Israel has launched numerous airstrikes on targets in Syria in an effort to interdict shipments of arms such as tactical ballistic missiles and air defence systems as well as arms production equipment to Syria and to Hizbullah in Lebanon.[81]

Interstate collaboration in arms interdiction is less common. The most prominent formal collaborative interdiction mechanism is the PSI. The Initiative, which is a multinational mechanism that was developed to address concerns over the proliferation of WMDs, encompasses delivery systems such as ballistic missiles as well. The PSI lacks a formal institutional framework but provides for high-level interstate collaboration. Its focus has been on disrupting WMD-related arms trafficking at sea by searching vessels suspected of transporting items of concern, but there is provision for preventing land

and air shipments, and for measures targeting production facilities and the entities that operate them.[82] Beyond this, a number of states now are collaborating through the contribution of naval forces in an effort to interdict Iranian maritime arms transfers to the Ansar Allah rebel movement in Yemen.[83]

## The Impact of Arms Transfer Controls

That arms transfer controls have had a significant impact on the diffusion of arms clearly is the case. Advanced arms in particular have proliferated less rapidly and less widely than would have been the case in the absence of national, multinational, and multilateral arms transfer controls. There are numerous cases where arms transfer controls have impeded advanced arms development programmes. The MTCR, for example, had a significant impact on missile development programmes in Argentina, Brazil, Egypt, Iraq, Libya, South Africa, South Korea, Syria, and Taiwan.[84] International sanctions also have slowed progress in Iran's ballistic missile programme.[85]

Some states have demonstrated considerable aptitude in circumventing arms transfer controls, however. Particularly noteworthy are South Africa, following the imposition of a mandatory arms embargo by the United Nations in 1977, and North Korea at the present time.[86] Even the MTCR failed to prevent thirty-five American and Western European firms from supporting Iraq's efforts to develop and produce tactical ballistic missiles.[87] It appears that there are limited prospects for arms transfer controls ultimately preventing the acquisition of arms by states where political authorities are determined to acquire them and are in a position to devote the resources necessary to this end. Where states possess comprehensive defence-industrial bases, supply-side controls may only be capable of delaying the introduction of specific types or new generations of arms.

While many arms transfer control efforts seem to have met only with moderate success in that they have not ultimately succeeded in preventing states from importing arms and arms related production inputs, it is important to consider how the success of arms transfer controls is measured. The ideal of arms transfer control generally is to prevent the supply of arms but often it is recognized that this may not be feasible. Arms transfer controls contribute significantly to non-proliferation efforts even where they fail to prevent target states from acquiring arms, by hindering the process and raising the cost—political if not financial—of arms programmes.[88] As a US State Department official noted of the MTCR, 'We have made them take longer, cost more and be less effective and less reliable than would otherwise be the case'.[89] And as one report noted, South Africa's efforts to develop an indigenous arms industry as means of overcoming the effects of the UN arms embargo resulted in 'a drain on the regime's resources and … a detrimental effect on the apartheid economy'.[90] Arms transfer controls have forced states such as North Korea and Russia to develop complex and costly procurement networks operating through intermediaries to meet their arms requirements.[91] Arms transfer controls can involve a high cost even for states with comprehensive defence-industrial bases through their effect of forcing them to source alternatives to components and sub-components required for local production and by denying access to sources of new technologies.[92] Effects such as this help to sustain support for arms transfer controls even where there ultimately is little prospect of preventing the acquisition of arms.

It also is important to note the important post-transfer effect of arms transfer controls. These can undermine the capacity of recipients to continue to operate arms they have succeeded in procuring. Denying states access to spares may force them to retire arms from service prematurely or to replace critical parts, potentially with unsatisfactory alternatives from other suppliers at considerable effort and cost. Iran, which has been subject to American arms sanctions for decades, has been forced to heavily modify aircraft of American origin to keep them operational.[93] Denying access to post-transfer MRO support can have a similar effect.

Growing international rivalry between major powers such as the United States, Russia, and China does not bode well for arms transfer control. The increasing politicization of arms transfer control issues will greatly complicate arms transfer control efforts, not least by rendering the exercise of developing an international consensus that much more difficult even where there appears to be common ground. This has the potential to compel greater reliance on national and multinational arms transfer control measures.

# 8 The Prospects for the International Arms Transfer System

Arms transfers will remain a prominent feature of the global security and economic landscape, though—as discussed below—it is important to approach arms transfers in more nuanced terms than often has been the case. The international arms transfer system will continue to be characterized by considerable complexity due to the importance of arms transfers in both security and economic terms; the dual imperatives driving many suppliers and recipients alike can compel difficult policy choices. Arms transfers and the control dilemmas that these entail will grow as the transformation outlined in Chapter 4 deepens.

How the international arms transfer system itself will evolve is less certain. The arms transfer system will continue to evolve as technological frontiers advance, economic forces further transform the defence-industrial landscape, and recipients' requirements evolve. The impact of trends and developments in these areas will be tempered by structural factors and suppliers' security concerns, however. Arms transfers can be expected to remain a sensitive and at times controversial issue in interstate relations and within many states. The developmental trajectory of the transformation of the international arms transfer system has significant implications on a number of levels. While it is not possible to predict with certainty either the shape or the pace of the system's transformation, not least because of the difficulty in predicting long-term industrial development trends, it is possible to identify key trends that compel close attention to how arms transfers are understood, and which can be expected to generate challenging policy demands.

## Whither the International Arms Transfer System?

The evolution of the international arms transfer system is being driven in large part by the structural transformation of processes of arms development and production. This transformation is having a particular impact on the demand for arms and the substance of international arms transfers. Deepening transnational defence-industrial integration, and the demand stemming from the development of emerging arms producers and the emergence of new arms producers, will generate increasing flows of arms related components, subcomponents, and technologies. These trends are mutually reinforcing. Transnational defence-industrial integration is contributing to the emergence and development of arms producers, and the emergence and development of producers is promoting a deepening of defence-industrial integration. The importance of emerging arms producers to arms development and production programmes based in established producers and the importance of established producers to programmes based in emerging producers will contribute to an increasingly complex network of transnational defence-industrial ties.

These processes are being facilitated by technical trends associated with the Fourth Industrial Revolution. The prospects for intangible technology transfer have improved considerably with the development of advanced means of data transfer, which enable more rapid and uncomplicated data transfers. The digital integration of value-chain partners has significant implications for the development, production, and ultimately the supply of arms. This process is particularly well advanced in high-technology industrial sectors such as aerospace and ICT. This will facilitate interfirm collaboration in arms R&D and production while complicating efforts by concerned authorities to exercise effective oversight of interfirm collaboration.

The development and widespread adoption of additive manufacturing (AM) technology and digital engineering are impacting at a more fundamental level. Though still in its infancy at this point, AM technology is developing rapidly and enables the onsite production of metal and plastic components using fewer parts through 3D scanning and printing. This offers obvious advantages for relatively low-cost, flexible production and also can help to reduce the time required for product development by enabling more rapid prototyping and integration of new technologies.[1] AM techniques also can be applied to the production of complete small arms, though the effectiveness is questionable.[2] Digital engineering techniques enable the creation of designs and models to test assumptions much more quickly and accurately than in the past.[3] In the case of the American T-7 Red Hawk training aircraft, digital engineering enabled designers to progress from a concept to first flight in a mere three years.[4]

The benefits of these technological breakthroughs apply quite generally but are unevenly distributed and are particularly important to states which have been disadvantaged in defence-industrial terms. These breakthroughs hold considerable promise in helping to offset the spiralling costs associated with the development and production of advanced arms. The revolution in arms development resulting from AM and digital engineering techniques is helping to reduce developmental and production costs and time frames. This is attractive to established and emerging arms suppliers alike but holds particular promise for states facing resource constraints and states which are subject to arms transfer controls. This potentially will help to narrow the capability gap between the established and emerging arms suppliers that results from their resource disparities. In enabling the production of parts required to maintain arms in service AM reduces the potential leverage of suppliers once arms have been transferred.[5]

This can be expected to facilitate the emergence and development of new arms suppliers that are in a position to successfully exploit the potential of these technological advances. It is important to note, however, that it will take some time to discern their potential; while the application of AM to the production of low-risk parts is spreading rapidly and its application to more critical parts is considered to have great potential, this only gradually is being demonstrated.[6]

Structural factors can be expected to continue to temper the impact of the transformation of the defence-industrial landscape, and thus the extent of change in the international arms transfer system, despite deepening industrial globalization. The levelling effect of transnational defence-industrial integration cannot necessarily compensate for interstate resource disparities. Some states will remain in a far better position to exploit the potential of defence-industrial globalization as a result of their industrial strengths. The international arms transfer system will remain highly asymmetric as a result. The difficulties inherent in developing and maintaining comprehensive defence-industrial capabilities ensure that even established arms producers will continue to be characterized by particular sectoral strengths and weaknesses and interstate arms flows will continue to reflect this.

It will be crucial to give due weight to transfers of items other than complete systems in analysing arms transfers. The transnational nature of arms production and the emergence of new arms producers render it important to approach arms transfers in terms of factors of production as well as complete systems. This represents a major departure for the analysis and control of arms transfers. Concerned authorities in many states struggle to address the challenges posed by arms transfers at this level, as demonstrated by the ongoing effort to prevent the supply of components, sub-components, and technologies to states of concern.

The increasing importance of the trade in components, sub-components, and technologies has significant implications. While the trade in complete systems will remain the focus of arms transfers and arms transfer control in most states, there will be states where the import of production inputs will be as important as that of complete systems. This will contribute to the growing role in the international arms transfer system of producers that are not necessarily in a position to provide complete systems, but which can supply components, sub-components, and technologies. This will strengthen the trend toward transnational defence-industrial integration and support the development of emerging arms producers by providing markets for their products.

States will remain central to the international arms transfer system in many respects, but the importance of sub-state actors will grow as their contribution to the development, production, and diffusion of arms expands and as arms production and transfer processes become more difficult for political authorities to influence. Firms and enterprises are playing a decisive role in shaping the form that arms production and transfers take. The evolving structure of the defence-industrial landscape, in which the dynamics are strongly influenced by industrial requirements, is accepted by political authorities in many states, though often not without considerable concern.

This concern is due in no small part to the perceived independence of firms and even enterprises. The pursuit of multi-domestic strategies and the distributed nature of core activities, as well as extensive reliance on offshore capability partners, is producing greater independence from individual states. As well as generally complicating relationships between states and between states and industry and contributing to the transformation of the international arms transfer system, this is providing increasing scope for sub-state actors to act in ways that conflict with the interests of the states in which they are based and operate. This is demonstrated by the difficulties experienced by governments such as those of the United States and other Western states in preventing firms from collaborating with counterparts in China in ways that challenge technology controls.

The international arms transfer system will grow more complex as transnational defence-industrial integration deepens. The system will be less static in terms of the relative position of states as suppliers develop their capabilities, new suppliers emerge, the capabilities of other suppliers decline, and as the relationship between suppliers evolves. This state of affairs will generate more demanding policy requirements in many states as the more flexible defence-industrial landscape will compel more extensive and sustained state intervention to ensure that transnational R&D and production processes serve national interests. In many states this will extend to strengthened intervention to ensure that defence-industrial processes do not contribute to defence-related R&D and production in states of concern.

The more complex policy requirements stemming from the transformation of the defence-industrial landscape and its impact on the international arms transfer system will encourage greater interstate collaboration. The requirements of collaboration will be quite complex in an environment of deepening industrial globalization and heightened strategic competition, however. This can be expected to lead to greater reliance in informal arrangements as formal interstate arrangements will be much more difficult to negotiate.

It is important to consider the future of arms transfer norms as the constellation of arms supplying states changes. There are strong indications of a preference for an alternative set of norms on the part of some states. Political authorities in some key arms producers are not entirely comfortable with the established norms or operate outside of them altogether. This alternative accepts without question the right of states to import arms, regardless of considerations such as the uses to which arms have been or are likely to be put. This set of norms contrasts with the prevailing trend whereby human security factors are assuming greater importance in arms supply decision making. Significantly, this group includes important established and emerging suppliers as well as 'rogue states'. While none of these states are revisionist in seeking to institutionalize these alternative norms at this point, the potential for this will grow as strategic competition deepens. This alternative to established norms would produce a far less restrictive arms transfer environment. The influence of major arms producers and suppliers such as the United States and Western European states such as France, Germany, and the United Kingdom renders such a fundamental transformation unlikely in the short to near term, but the impetus for change is likely to strengthen over time as arms suppliers such as China grow in importance.

There are several general factors that potentially will influence how political authorities approach the international arms transfer system going forward. One factor that has the potential to significantly disrupt the present trend toward deepening defence-industrial integration and the relatively free flow of production inputs that accompanies this is the outbreak of an international conflict or a protracted period of heightened international tension between states that have developed extensive industrial interdependence. This would serve to highlight the strategic implications of defence-industrial interdependence, particularly in terms of the integrity of national defence-industrial bases and the vulnerability of arms production processes stemming from transnational supply chains. This has the potential to generate a level of state intervention in R&D and production processes sufficient to threaten the path forged by firms and enterprises in their quest for greater efficiencies. This could over time produce a return to the state of affairs that prevailed prior to the emergence of defence-industrial globalization, with a reduction in the number of arms suppliers and the re-emergence of a much more clearly defined international division of labour in the supply as well as the production of arms. Such an outcome is possible even in the event that conflict or tension did not directly impact on key states or was relatively limited in scope, due to the extent and depth of transnational industrial integration.

The international arms transfer system is sensitive to trends and developments on the part of key states as well as those of a systemic nature. Particular states are quite influential as a result of their position as arms producers and suppliers and their structural role. Typically, it is the established suppliers that occupy such a position. This potential is demonstrated by recent developments in the United States. The position of this key arms supplier and advocate of arms transfer control, which often has served as the gatekeeper for formal and informal arms control arrangements, changed dramatically under the presidency of Donald Trump. His avowed intention to withdraw the United States from the ATT sent an important signal at a time when there was increasing concern over the diffusion of advanced arms, threatening arms transfer control norms and undermining efforts to develop more effective controls on international arms transfers. China's development as an international actor and its assumption of a more prominent role in the global political landscape will increase its influence on the shape of the arms transfer system.

## Understanding Arms Transfers

As this volume demonstrates, the international arms transfer system is complex and arms transfers are far from straightforward. This is the case with respect to the imperatives driving arms exports and imports, the form that arms transfers take, and arms transfer processes. This complexity reflects the importance and sensitivity of arms transfers in security and economic terms and the distinct interests and contribution of the various state and sub-state actors that contribute to the development, production, and supply of arms. International arms transfers are a product of a highly asymmetrical global industrial landscape. Arms transfers effectively are a levelling instrument; they represent a key means by which political authorities seek to overcome insecurity by addressing significant interstate disparities in defence capabilities. Arms transfers demonstrate the extent to which defence capabilities are transferrable. In some cases, arms transfers represent a means of establishing military ascendancy over rival states or local insurgent groups rather than levelling the uneven ground of the global military order.

Arms transfers as a category remains valid despite the need to situate trends and developments in broader industrial processes. Arms transfers represent one facet among many of the processes inherent to the global economic landscape. While arms transfers present a comparatively minor segment of the international economy, their local importance can be considerable.

The growing significance of economic considerations and processes highlights the importance of examining arms transfers through economic as well as security lenses. It is imperative to bear in mind the strength of economic processes in examining the role played by sub-state actors in international arms transfers. It is not necessarily the case that firms and enterprises fail to recognize and support the security interests of the states in which they are based and in which they operate, but this generally does not represent their primary objective; responsible stakeholders in firms and enterprises may not value this at all. Where there is acknowledgement of the importance of security interests, this can be complicated by the question of which security interests should be served. This is such an important issue because of the extent to which many firms and enterprises are structured transnationally and have developed local identities in the course of globalizing their operations. Firms and enterprises increasingly are operating with less regard for the interests of their 'home' states.

It is not necessarily the case that different states' security interests are incompatible, particularly where the states concerned are allies or otherwise enjoy close political relations. This is not always the case, however, potentially requiring difficult choices or a careful balancing act on the part of industry executives. Where firms and enterprises engage in proscribed activities this should not necessarily be assumed as indicating official direction or even acquiescence in other states where they operate.

There are limits on the utility of focusing on arms transfers as economic phenomena. The strength of economic imperatives in arms transfer decision making may be increasing relative to security imperatives and industry may be playing a more decisive role in shaping arms transfer processes, but political authorities still generally view arms transfers through the lens of national security and approach them accordingly. Where there is tension between security and economic requirements, authorities generally prioritize the former. This remains the case even as the economic importance of arms transfer grows and defence-industrial processes become more transnational. It is crucial as a result not to lose sight of arms transfers as facets of the pursuit of national security, even if it is important to consider economic factors when analysing arms transfers and the processes which are transforming the international arms transfer system are likely to prove enduring.

## Arms Transfers and Policy Requirements

Arms transfers are growing increasingly complex as the economic processes involved become more globalized. Only in exceptional cases are national defence-industrial bases truly national in the sense that they can operate independently of offshore capability partners and national supply chains generally well beyond the state concerned. Several key issues confront concerned authorities as the international arms transfer system evolves. The policy challenge involved will vary, depending on the security and economic requirements and agendas of political authorities and the extent to which arms transfer trends are understood to impact on these.

The tension between the supply and control of arms can be expected to increase, complicating the task facing policy communities. The importance of arms exports in both security and economic terms will endure. The balance between them often will be unequal, but political authorities in many states will be confronted by the dilemma resulting from the perceived need to address security and economic requirements in tandem. In many cases this will generate demands to export arms while encouraging arms transfer controls. Political authorities in states where security is not a prominent priority may not be confronted by a significant dilemma but where security concerns are more salient, this will be more of an issue. Such a distinction is evident at the present time. There is considerable tension between the United States and a number of Western European states over arms transfer control; while they share similar concerns in wanting to control transfers to states of concern, Western European states generally are far less willing to sacrifice economically in order to achieve this. It remains to be seen if concerns arising from the Russo-Ukrainian War will bridge this divide. The potential of trends and developments in the international security environment to influence the relative prioritization of security and economic requirements was demonstrated by the expansion of international support for the MTCR in the wake of Iraq's invasion of Kuwait in 1990.

The evolution of the global defence-industrial landscape can be expected to influence how states approach the conflicting demands of the supply and control of arms. Its ongoing transformation with respect to how arms are developed and produced will help to determine both what concerned authorities need to do to ensure access to the arms they require and to ensure that arms do not proliferate in ways that undermine national security. The established arms transfer system developed in a particular structural environment. This environment was defined by a global industrial landscape that was highly asymmetric and centred around a relatively small group of arms producing states. The result was a highly stratified structure of arms producers and suppliers. There was limited structural change; while the position of suppliers changed as new suppliers emerged and established ones faded, the structure itself proved quite resilient. This structure now is waning. The trends discussed in this volume are producing a structure that is both less hierarchical and more flexible. This transformation will influence how political authorities approach arms exports. The increasing importance of offshore industry to domestic arms development and production programmes generally will render it more difficult for them to approach their security and economic objectives in isolation. The impact of the transformation of the defence-industrial structure on the international arms transfer system and policy requirements will grow as this transformation deepens.

The extent of official concern in many states should not be underestimated; political authorities continue to struggle with addressing issues arising from transnational defence-industrial integration. Despite growing attention being given to managing arms transfers, including in terms of the norms against their indiscriminate supply, international arms transfers will prove increasingly resistant to effective state control. This will be to the great advantage of states and NSAGs which are the subject of arms transfer controls. It will also represent a major issue for states that have an interest in maintaining qualitative military advantages or in preventing politico-military rivals from developing their military capabilities. All this will generate heightened official attention to the international arms trade.

# Notes

## 1 Arms Transfers Between State and Industry

## 2 The Imperatives of Arms Supply

1 Nicholas Fiorenza, 'Zelensky's European Tour Yields More Weapons for Kyiv', *Jane's Defence Weekly*, 60 (24 May 2023), p. 15.

2 See H.C. Engelbrecht and F.C. Hanighen, *Merchants of Death: A Study of the International Armament Industry* (New York: Dodd, Mead & Co., 1934), pp. 262–63.

3 Quoted in Clive Trebilcock, 'The British Armaments Industry 1890–1914: False Legend and True Utility', in *War, Economy and the Military Mind*, ed. by Geoffrey Best and Andrew Wheatcroft (London: Croom Helm, 1976), pp. 89–107 (p. 90).

4 Gerald Howson, *Arms for Spain: The Untold Story of the Spanish Civil War* (New York: St. Martin's Press, 1998), p. 82.

5 See, for example Francesco Strazzari and Simone Tholens, 'Another Nakba: Weapons Availability and the Transformation of the Palestinian National Struggle, 1987–2007', *International Studies Perspectives*, 11 (2010), pp. 112–30 (pp. 114–15).

6 Chris Hughes, 'Japan's Emerging Arms Transfer Strategy: Diversifying to Re-centre on the US-Japan Alliance', *The Pacific Review*, 31 (2018), pp. 424–40 (p. 431).

7 See United States Congress, Office of Technology Assessment, 'Global Arms Trade: Commerce in Advanced Military Technology and Weapons' (Washington: Office of Technology Assessment, 1991), p. 1; and Mark Kramer, 'The Global Arms Trade After the Persian Gulf War,' *Security Studies*, 2 (Winter 1992), pp. 260–309 (p. 260).

8 See Steven W. Hook and David B. Rothstein, 'New Rationales and Old Concerns About U.S. Arms-Export Policy', in *Guns and Butter: The Political Economy of National Security*, ed. by Peter Dombrowski (Boulder: Lynne Rienner Publishers, 2005), pp. 153–78 (pp. 169–70).

9 See Paul A.C. Koistinen, *Beating Plowshares into Swords: The Political Economy of American Warfare, 1606–1865* (Lawrence: University Press of Kansas, 1996), pp. 78–79.

10 See, for example Gareth Jennings, 'UK Throws Weight Behind Saab's Gripen F-X2 Bid', *Jane's Defence Weekly*, 46 (18 November 2009), p. 13.

11 Michael S. Chase, '"Strong Indignation," but Limited Retribution: China's Response to U.S. Arms Sales to Taiwan', *China Brief*, 11 (14 October 2011), pp. 3–6; Associated Press, 'China Sanctions Lockheed Martin, Raytheon for Taiwan Sales' (17 February 2023), <www.voanews.com/a/china-sanctions-lockheed-martin-raytheon-for-taiwan-sales/6967494.html> [accessed 18 February 2023].

12 See George Thayer, *The War Business: The International Trade in Armaments* (London: Weidenfeld and Nicolson, 1969), pp. 273–74.

13 AIR International, 'The Ayatolllahs' Air Force', *AIR International*, 26 (June 1984), pp. 277–80 (p. 278). See also Andrew Hull and David Markov, 'Trends in the Arms Market: Part Two', *Jane's Intelligence Review*, 9 (May 1997), pp. 232–38 (p. 236).

14 See Kim Cragin and Bruce Hoffman, *Arms Trafficking and Colombia* (Santa Monica: RAND Corporation, 2003), p. 15.

15 Hull and Markov, 'Trends in the Arms Market', p. 236.

16 Kenneth Boutin, 'Feeding the Lion: China and Defence Development in African States', *Defense & Security Analysis*, 34 (2018), pp. 232–48 (p. 241).

17 Reuben F. Johnson, 'Losses, Gains Emerge as Talent Pool Heads Home', *Jane's Defence Weekly*, 46 (4 March 2009), p. 24.

18 Stephen Blank, 'Russia's Clearance Sale', *Jane's Intelligence Review*, 9 (November 1997), pp. 517–22 (pp. 520–21); Hull and Markov, 'Trends in the Arms Market', p. 233; Robert Sae-Liu, 'Second Song Submarine Vital to China's Huge Programme', *Jane's Defence Weekly*, 32 (18 August 1999), p. 17.

19 Steven J. Zaloga, *Superguns 1854–1991: Extreme Artillery from the Paris Gun and the V-3 to Iraq's Project Babylon* (Oxford: Osprey Publishing, 2018), pp. 39–40.

20 Ian Kemp, 'The Execution of Project "Babylon"', *Jane's Defence Weekly*, 14 (24 November 1990), p. 1010.

21 Gordon Arthur, 'Fincantieri Inks $1.3B Deal with Indonesia for Two Patrol Ships', *Defense News* (30 March 2024), <https://defensenews.com/naval/2024/03/29/fincantieri-inks-13b-deal-with-indonesia-for-two-patrol-ships> [accessed 30 March 2024].

22 Max Hastings and Simon Jenkins, *The Battle for the Falklands* (London: Pan Books, 2022), p. 401.

23 Ronen Bergman, *Rise and Kill First: The Secret History of Israel's Targeted Assassinations*, trans by Ronnie Hope (London: John Murray, 2018), pp. 612 and 624–25.

24 See Andrew J. Pierre, *The Global Politics of Arms Sales* (Princeton: Princeton University Press, 1982), p. 112.

25 Peter A. Wilson and John V. Parachini, 'Russia's Military Aircraft Exports Are Headed for a Nosedive', *Defense News* (21 October 2022), <www.defensenews.com/opinion/commerntary/2022/10/20/russias-military-aircraft-exports-are-headed-for-a-nosedive> [accessed 21 October 2022].

26 See Jon Grevatt, 'Thailand Makes Defence Development a Priority', *Jane's Defence Weekly*, 53 (22 June 2016), p. 21.

27 Thayer, *The War Business*, p. 343.

28 *Jane's Defence Weekly*, 'Industry', *Jane's Defence Weekly*, 57 (9 December 2020), pp. 42–46 (p. 43); Ian Taylor, *China's New Role in Africa* (Boulder: Lynne Rienner Publishers, 2009), p. 123.
29 Pierre, *The Global Politics of Arms Sales*, p. 23.
30 Patrick Brogan and Albert Zarca, *Deadly Business: Sam Cummings, Interarms, and the Arms Trade* (New York: W.W. Norton & Co., 1983), pp. 196–97.
31 Gareth Jennings, 'Afghan Air Force to Field Black Hawk Helicopters in Place of Mi-17s', *Jane's Defence Weekly*, 53 (30 November 2016), p. 6.
32 Paul Jackson, *Mirage* (Shepperton: Ian Allan, 1985), p. 51. See also Charles Forrester, 'Paris, Riyadh Agree New Procurement Deal', *Jane's Defence Weekly*, 55 (18 April 2018), p. 21.
33 Brogan and Zarca, *Deadly Business*, pp. 241–42.
34 AIR International, 'The Ayatollahs' Air Force', p. 280.
35 Agathe Demarais, 'Why China Hasn't Come to Russia's Rescue', *Foreign Affairs* (28 April 2023), <www.foreignaffairs.com/china/why-china-hasnt-come-russias-rescue> [accessed 2 May 2023].
36 Thayer, *The War Business*, p. 317.
37 Christian Le Mière, Gary Li and Nigel Inkster, 'China', in *Afghanistan: To 2015 and Beyond*, ed. by Toby Dodge and Nicholas Redman (London: The International Institute for Strategic Studies, 2011), pp. 219–30 (p. 219).
38 Anthony Sampson, *The Arms Bazaar: From Lebanon to Lockheed* (New York: The Viking Press, 1977), p. 173; Thayer, *The War Business*, pp. 217–18.
39 Alexander Rose, *The Lion and the Fox: Two Rival Spies and the Secret Plot to Build a Confederate Navy* (New York: Mariner Books, 2022), pp. 83–94.
40 Peter Lewis Young, 'Clandestine Trade in Arms: A Matter of Ways and Means', *Jane's Intelligence Review*, 12 (May 2000), pp. 48–51 (p. 49).
41 Ibid., pp. 50–51.
42 See Joseph S. Bermudez, Jr., *Shield of the Great Leader: The Armed Forces of North Korea* (St. Leonards: Allen & Unwin, 2001), p. 186.
43 Yu-Chin Lee, 'Implications of China's Aircraft Carrier Development' (Carlisle: US Army War College, 2012), pp. 6–7.
44 Hastings and Jenkins, *The Battle for the Falklands*, p. 211.
45 Howson, *Arms for Spain*, pp. 260–305.
46 See, for example Rudy Ruitenberg, 'KNDS Will Set Up Shop in Ukraine to Repair Heavy Weapons, Make Ammo', *Defense News* (8 June 2024), <www.defensenews.com/global/europe/2024/06/07/knds-will-set-up-shop-in-ukraine-to-repair-heavt-weapons-make-ammo> [accessed 8 June 2024].
47 Brogan and Zarca, *Deadly Business*, pp. 95–96.
48 See Wang Zhengyi, 'China Confronts Globalization: Conceptualizing Economic Security and Governance', in *Globalisation and Economic Security in East Asia: Governance and Institutions*, ed. by Helen E.S. Nesadurai (London: Routledge, 2006), pp. 62–84 (pp. 76–77).
49 Zhang Qingmin, 'Harmonising the Management of Foreign and Domestic Affairs in Chinese Foreign Policy', in *China Under Xi Jinping: Its Economic Challenges and Foreign Policy Initiatives*,

ed. by Shao Binhong (Leiden: Brill Publishing, 2015), pp. 143–66 (pp. 155–57); James Hardy, 'UNSC Investigates Chinese Link to North Korean TEL', *Jane's Defence Weekly*, 49 (25 April 2012), p. 6.

50 Bai Si Yeng, 'Understanding the Chinese Defence Industry', *Military Technology*, 11 (March 1987), pp. 36–53 (pp. 47–49).

51 Paradorn Rangsimaporn, 'Russia's Debate on Military-Technological Cooperation with China', *Asian Survey*, 46 (2006), pp. 477–95 (pp. 478–79). See also Blank, 'Russia's Clearance Sale', p. 518.

52 Roderic Alley, 'Small Arms and Light Weapons: The Disjunction Problem', *Conflict, Security & Development*, 19 (2019), pp. 143–72 (p. 143). For other examples of diversion, see Kua Kia Soong, *Questioning Arms Spending in Malaysia: From Altantuya to Zikorsky* (Petaling Jaya: Suara Rakyat Malaysia, 2010), pp. 102–04; and Matt Potter, *Outlaws Inc.: Flying with the World's Most Dangerous Suppliers* (London: Sidgwick & Jackson, 2011), pp. 34–36.

53 Jim Dorschner, 'Conflict Zone', *Jane's Defence Weekly*, 56 (27 March 2019), pp. 20–25 (p. 21).

54 Voice of America, 'Taliban Hand in Smuggling of US Arms Clear, Despite Denials' (17 July 2023), <www.voanews.com/a/fact-check-/7184125.html> [accessed 20 July 2023].

55 See, for example Howson, *Arms for Spain*, pp. 75–80.

56 Young, 'Clandestine Trade in Arms', p. 49.

57 Denise Garcia, 'Arms Transfers beyond the State-to-State Realm', *International Studies Perspectives*, 10 (May 2009), pp. 151–68 (pp. 158–59).

58 Jeremy Binnie, 'Saudis Unveil DF-3 Ballistic Missiles', *Jane's Defence Weekly*, 51 (7 May 2014), p. 19.

59 See Ian Anthony, 'The "Third Tier" Countries: Production of Major Weapons', *Arms Industry Limited*, ed. by Herbert Wulf (Oxford: Oxford University Press, 1993), pp. 362–83 (pp. 362–63).

60 Andrew L. Ross, *Arms Production in Developing Countries: The Continuing Proliferation of Conventional Weapons* (RAND Note N-1615-AF) (Santa Monica: RAND Corporation, 1981), p. 6.

1 Thayer, *The War Business*, p. 214.

2 United States, Office of the White House, 'National Security Presidential Memorandum Regarding U.S. Conventional Arms Transfer Policy' (Washington: Office of the White House, 19 April 2018), Section 2.

3 Guy Anderson et al., 'Exports and Global Influence', *Jane's Industry Quarterly*, 1 (July 2008), pp. 3–9 (p. 5).

4 Reuters, 'US Tries to Woo India Away From Russia With Aircraft' (17 February 2023), <www.voanews.com/a/6967153.html> [accessed 18 February 2023].

5 Howson, *Arms for Spain*, p. 85.

6 Yaakov Katz and Amir Bohbot, *The Weapon Wizards: How Israel Became a High-Tech Military Superpower* (New York: St. Martin's Press, 2017), p. 236.

7 Andrew J. Pierre, 'Toward an International Regime for Conventional Arms Sales', in *Cascade of Arms: Managing Conventional Weapons Proliferation*, ed. by Andrew J. Pierre (Washington: Brookings Institution Press; and Cambridge: The World Peace Foundation, 1997), pp. 369–436 (p. 406).

8 Michael Mihalka, *The Measurement and Modelling of Arms Accumulation: The Middle East as a Case Study* (Cambridge: Center for International Studies, Massachusetts Institute of Technology, 1975), pp. 11–12.

9 Burak Ege Bekdil, 'Turkey seeks to Repair Ties With Western Procurement Club', *Defense News* (6 June 2022), <www.defensenews.com/global/europe/2022/06/06/turkey-seeks-to-repair-ties-with-western-procurement-club> [accessed 7 June 2022]; Jeremy Binnie, 'US Aircraft "On the Table" for UAE After Normalising Relations with Israel', *Jane's Defence Weekly*, 57 (2 September 2020), p. 16.

10 Joe Maiolo, *Cry Havoc: The Arms Race and the Second World War, 1931–41* (London: John Murray, 2010), pp. 370–71.

11 Thayer, *The War Business*, p. 35.

12 Duncan L. Clarke, Daniel B. O'Connor and Jason D. Ellis, *Send Guns and Money: Security Assistance and U.S. Foreign Policy* (Westport: Praeger Publishers, 1997), pp. 13–14.

13 Bryant Harris, 'Congress Passes Bill to Loan U.S. Military Equipment to Ukraine and Allies', *Defense News* (29 April 2022), <www.defensenews.com/congress/2022/04/28/congress-passes-bill-to-loan-us-military-equipment-to-ukraine-and-allies> [accessed 29 April 2022].

14 See, for example Rudy Ruitenberg, 'Norway's View on Long War in Ukraine Drives Easing of Arms Export Rule', *Defense News* (18 January 2024), <www.defensenews.com/global/europe/2024/01/17/norways-view-on-long-war-in-ukraine-drives-easing-of-arms-export-rule> [accessed 18 January 2024].

15 Joe Gould, 'Here's What Global Weapons Chiefs Will Discuss this Month in Brussels', *Defense News* (10 September 2022), <www.defensenews.com/pentagon/2022/09/09/heres-what-global-weapons-chiefs-will-discuss-this-month-in-brussels> [accessed 10 September 2022]; Noah Robertson, 'With Pause in US Aid, Ukraine's Allies Rally to Ponder What's Next', *Defense News* (19 March 2024), <www.defensenews.com/pentagon/2024/03/19/with-pause-in-us-aid-ukraines-allies-rally-to-ponder-whats-next> [accessed 20 March 2024].

16 Carla Babb, 'Austin Hosts First In-Person Ukraine Defense Contact Group of 2024' (18 March 2024), <www.voanews.com/a/austin-hosts-first-in-person-ukraine-defense-contact-group-of-2024/7533349.html> [accessed 19 March 2024].

17 Joe Gould and Sebastian Sprenger, 'Ukraine Weapon Switcheroos are Flushing Soviet Arms Out of Europe', *Defense News* (29 April 2022), <www.defensenews.com/global/europe/2022/04/28/ukraine-weapon-switcheroos-are-flushing-soviet-arms-out-of-europe> [accessed 29 April 2022].

18 Jeff Seldin, 'US Pushing Central, South American Countries to Give Ukraine Quick Military Boost' (20 January 2023), <www.voanews.com/us-pushing-central-south-american-countries-to-give-ukraine-quick-military-boost-/6927591.html> [accessed 21 January 2023].

19 Vivienne Machi, 'Czech Army to Get Leopard Tanks Under Berlin-Prague Arms Swap', *Defense News* (12 October 2022), <www.defensenews.com/global/europe/2022/10/11/czech-army-to-get-leopard-tanks-under-berlin-prague-arms-swap> [accessed 12 October 2022].

20 Stockholm International Peace Research Institute, *The Arms Trade with the Third World* (Harmondsworth: Penguin Books, 1975), p. 159.

21 Clarke, O'Connor and Ellis, *Send Guns and Money*, pp. 53–54.

22 Rahul Bedi, 'India, Pakistan Look to Ease Tensions after Dogfights Over Kashmir's LoC', *Jane's Defence Weekly*, 56 (6 March 2019), pp. 4–5 (p. 5).

23 Bruce Jones, 'Putin Backs Ankara-Moscow S-400 Sales Negotiations', *Jane's Defence Weekly*, 54 (14 June 2017), p. 17.

24 Meredith Roaten, 'US to Send Second Patriot Air-Defence Battery to Ukraine', *Jane's Defence Weekly* 61 (24 July 2024), p. 4.

25 Michael Axworthy, *Revolutionary Iran: A History of the Islamic Republic* (Second Edition) (London: Penguin Books, 2019), pp. 84–85; Sebastian Sprenger, 'The Race to Arm Ukraine Highlights West's Worry of Losing Tech Secrets', *Defense News* (9 June 2022), <www.defensenews.com/global/europe/2022/06/08/the-race-to-arm-ukraine-highlights-wests-worry-of-losing-tech-secrets> [accessed 9 June 2022].

26 Ridzwan Rahmat, 'Japan to Boost Defence Sales in Asia as Part of Diplomatic Strategy', *Jane's Defence Weekly*, 54 (25 January 2017), p. 7.

27 See Associated Press, 'China Makes Semi-Secret Delivery of Missiles to Serbia' (10 April 2022), <www.voanews.com/a/china/china-makes-semi-secret-delivery-of-missiles-to-serbia/6523269.html> [accessed 11 April 2022].

28 Keren Yarhi-Milo, Alexander Lanoszka and Zack Cooper, 'To Arm or to Ally? The Patron's Dilemma and the Strategic Logic of Arms Transfers and Alliances', *International Security*, 41 (Fall 2016), pp. 90–139 (p. 96).

29 Hughes, 'Japan's Emerging Arms Transfer Strategy', p. 432.

30 Axworthy, *Revolutionary Iran*, p. 208.

31 Xiaobing Li, *A History of the Modern Chinese Army* (Lexington: University Press of Kentucky, 2007), p. 124.

32 Gabriel Dominguez, 'Russia to Deliver First Four Su-35s to China in 2016', *Jane's Defence Weekly*, 53 (28 September 2016), p. 6; Reuben F. Johnson, 'PLA May Finally Receive S-400 SAMs', *Jane's Defence Weekly*, 51 (16 April 2014), p. 8.

33 Peter Kazimiroff, 'Russian Industry Wary of Su-35 Sale to China', *Jane's Defence Weekly*, 49 (21 March 2012), p. 5.

34 Yaakov Katz, 'Israel Offered F-35s in Return for West Bank Deal', *Jane's Defence Weekly*, 47 (24 November 2010), p. 6.

35 Steven J. Zaloga, *The M47 and M48 Patton Tanks* (Oxford: Osprey Publishing, 1999), pp. 36–37.

36 See Gareth Jennings, 'US Looks to Contain Iran with Arms Sales to Allies', *Jane's Defence Weekly*, 50 (1 May 2013), p. 4.

37 Katz and Bohbot, *The Weapon Wizards*, p. 227. See also Yaakov Katz, 'Israel Seeks Rapport with China Over Iran', *Jane's Defence Weekly*, 48 (22 June 2011), p. 19.

38 Jon Grevatt, 'US Senate Committee Approves Proposed Taiwan Policy Law', *Jane's Defence Weekly*, 59 (28 September 2022), p. 4.

39 See Benjamin Lai, *The Chinese People's Liberation Army Since 1949: Ground Forces* (Oxford: Osprey Publishing, 2012), p. 11.

40 Jeff Seldin, 'US Security Aid to Israel to Arrive in Coming Days' (8 October 2023), <www.voanews.com/a/us-to-send-carrier-striker-group-to-mediterraneran-in-support-of-israel/7301975.html> [accessed 9 October 2023].

41 Stockholm International Peace Research Institute, *The Arms Trade with the Third World*, p. 216; Thayer, *The War Business*, pp. 323–26.

42 R.T. Naylor, *Patriots and Profiteers: Economic Warfare, Embargo Busing, and State-Sponsored Crime* (Second Edition) (Montreal and Kingston: McGill-Queen's University Press, 2008), p. 220.

43 Bryant Harris, 'Biden Arms Deal Policy Seeks to Balance Human Rights and Competition', *Defense News* (24 February 2023), <www.defensenews.com/pentagon/2023/02/23/biden-arms-deal-policy-seeks-to-balance-human-righys-and-competition> [accessed 24 February 2023].

44 Ryan Brobst, John Hardie and Bradley Bowman, 'World Leaders Should Press Switzerland on Arms Deliveries to Ukraine', *Defense News* (18 January 2023), <www.defensenews.com/opinion/commentary/2023/01/17/world-leaders-should-press-switzerland-on-arms-deliveries-to-ukraine> [accessed 18 January 2023]. See also William Gallo, 'Ukraine's Call for Weapons Remains Tough Sell in South Korea' (1 March 2023), <www.voanews.com/a/ukraine-call-for-weapons-remains-tough-sell-in-south-korea/6985407.html> [accessed 3 March 2023].

45 Sean Monaghan, 'Challengers and Challenges: The Promise and Perils of UK Leadership', *Defense News* (20 January 2023), <www.defensenews.com/opinion/commentary/2023/01/19/challengers-and-challenges-the-promise-and-perils-of-uk-leadership> [accessed 20 January 2023].

46 See Bruce E. Bechtol, Jr., *North Korean Military Proliferation in the Middle East and Africa: Enabling Violence and Instability* (Lexington: The University Press of Kentucky, 2018), p. 33.

47 Steve Coll, *Directorate S: The C.I.A. and America's Secret Wars in Afghanistan and Pakistan, 2001–2016* (London: Allen Lane, 2018), p. 138.

48 Sebastian Sprenger and Joe Gould, 'US Officials Balance Arms Sales Push Against Securing Tech Secrets', *Defense News* (8 September 2022), <www.defensenews.com/pentagon/2022/09/07/us-officials-balance-arms-sales-push-against-tech-protection-needs> [accessed 8 September 2022].

49 Alon Ben-David, 'China Issue Undermines US-Israeli Defence Ties', *Jane's Defence Weekly*, 42 (27 April 2005), p. 6.

50 Jon Grevatt, 'US "Normalises" Defence Trade with Taiwan', *Jane's Defence Weekly*, 56 (10 July 2019), p. 5; J. Michael Cole, 'Taiwan's Surveillance Radar "Will Not Track Satellites"', *Jane's Defence Weekly*, 49 (29 February 2012), p. 10.

51 Ashley Roque, 'New Truck-Mounted Harpoon Launchers Headed to Ukraine', *Jane's Defence Weekly*, 59 (29 June 2022), p. 5; Stephen Losey, 'F-16s Key Step for Ukraine, but Won't be "Game-Changer", SECAF Says', *Defense News* (23 May 2023), <www.defensenews.com/air/2023/05/22/f-16s-key-step-for-ukraine-but-wont-be-game-changer-secaf-says> [accessed 23 May 2023].

52 Quoted in Ralph Sanders, *Arms Industries: New Suppliers and Regional Security* (Washington: National Defense University, 1990), p. 17.

53 See Taylor, *China's New Role in Africa*, pp. 114–15.

54 Daniel Todd, 'Naval Shipbuilding: Prerequisite for Rising Powers?', *International Defense Review*, 24 (March 1991), pp. 229–34 (p. 230); James Elliot and Ezio Bonsignore, 'Asia's "New" Aerospace Industry: At the Turning Point?', *Military Technology*, 22 (February 1998), pp. 24–32 (p. 24).

55 Richard Scott, 'Refreshed or Rehashed?', *Jane's Defence Weekly*, 59 (6 April 2022), pp. 18–21 (p. 21).

56 See, for example Katz and Bohbot, *The Weapon Wizards*, p. 236.

57 Hook and Rothstein, 'New Rationales and Old Concerns About U.S. Arms-Export Policy', p. 154; Paul A.C. Koistinen, *State of War: The Political Economy of American Warfare, 1945–2011* (Lawrence: University Press of Kansas, 2012), p. 184.

58 Marina Malenic, 'US Targets Exportability as Part of Acquisition Overhaul', *Jane's Defence Weekly*, 49 (21 November 2012), p. 10; see also Richard Scott, 'Intrinsically Exportable', *Jane's Defence Weekly*, 56 (2 October 2019), pp. 22–27 (p. 23).

59 Kenneth Boutin, *Economic Security and Sino-American Relations: Progress Under Pressure* (Cheltenham: Edward Elgar, 2019), p. 57.

60 Stephen Losey, 'US Air Force, Boeing Reach Deal on Prototype E-7', *Defense News* (22 July 2024), <www.defensenews.com/air/2024/07/22/us-air-force-boeing-reach-deal-on-prototype-e-7> [accessed 13 August 2024].

61 See Boutin, 'Feeding the Lion', p. 241.

62 Gabriel Dominguez, 'UN Report Highlights Role of Foreign Players in North Korean Arms Sales', *Jane's Defence Weekly*, 56 (20 March 2019), p. 4.

63 Bermudez, *Shield of the Great Leader*, p. 116.

64 Peter H. Wilson, 'European Warfare 1815–2000', in *War in the Modern World Since 1815*, ed. by Jeremy Black (London: Routledge, 2003), pp. 192–216 (p. 200).

65 Andrew Hull and David Markov, 'A Changing Market in the Arms Bazaar', *Jane's Intelligence Review*, 9 (March 1997), pp. 140–42 (p. 140). See also Blank, 'Russia's Clearance Sale', p. 517.

66 Hull and Markov, 'A Changing Market in the Arms Bazaar', p. 140. See also Hook and Rothstein, 'New Rationales and Old Concerns About U.S. Arms-Export Policy', pp. 153–54; and Carol Reed and Barbara Starr, 'Defending the Industrial Realm', *Jane's Defence Weekly*, 17 (11 April 1992), pp. 629–30.

67 See, for example Gareth Jennings, 'Rotary Recap', *Jane's Defence Weekly*, 59 (14 September 2022), pp. 16–23 (p. 22).

68 Alessandra Giovanzanti, 'Supercharged in the Sky', *Jane's Defence Weekly*, 59 (2 March 2022), pp. 22–29 (p. 29).

69 See United States Congress, Office of Technology Assessment, *Arming Our Allies: Cooperation and Competition in Defense Technology* (Washington: US Government Printing Office, 1990), p. 112.

70 Jon Grevatt, 'Japan Export Ban Leaves Industry "at a Standstill"', *Jane's Defence Weekly*, 46 (4 March 2009), p. 23.

71 See, for example Blank, 'Russia's Clearance Sale', pp. 517–18.

72 David J. Louscher and Anne Naylor Schwarz, 'Patterns of Third World Military Technology Acquisition', in *The Dilemma of Third World Defense Industries: Supplier Control or Recipient Autonomy?*, ed. by Kwang-Il Baek, Ronald D. McLaurin and Chung-in Moon (Boulder: Westview Press, 1989), pp. 33–56 (p. 35).

73 Chris McNab, *Armies of the Iran-Iraq War 1980–88* (Oxford: Osprey Publishing, 2022), p. 30.

74 Michael Wilson, 'European Avionics into the 1990s and Beyond', *Jane's Defence Weekly*, 2 (1 September 1984), pp. 335–43 (p. 343).

75 Rangsimaporn, 'Russia's Debate on Military-Technological Cooperation with China', p. 479.

76 Ezio Bonsignore and Eugene Kogan, 'Fatal Attraction: The EU Defence Industry and China', *Military Technology*, 29 (June 2005), pp. 8–15 (pp. 8–9).

77 See Steven Gunn, 'War and the Emergence of the State: Western Europe, 1350–1600', in *European Warfare 1350–1750*, ed. by Frank Tallett and D.J.B. Trim (Cambridge: Cambridge University Press, 2010), 50–73 (p. 55).

78 Geoffrey Parker, *The Military Revolution: Military Innovation and the Rise of the West, 1500–1600* (Second Edition) (Cambridge: Cambridge University Press, 1996), p. 131.

79 See, for example Axworthy, *Revolutionary Iran*, p. 292.

80 Kenneth Boutin, 'Arms and Autonomy: The Limits of China's Defense-Industrial Transformation', in *The Modern Defense Industry: Political, Economic, and Technological Issues*, ed. by Richard A. Bitzinger (Santa Barbara: Praeger Security International, 2009), pp. 212–26 (pp. 218–20).

81 See Thayer, *The War Business*, pp. 26–28.

82 Brogan and Zarca, *Deadly Business*, p. 27. See also Paddy Ashdown, *Nein: Standing Up to Hitler 1935–1944* (London: William Collins, 2018), p. 19.

83 Philip S. Jowett, *Modern African Wars (5): The Nigerian-Biafran War 1967–70* (Oxford: Osprey Publishing, 2016), pp. 18–19.

84 See Douglas Farah and Stephen Braun, *Merchant of Death: Money, Guns, Planes, and the Man Who Makes War Possible* (Hoboken: John Wiley & Sons, 2007); Juan C. Zarate, *Treasury's War: The Unleashing of a New Era of Financial Warfare* (New York: Public Affairs, 2013), pp. 119–21; and Joseph C. Goulden with Alexander W. Raffio, *The Death Merchant: The Rise and Fall of Edwin P. Wilson* (London: Sidgwick & Jackson, 1984), pp. 123–30.

85 See Cragin and Hoffman, *Arms Trafficking and Colombia*, pp. 22–23.

## 3 The Imperatives of Arms Imports

1 See David B. Ralston, *Importing the European Army: The Introduction of European Military Techniques and Institutions into the Extra-European World, 1600–1914* (Chicago: University of Chicago Press, 1996).

2 See Michael Smith, *The Real Special Relationship: The True Story of How the British and US Secret Services Work Together* (London: Simon & Schuster, 2022), pp. xviii–xix.

3 See Barry Buzan and Eric Herring, *The Arms Dynamic in World Politics* (Boulder: Lynne Rienner Publishers, 1998), p. 51.

4 Amitav Acharya, *An Arms Race in Post-Cold War Southeast Asia: Prospects for Control* (Singapore: Institute of Southeast Asian Studies, 1994); Muthiah Alagappa, 'Asian Practice of Security: Key Features and Explanations', in *Asian Security Practice: Material and Ideational Influences*, ed. by Muthiah Alagappa (Stanford: Stanford University Press, 1998), pp. 611–76 (p. 631); Buzan and Herring, *The Arms Dynamic in World Politics*, p. 76.

5 See Stockholm International Peace Research Institute, *The Arms Trade with the Third World*, p. 39.

6 See Buzan and Herring, *The Arms Dynamic in World Politics*, pp. 76–77.

7 Thayer, *The War Business*, p. 324.

8 Joshua Pollack, 'Ballistic Trajectory: The Evolution of North Korea's Ballistic Missile Market', *The Nonproliferation Review*, 18 (July 2011), pp. 411–29 (p. 419).

9 Mike Stone, 'Ukraine War Spurs European Demand for U.S. Arms, But Not Big-Ticket Items' (17 February 2023), <www.reuters.com/world/europe/ukraine-war-spurs-european-demand-us-arms-not-big-ticket-items-2023-02-17> [accessed 18 February 2023].

10 Brooks Tigner, 'More Nations Join Danish-Led NATO Group to Bulk-Buy PGMs', *Jane's Defence Weekly*, 54 (15 November 2017), p. 12.

11 *Jane's Defence Weekly*, 'New Interests Spur Force Development', *Jane's Defence Weekly*, 25 (22 May 1996), pp. 23–26 (p. 24).

12 Vivienne Machi, 'How the F-35 Swept Europe, and the Competition it Could Soon Face', *Defense News* (4 September 2022), <www.defensenews.com/global/europe/2022/09/04/how-the-f-35-swept-europe-and-the-competition-it-could-soon-face> [accessed 5 September 2022].

13 Gareth Jennings, 'UAE Set to Upgrade Mirage 2000 Fighters', *Jane's Defence Weekly*, 54 (22 November 2017), p. 7.

14 Karl Soper, 'Russia Completes Assembly of Iveco LMV 4x4s', *Jane's Defence Weekly*, 51 (19 November 2014), p. 14.

15 Adam Tooze, *The Wages of Destruction: The Making and Breaking of the Nazi Economy* (London: Allen Lane, 2006), p. 404.

16 See Stockholm International Peace Research Institute, *The Arms Trade with the Third World*, pp. 78–79.

17 Cynthia Cook, 'Friends Over Factories', *Foreign Affairs* (27 March 2023), <www.foreignaffairs.com/united-states/firiends-over-factories> [accessed 28 March 2023].

18 Tom Keatinge, *Developing Bad Habits: What Russia Might Learn from Iran's Sanctions Invasion* (London: Royal United Services Institute, 2023), pp. 23–26.

19 Stone, 'Ukraine War Spurs European Demand for U.S. Arms, But Not Big Ticket Items'.

20 See Keith Krause, *Arms and the State: Patterns of Military Production and Trade* (Cambridge: Cambridge University Press, 1992), p. 174 for this concept.

21 Quoted in Gavin Kennedy, *The Military in the Third World* (New York: Charles Scribner's Sons, 1974), p. 304.

22 Ibid., p. 284.

23 Reuben F. Johnson, 'Russian Industry Makes Push into the Iranian Market', *Jane's Defence Weekly*, 53 (23 November 2016), p. 9.

24 Hamburg Institute for Economic Research, Kiel Institute for World Economics, and National Research Council, *Conflict and Cooperation in National Competition for High-Technology Industry* (Washington: National Academy Press, 1996), p. 106.

25 Brooks Tigner, 'EDA Warns Europe to Address Critical Defence Dependencies', *Jane's Defence Weekly*, 48 (27 April 2011), p. 15; Matthew Smith and Guy Anderson, 'European A&D Giants Call for MALE UAS Programme', *Jane's Defence Weekly*, 50 (26 June 2013), p. 23.

26 John M. Deutch and Ernest J. Moniz, 'How America Can Make Industrial Policy Work', *Foreign Affairs* (7 September 2022), <www.foreignaffairs.com/united-states/how-america-can-make-industrial-policy-work> [accessed 17 August 2023].

27 Charles Stafrace, *Arab Air Forces* (Carrollton: Squadron/Signal Publications, 1994), p. 14.

28 H.M.F. Howarth, 'The Malaysian Armed Forces,' *International Defense Review*, 16 (September 1983), pp. 1225–31 (p. 1226); Jon Grevatt, 'Slow and Steady', *Jane's Defence Weekly*, 56 (31 July 2019), pp. 24–30 (p. 28).

29 Rahul Bedi, 'US Overtakes Russia as India's Main Materiel Supplier', *Jane's Defence Weekly*, 51 (20 August 2014), p. 6.

30 See Benedict Anderson, *Imagined Communities: Reflections on the Origin and Spread of Nationalism* (Revised Edition) (London: Verso, 1991), pp. 4–6.

31 Hsi-Sheng Ch'i, *Warlord Politics in China 1916–1928* (Stanford: Stanford University Press, 1976), p. 117.

32 Lauren Gelfand, 'Delivery of Su-30MKAs to Algeria Revives Arms Deal', *Jane's Defence Weekly*, 45 (11 June 2008), p. 21.

33 Tom Martin and Rachel Scmidt, *A Case Study of the F-20 Tigershark* (Report P-7495-RGS) (Santa Monica: RAND Corporation, 1987), p. 21.

34 Coll, *Directorate S*, p. 454.

35 Lauren Gelfand, 'South Sudan Set to Buy Mi-17 Transport Helos', *Jane's Defence Weekly*, 47 (15 September 2010), p. 18.

36 Gavin Phipps and James Hardy, 'But Taipei Will Still Push for F-16C/D Purchase', *Jane's Defence Weekly*, 48 (28 September 2011), p. 6.

37 See AIR International, 'Singapore', *AIR International*, 26 (March 1984), p. 110.

38 Ryan K. Noppen, *Ottoman Navy Warships 1914–18* (Oxford: Osprey Publishing, 2015), pp. 7 and 14–15.

39 Rahul Bedi, 'India Asks Japan to Offer Soryu Subs for Project 75I', *Jane's Defence Weekly*, 52 (4 February 2015), p. 25.

40 Elisabeth Gosselin-Malo, 'Rafales on the Upswing? French Fighter Eyes Additional Mideast Sales', *Defense News* (7 September 2023), <www.defensenews.com/air/2023/09/07/rafales-on-the-upswing-french-fighter-eyes-additional-mideast-sales> [accessed 8 September 2023].

41 Michael S. Chase, *Taiwan's Security Policy: External Threats and Domestic Policies* (Boulder: Lynne Rienner Publishers, 2008), p. 140.

42 Robert Karniol, 'Taiwan to Slash Its IDF Fighter Production', *Jane's Defence Weekly*, 19 (3 April 1993), p. 5; Hu Hsun, 'Building Up the Island Nation', *Jane's Defence Weekly*, 21 (22 January 1994), pp. 24–25 (p. 25).

43 Robert Forczyk, *Case Red: The Collapse of France, 1940* (Oxford: Osprey Publishing, 2017), p. 31.

44 Gabriel Dominguez, 'N Korean "Scuds" "Can Hit USN in Japan"', *Jane's Defence Weekly*, 53 (6 July 2016), p. 8.

45 Bruce E. Arlinghaus, 'Social Versus Military Development: Positive and Normative Dimensions', in *Arms Production in Developing Countries: An Analysis of Decision Making*, ed. by James Everett Katz (Lexington: D.C. Heath and Co., 1984), pp. 39–50 (pp. 43–44).

46 Tom Kington, 'Italy Readies Quick Sale of Patrol Ships to Indonesia Amid China Fears', *Defense News* (27 October 2023), <www.defensenews.com/global/europe/2023/10/27/italy-readies-quick-sale-of-patrol-ships-to-indonesia-amid-china-fears> [accessed 28 October 2023].

47 Jeremy Binnie, 'Riyadh and Moscow Sign S-400 MOU', *Jane's Defence Weekly*, 54 (11 October 2017), p. 4.

48 See, for example Barbara Starr, 'S Koreans Cool Hornet Deal', *Jane's Defence Weekly*, 14 (10 November 1990), p. 921.

49 United States, Congress, Office of Technology Assessment, *Arming Our Allies*, p. 111. See also Dong Joon Hwang, 'Industry: Into a New Era', *Jane's Defence Weekly*, 16 (16 November 1991), pp. 965–67 (p. 967).

50 James Hardy, 'South Korea Signs Up for 40 F-35As', *Jane's Defence Weekly*, 51 (1 October 2014), p. 9; Jon Grevatt, 'S Korea Considers Offset Changes in Bid for Investment', *Jane's Defence Weekly*, 47 (17 March 2010), p. 18.

51 Charles Forrester, 'Algeria Aims to Expand its Defence Industrial Output', *Jane's Defence Weekly*, 51 (17 September 2014), p. 22.

52 See Robert Karniol, 'Linking Defence with Economic Progress', *Jane's Defence Weekly*, 24 (25 November 1995), p. 40. See also Sanders, *Arms Industries*, p. 16.

53 Riad Kahwaji, 'Making Headway', *Defense News* (26 May 2003), p. 20.

54 See Jon Grevatt, 'Taiwan Starts Offset Negotiations Over F-16', *Jane's Defence Weekly*, 48 (12 October 2011), p. 20; and *Jane's Defence Weekly*, 'Climbing the Industrial Ladder', *Jane's Defence Weekly*, 20 (31 July 1993), pp. 20–25 (pp. 20–23).

55 Jon Grevatt, 'Indonesia Announces Offset Programme', *Jane's Defence Weekly*, 51 (16 April 2014), p. 20; Ron Matthews, 'Indonesian Strategy is Put to the Test', *Jane's Defence Weekly*, 19 (20 March 1993), pp. 29–30.

56 See, for example Nicholas Fiorenza, 'Belgium Chooses F-35, Invests in Armoured Vehicles and MALE UAVs', *Jane's Defence Weekly*, 55 (31 October 2018), p. 4.

57 Yefim Gordon and Dmitry Komissarov, *Soviet and Russian Military Aircraft in Asia* (Manchester: Hikoki Publications, 2014), p. 290; Samuel Cranny-Evans, 'Big Spenders', *Jane's Defence Weekly*, 57 (27 May 2020), pp. 25–29 (p. 29); Nikolai Novichkov, 'Tor-M1s Help Pay Debt to Beijing', *Jane's Defence Weekly*, 33 (15 March 2000), p. 13.

58 See Brogan and Zarca, *Deadly Business*, pp. 49–54.

59 Bermudez, *The Shield of the Great Leader*, p. 116.

60 Jon Grevatt, 'Thai Offset Plans Could be Derailed by Moves to Reinstate Countertrade', *Jane's Defence Weekly*, 49 (5 December 2012), p. 17.

61 Bergman, *Rise and Kill First*, p. 128.

62 Tim Fish, 'LTTE Navy is "Defunct" Says Sri Lankan MoD', *Jane's Defence Weekly*, 44 (26 September 2007), p. 14.

63 See Simon Pepper, 'Aspects of Operational Art: Communications, Cannon, and Small War', in *European Warfare 1350–1750*, ed. by Frank Tallett and D.J.B. Trim (Cambridge: Cambridge University Press, 2010), pp. 181–202 (pp. 194–95).

## 4 Transnational Industry and the International Arms Transfer System

1 Jacques S. Gansler, *The Defense Industry* (Cambridge: The MIT Press, 1980), p. 204.

2 Boutin, *Economic Security and Sino-American Relations*, pp. 81–82. See also Guy Anderson, 'GAO Reports on Counterfeit Parts Probe', *Jane's Defence Weekly*, 49 (4 April 2012), p. 15.

3 Mark A. Lorell et al., *Going Global? U.S. Government Policy and the Defense Aerospace Industry* (Santa Monica: RAND Corp., 2002), p. 77.

4 Marc Lohnstein, *Royal Netherlands East Indies Army 1936–42* (Oxford: Osprey Publishing, 2018), p. 11.

5 Kenneth Boutin, *American Technology Policy: Evolving Strategic Interests after the Cold War* (Dulles: Potomac Books, 2013), p. 46.

6 See Thayer, *The War Business*, p. 33.

7 Stephen D. Bryen, *Technology Security and National Power: Winners and Losers* (New Brunswick: Transaction Publishers, 2016), pp. 21–22.

8 Edward Hallett Carr, *German–Soviet Relations Between the Two World Wars, 1919–1939* (New York: Harper & Row, 1966), pp. 57–61.

9 Angus Konstam, *British Motor Gun Boat 1939–45* (Oxford: Osprey Publishing, 2010), p. 15.

10 See Theodore H. Moran and David C. Mowery, 'Aerospace and National Security in an Era of Globalization', in *Techno-Security in an Age of Globalization: Perspectives from the Pacific Rim*, ed. by Denis Fred Simon (Armonk: M.E. Sharpe, 1997), pp. 226–50 (pp. 229–32).

11 Franz Tödtling, 'The Uneven Landscape of Innovation Poles: Local Embeddedness and Global Networks', in *Globalization, Institutions, and Regional Development in Europe*, ed. by Ash Amin and Nigel Thrift (Oxford: Oxford University Press, 1994), pp. 68–90 (p. 70); Vicki L. Golich, 'From Competition to Collaboration: The Challenge of Commercial-Class Aircraft Manufacturing', *International Organization*, 46 (Autumn 1992), pp. 899–934 (pp. 903–06).

12 Wong Poh-Kam, 'The Proliferation of Technology-Based International Strategic Alliances: Contrasting Perspectives', in *Techno-Security in an Age of Globalization: Perspectives from the Pacific Rim*, ed. by Denis Fred Simon (Armonk: M.E. Sharpe, 1997), pp. 165–85 (pp. 166–69).

13 David Mulholland, Interview with Richard Moon, Chief Executive of Thales Defence, *Jane's Defence Weekly*, 35 (18 April 2001), p. 40.

14 Theodore H. Moran and David C. Mowery, 'Aerospace', *Daedalus*, 120 (1991), pp. 135–54 (pp. 140–41). See also Vicki Golich, 'Aviation's Technology Imperative and the Transformation of the Global Political Economy', in *Technology, Culture and Competitiveness: Change and the World Political Economy*, ed. by Michael Talalay, Chris Farrands and Roger Tooze (London: Routledge, 1997), pp. 180–95 (pp. 187–90).

15 Boutin, *Economic Security and Sino-American Relations*, p. 27.

16 See Son Key-young, 'N. Korea to Use Shanghai as Benchmark for SEZ', *The Korea Times* (26 January 2001), <www.koreatimes.co.kr/times/200101/t2001012617322840111184.htm> [accessed 28 August 2002].

17 See Bryan Mabee, *The Globalization of Security: State Power, Security Provision and Legitimacy* (Basingstoke: Palgrave Macmillan, 2009), p. 91.

18 See Richard Bitzinger, *Arming Asia: Technonationalism and its Impact on Local Defense Industries* (London: Routledge, 2017); and Theodore H. Moran and David C. Mowery, 'Aerospace and National Security in an Era of Globalization', pp. 226–27.

19 O. Shawn Cupp, 'Defence Consolidation in the US', in *Handbook of Defence Politics: International and Comparative Perspectives*, ed. by Isaiah Wilson III and James J.F. Forest (London: Routledge, 2008), pp. 361–69 (p. 363).

20 See, for example Michael Oden, 'Cashing In, Cashing Out, and Converting: Restructuring of the Defense Industrial Base in the 1990s', in *Arming the Future: A Defense Industry for the 21st Century*, ed. by Ann R. Markusen and Sean S. Costigan (New York: Council on Foreign Relations Press, 1999), pp. 74–105 (pp. 82–83).

21 See Stephanie G. Neuman, 'Defense Industries and Global Dependency', *Orbis*, 50 (Summer 2006), pp. 429–51 (p. 432).

22 Linda Deer Richardson, 'COTS Conundrum', *Jane's Defence Weekly*, 49 (25 January 2012), pp. 29–32.

23 The International Institute for Strategic Studies, *The Military Balance 1987–1988* (London: International Institute for Strategic Studies, 1987), p. 239.

24 Bill Sweetman, 'The Big US Seven Vie for Survival', *Jane's Defence Weekly*, 16 (14 September 1991), pp. 476–79 (p. 478).

25 Tom Kington, 'German-Italian Tank Kerfuffle Dings Vision of Europeanized Arms', *Defense News* (14 June 2024), <www.defensenews.com/global/europe/2024/06/14/german-italian-tank-kerfuffle-dings-vision-of-europeanized-arms> [accessed 15 June 2024].

26 Roy Braybrook, 'The Shape of Things to Come', *AIR International*, 27 (September 1984), pp. 143–49 (p. 145).

27 Lorell et al., *Going Global?*, pp. 5–7.

28 Charles Grant, 'Global Defence Industry', *The Economist*, 343 (14 June 1997), pp. 3–18 (p. 6).

29 The International Institute for Strategic Studies, 'Consolidating Europe's Defence Industries: Big Rewards, Big Obstacles', *Strategic Comments*, 11 (June 2005), pp. 1–2 (p. 1).

30 Koistinen, *State of War*, p. 184.

31 Keri Wagstaff-Smith, 'PFI: Unfairly Maligned?' *Jane's Defence Weekly*, 48 (2 March 2011), pp. 28–31.

32 Jon Grevatt, 'United States, India Advance Trade and Technology Initiative', *Jane's Defence Weekly*, 56 (27 March 2019), p. 18.

33 Boutin, *Economic Security and Sino-American Relations*, pp. 40–41.

34 See Jon Grevatt, 'China's AVIC Begins Sale of Shipbuilding Arm', *Jane's Defence Weekly*, 56 (8 May 2019), p. 20.

35 Daniel Alderman et al., 'The Rise of Chinese Civil-Military Integration', in *Forging China's Military Might: A New Framework for Assessing Innovation*, ed. by Tai Ming Cheung (Baltimore: Johns Hopkins University Press, 2014), pp. 109–35 (p. 109).

36 Keith Hayward, 'The Globalisation of Defence Industries', *Survival*, 43 (Summer 2001), pp. 115–32 (p. 118).

37 Raymond Vernon and Ethan B. Kapstein, 'National Needs, Global Resources', in *Defense and Dependence in a Global Economy*, ed. by Raymond Vernon and Ethan B. Kapstein (Washington: Congressional Quarterly, 1992), pp. 1–22 (p. 5).

38 See Artis Pabriks, 'Latvia's Defense Minister: The Security of Supply Can Solve Crises', *Defense News* (8 December 2022), <www.defensenews.com/outlook/2022/12/05/latvias-defense-minister-the-security-of-supply-can-solve-crises> [accessed 9 December 2022].

39 Jen Judson, 'Rafael Pitches Latest Spike Variant for US Army's Long-Range Weapon for Helos', *Defense News* (17 June 2022), <www.defensenews.com/digital-show-dailies/eurosatory/2022/06/17/rafael-pitches-spike-variant-for-us-armys-long-range-weapon-for-helos> [accessed 20 June 2022].

40 Mark Hewish, 'Re-directing the Defense R&D Pipeline', *International Defense Review*, 26 (July 1993), p. 555.

41 See James Heitz Jackson, 'Reshaping of the Defence Industry', *Jane's Defence Weekly*, 12 (25 November 1989), pp. 1153–55 (p. 1154) for a useful overview of interfirm collaborative approaches.

42 Shaun Connors, interview with Shane O'Neill, CEO of Timoney Technology Limited, *Jane's Defence Weekly*, 53 (9 November 2016), p. 34; Richard Scott, 'Steller Systems Trials Scaled Offshore Insertion Craft', *Jane's Defence Weekly*, 61 (10 April 2024), p. 13.

43 See Gary M. Shiffman, *Economic Instruments of Security Policy: Influencing Choices of Leaders* (London: Palgrave Macmillan, 2006), pp. 93–94.

44 Tim Robinson, 'Getting a Slice of the Cake', *Military Technology*, 30 (November 2006), pp. 8–17.

45 Daniel Wasserbly, 'Brazil to Make F-X2 Decision in "April or May"', *Jane's Defence Weekly*, 47 (21 April 2010), p. 10; Jon Grevatt, 'South Korea, US to Sign Industry Sharing Accord', *Jane's Defence Weekly*, 53 (30 November 2016), p. 19.

46 Jon Grevatt, 'Toughening Up', *Jane's Defence Weekly*, 56 (24 April 2019), pp. 20–25 (p. 22).

47 Jon Grevatt, 'Japan Paves Way for Defence Sales in Southeast Asia', *Jane's Defence Weekly*, 54 (15 November 2017), p. 18.

48 Thomas R. Meagher, 'The Future of the Global Defense-Industrial Base: A Case Study of the LTV Sale', *International Defense Review*, 26 (January 1993), pp. 71–73 (p. 71).

49 See Howard Wheeldon, 'JSF Technology Transfer Remains an Unproven Art', *Jane's Defence Weekly*, 44 (16 May 2007), p. 21; and James Murphy, 'DIS "Incompatible" with US Policy, Says UK Official', *Jane's Defence Weekly*, 43 (12 April 2006), p. 21.

50 Boutin, *Economic Security and Sino-American Relations*, pp. 138–41.

51 Ibid., p. 145.

52 See Guy Anderson, 'Partnerships of Equality', *Jane's Defence Weekly*, 47 (20 January 2010), pp. 28–31 (p. 29).

53 Boutin, *Economic Security and Sino-American Relations*, p. 146.

54 Quoted in Sharon Hobson, 'Picking Your Partner', *Jane's Defence Weekly*, 18 (4 July 1992), pp. 43–46 (p. 43).

55 Robert Wall, 'Export Issues Bedevil JSF', *Aviation Week & Space Technology*, 158 (3 March 2003), pp. 36–37.

56 Boutin, *American Technology Policy*, p. 34.

57 Boutin, *Economic Security and Sino-American Relations*, p. 42.

58 *International Defense Review*, 'Matra's International Strategy', *International Defense Review*, 22 (July 1989), p. 887; Richard Scott, 'Global Matrix', *Jane's Defence Weekly*, 43 (19 April 2006), pp. 24–28 (pp. 24–25); Guy Anderson, 'QinetiQ Reveals Push for Fourth "Home" Market', *Jane's Defence Weekly*, 45 (23 July 2008), p. 22.

59 Martin Carnoy, 'Multinationals in a Changing World Economy: Whither the Nation-State?' in *The New Global Economy in the Information Age: Reflections on Our Changing World*, ed. by Martin Carnoy, Manuel Castells, Stephen S. Cohen and Fernando Henrique Cardoso (University Park: Pennsylvania State University Press, 1993), pp. 45–96 (p. 77). See also Richard Bassett, Interview with Dan Burnham, Raytheon Chief Executive, *Jane's Defence Weekly*, 31 (31 March 1999), p. 32.

60 Guy Anderson, 'US Aerospace and Defence Exports Facing "Headwinds"', *Jane's Defence Weekly*, 56 (15 May 2019), p. 20. See also Damian Kemp, 'Spotlight Falls on UK, US Export Controls', *Jane's Defence Weekly*, 41 (3 March 2004), p. 8.

61 Pollack, 'Ballistic Trajectory', p. 415.

## 5 The Emerging Arms Supplier States

1 See Robert Hewson, 'Cruise Missile Technology Proliferation Takes Off', *Jane's Intelligence Review*, 17 (October 2005), pp. 41–45 (p. 41).

2 Sanders, *Arms Industries*, pp. 6–7.

3 Bechtol, *North Korean Military Proliferation in the Middle East and Africa*, pp. 1–2.

4 Joseph S. Bermudez, Jr., Victor Cha and Jennifer Jun, 'Major Munitions Transfers from North Korea to Russia' (28 February 2024), <https://beyondparallel.csis.org/major-munitions-transfers-from-north-korea-to-russia> [accessed 4 March 2024].

5 John Boatman, 'USA's Growing Concern Over Co-operation', *Jane's Defence Weekly*, 12 (29 July 1989), p. 165.

6 Janne E. Nolan, *Military Industry in Taiwan and South Korea* (Houndmills: Macmillan Press, 1986), pp. 87–89 and 101.

7 Jon Grevatt, 'Powering Up', *Jane's Defence Weekly* 58 (26 May 2021), pp. 18–23 (p. 18).

8 Lindsey Shanson, 'Building on Offsets', *Jane's Defence Weekly*, 14 (15 December 1990), pp. 1248–49.

9 *Jane's Defence Weekly*, 'New Interests Spur Force Development', p. 24.

10 See David J. Louscher and Michael D. Salomone, *Technology Transfer and U.S. Security Assistance: The Impact of Licensed Production* (Boulder: Westview Press, 1987), pp. 168–69.

11 James Elliot, 'The "Other" Military Aircraft Programmes', *Military Technology*, 22 (July 1998), pp. 54–61 (p. 58).

12 Arun Sasidharan, 'Kaveri to be Revived with French Assistance', *Jane's Defence Weekly*, 54 (22 February 2017), p. 7.

13 See *Jane's Defence Weekly*, 'Climbing the Industrial Ladder', p. 20.

14 See Sanders, *Arms Industries*, pp. 12–14; and Anthony, 'The "Third Tier" Countries', p. 364.

15 Kerry Herschelman, 'Independence Through Industry', *Jane's Defence Weekly*, 56 (3 April 2019), pp. 20–30 (p. 24).

16 See Ashok Sharma, 'India to Boost Arms Output, Fearing Shortfall from Russia', *Defense News* (8 April 2022), <www.defensenews.com/global/asia-pacific/2022/04/07/india-to-boost-arms-output-fearing-shortfall-from-russia> [accessed 8 April 2022].

17 Young-Sun Ha, 'South Korea', in *Arms Production in Developing Countries: An Analysis of Decision Making*, ed. by James Everett Katz (Lexington: D.C. Heath and Co., 1984), pp. 225–33 (pp. 227–28).

18 Helmoed-Römer Heitman, 'South Africa "Seeks Defence Self-Reliance"', *Jane's Defence Weekly*, 48 (30 March 2011), p. 16.

19 See Karniol, 'Taiwan to Slash its IDF Fighter Production', p. 5.

20 Nicole Ball, *Security and Economy in the Third World* (Princeton: Princeton University Press, 1988), p. 355.

21 Ibid.

22 *Jane's Defence Weekly*, 'Nigeria Unveils Indigenous Ship', *Jane's Defence Weekly*, 49 (13 June 2012), p. 16.

23 See Ken Conca, 'Third World Military Industrialization and the Evolving Security System', in *The Highest Stakes: The Economic Foundations of the Next Security System*, ed. by Wayne Sandholtz et al. (New York: Oxford University Press, 1992), pp. 141–64 (p. 148).

24 Grevatt, 'Toughening Up', p. 21.

25 Brogan and Zarca, *Deadly Business*, p. 185.

26 Jon Grevatt, 'DAPA Unveils Plan to Develop Industrial Base', *Jane's Defence Weekly*, 55 (26 September 2018), p. 24; Grevatt, 'Slow and Steady', p. 30.

27 Conca, 'Third World Military Industrialization and the Evolving Security System', p. 144.

28 Robert E. Looney, *Third-World Military Expenditure and Arms Production* (Houndmills: Macmillan Press, 1988), p. 84.

29 Jon Grevatt and Guy Anderson, 'Seoul Outlines Policy Shift Towards Industrial Collaboration', *Jane's Defence Weekly*, 56 (15 May 2019), p. 21; Jon Grevatt, 'Seoul Expands Import Substitution Drive', *Jane's Defence Weekly*, 56 (20 March 2019), p. 18.

30 See Tai Ming Cheung, *Fortifying China: The Struggle to Build a Modern Defense Economy* (Ithaca: Cornell University Press, 2009), pp. 31–35.

31 Thayer, *The War Business*, p.281; Bergman, *Rise and Kill First*, pp. 61–62.

32 Mike Yeo, 'Taiwan Launches its First Homemade Submarine', *Defense News* (29 September 2023), <www.defensenews.com/global/asia-pacific/2023/09/29/taiwan-launches-its-first-homemade-submarine> [accessed 30 September 2023].

33 Bergman, *Rise and Kill First*, pp. 356–57.

34 See AIR International, 'Egypt', *AIR International*, 10 (May 1976), p. 210.

35 James Bingham, 'UN Report Reveals Extent of North Korean Arms Sales', *Jane's Defence Weekly*, 55 (11 April 2018), p. 8.

36 Robert Hewson, 'Chinese Su-27 Upgrade Funds Russian Project', *Jane's Defence Weekly*, 40 (8 October 2003), p. 5.

37 Kenneth Boutin, 'Emerging Defense Industries: Prospects and Implications', in *The Modern Defense Industry: Political, Economic, and Technological Issues*, ed. by Richard A. Bitzinger (Santa Barbara: Praeger Security International, 2009), pp. 227–40 (p. 228).

38 David Saw, 'The Emergence of the Third World Aircraft Industry', *Military Technology* 12 (April 1988), pp. 42–52 (pp. 49–50).

39 See, for example, ibid., p. 49.

40 Jon Grevatt, 'Indonesia Bails Out Defence Groups with $1bn of Funding', *Jane's Defence Weekly*, 48 (13 July 2011), p. 19.

41 Iris Chang, *Thread of the Silkworm* (New York: Basic Books, 1995), pp. 215–17.

42 See Andrew Moravcsik, 'Arms and Autarky in Modern European History', *Daedalus*, 120 (1991), pp. 23–45 (pp. 24–26).

43 Conca, 'Third World Military Industrialization and the Evolving Security System', p. 155.

44 Richard A. Bitzinger, *Towards a Brave New Arms Industry?* (Adelphi Paper No.356) (London: International Institute for Strategic Studies, 2003), p. 60.

45 Stephanie G. Neuman, 'Third World Arms Production and the Global Arms Transfer System', in *Arms Production in Developing Countries: An Analysis of Decision Making*, ed. by James Everett Katz (Lexington: D.C. Heath and Co., 1984), pp. 15–37 (p. 26).

46 Patsy Widakuswara, 'Russia Receiving Hundreds of Iranian Drones, Plans to Produce Them: White House', <www.voanews.com/a/7130137.html> [accessed 10 June 2023]; Associated Press, 'US: Russia to Buy Rockets, Artillery Shells from North Korea' (6 September 2022), <www.voanews.com/a/us-russia-to-buy-rockets-artillery-shells-from-north-korea/6733042.html> [accessed 7 September 2022].

47 Maximilian Hess, *Economic War: Ukraine and the Global Conflict between Russia and the West* (London: Hurst & C., 2023), p. 157.

48 See Bermudez, *Shield of the Great Leader*, p. 290.

49 Hewson, 'Cruise Missile Technology Proliferation Takes Off', pp. 41–43.

50 Andrea Berger, 'Disrupting North Korea's Military Markets', *Survival*, 58 (June–July 2016), pp. 101–30 (pp. 108–09 and 112–13); Mark Fitzpatrick, 'Iran and North Korea: The Proliferation Nexus', *Survival*, 48 (Spring 2006), pp. 61–80 (pp. 62–64); Joshua Pollack, 'Ballistic Trajectory', p. 416.

51 Pollack, 'Ballistic Trajectory', p. 414; Steve Rodan, 'Israel, USA Claim Egyptian Missile Links with N Korea', *Jane's Defence Weekly*, 33 (23 February 2000), p. 18.

52 Jeremy Binnie, 'Analysis: Iraq's Shia Militias Roll Out Heavy Rockets for IS Offensive', *Jane's Defence Weekly*, 52 (1 April 2015), p. 18.

53 See Jeffrey Lewis, 'North Korea's Juche Rocket' (23 January 2013), <http://lewis.armscontrolwonk.com/archive/6177/north-koreas-juche-rocket> [accessed 25 January 2013].

54 Andrew L. Ross, 'World Order and Arms Production in the Third World', in *The Implications of Third World Military Industrialization: Sowing the Serpents' Teeth*, ed. by James Everett Katz (Lexington: D.C. Heath and Co., 1986), pp. 277–92 (pp. 277–79).

## 6 International Arms Transfer Patterns

1 Jon Grevatt, 'US Voices Concerns About Indian S-400 Buy', *Jane's Defence Weekly*, 56 (26 June 2019), p. 17.

2 J.W. Kehoe and K.S. Brower, 'US and Soviet Weapon System Design Practices', *International Defense Review*, 15 (June 1982), pp. 705–12 (pp. 705–06).

3 Rahul Bedi, 'India Reverts to Russia for Defence Equipment Needs', *Jane's Defence Weekly*, 56 (3 July 2019), p. 23.

4 Reuben F. Johnson, 'Users of Russian Hardware Facing Spare Parts Dilemma', *Jane's Defence Weekly*, 53 (15 June 2016), p. 22.

5 AIR International, 'Egypt', p. 210.

6 Axworthy, *Revolutionary Iran*, p. 166.

7 See Saw, 'The Emergence of the Third World Aircraft Industry', p. 42.

8 See Anthony Davis, 'Myanmar Air Force Inducts New FTC-2000Gs to Replace K-8s', *Jane's Defence Weekly*, 59 (21 December 2022), p. 16.

9 Pierre, *The Global Politics of Arms Sales*, p. 166.

10 Farhan Bokhari and Nikolai Novichkov, 'Pakistan, Russia Sign Defence Co-operation Accord', *Jane's Defence Weekly*, 51 (3 December 2014), p. 6.

11 Ashley Roque and Kerry Herschelmann, 'SACEUR Warns Against Selling F-35 to Turkey if Ankara's S-400 Buy Proceeds', *Jane's Defence Weekly*, 56 (13 March 2019), p. 4.

12 See Georg Mader, 'Austrian Typhoon Delay Possible', *Jane's Defence Weekly*, 44 (16 May 2007), p. 11.

13 Matthew Bell, Mark Bobbi and Keri Wagstaff-Smith, 'JSF: Weighing Up the Partner Nation Benefits', *Jane's Defence Weekly*, 47 (3 February 2010), p. 23. See also Lale Sariibrahimoglu, 'Strategic Operator', *Jane's Defence Weekly*, 48 (27 April 2011), pp. 24–31 (p. 30); and Alon Ben-David, 'Israel Cannot Fit Local EW Systems to its F-35s, Says US', *Jane's Defence Weekly*, 46 (2 December 2009), p. 16.

14 Martin J. Dougherty, *Chinese Tanks & AFVs: 1950–Present* (London: Amber Books, 2019), p. 19; Gabriel Dominguez, 'Type 15 Light Tank Enters Service in Xinjiang', *Jane's Defence Weekly*, 58 (10 February 2021), p. 15.

15 Boutin, 'Feeding the Lion', p. 238; Jon Grevatt, 'Good Enough', *Jane's Defence Weekly*, 56 (20 November 2019), pp. 22–27 (p. 25).

16 Berger, 'Disrupting North Koreas Military Markets', pp. 105 and 112–13.

17 Neil Grant, *Mauser Military Rifles* (Oxford: Osprey Publishing, 2015), p. 78.

18 Thomas G. Mahnken, *Uncovering Ways of War: U.S. Intelligence and Foreign Military Innovation, 1918–1941* (Ithaca: Cornell University Press, 2002), pp. 98–99 and 115–16.

19 Boutin, 'Feeding the Lion', p. 239. See also Taylor, *China's New Role in Africa*, p. 115.

20 Berger, 'Disrupting North Korea's Military Markets', pp. 110–13.

21 Australian Broadcasting Corporation, 'Russia Seeks Arms-for-Food Deal with North Korea, US Says' (31 March 2023), <www.abc.net.au/news/2023-03-31/us-russia-seeks-arms-for-food-deal-with-north-korea/102169302> [accessed 31 March 2023].

22 Thayer, *The War Business*, pp. 214 and 239–40.

23 Rahul Bedi and Jon Grevatt, 'Panetta to Talk Defence Sales on Trip to India', *Jane's Defence Weekly*, 49 (30 May 2012), p. 21.

24 Nicholas Fiorenza, 'Belgium Procures SPHs and Mortar Carriers from France', *Jane's Defence Weekly*, 60 (20 December 2023), p. 15.

25 See Farhan Bokhari, 'Pakistan Takes Delivery of Home Produced JF-17', *Jane's Defence Weekly*, 46 (2 December 2009), p. 8.

26 See Stockholm International Peace Research Institute, *The Arms Trade with the Third World*, p. 216.

27 Bermudez, *The Shield of the Great Leader*, pp. 115–16.

28 Thayer, *The War Business*, p. 275.

29 Ibid., p. 276.

30 Wyn Q. Bowen, *The Politics of Ballistic Missile Nonproliferation* (Houndmills: Macmillan Press, 2000), p. 18.

31 See Stephen Losey, 'Russia Burning Through Ammunition in Ukraine at "Extraordinary" Rate', *Defense News* (5 December 2022), <www.defensenews.com/smr/reagan-defense-forum/2022/12/04/russia-burning-through-ammunition-in-ukraine-at-extraordinary-rate> [accessed 5 December 2022].

32 Pollack, 'Ballistic Trajectory', p. 416.

33 Oishee Majumdar, 'Bangladesh to Procure Bayraktar TB2 But Remains Silent On Numbers', *Jane's Defence Weekly*, 59 (10 August 2022), p. 16; Vivienne Machi, 'Lockheed, Rheinmetall Pair Up to Build Europe-made Rocket Launcher', *Defense News* (24 June 2023), <www.defensenews.com/global/europe/2023/06/23/lockheed-rheinmetall-pair-up-to-build-europe-made-rocket-launcher>[accessed 24 June 2023].

34 See Saibal Dasgupta, 'China Boosts Military Spending Amid Ukraine Uncertainties' (5 March 2022), <www.voanews.com/a/china-boosts-military-spending-amid-ukraine-uncertainties/6471773.html> [accessed 6 March 2022].

35 Frédéric Lert and Nikolai Novichkov, 'Egypt to Buy the Two Ex-Russian Mistral-class Helicopter Carriers', *Jane's Defence Weekly*, 52 (30 September 2015), p. 5.

36 Joe Gould, 'US Pledges $391 Million for Euro Allies to Buy American to Backfill Weapons Donations to Ukraine', *Defense News* (26 April 2022), <www.defensenews.com/global/europe/2022/04/25/us-pledges-391-million-for-euro-allies-to-buy-american-to-backfill-weapons-donations-to-ukraine> [accessed 26 April 2022].

37 Buzan and Herring, *The Arms Dynamic in World Politics*, p. 88.

38 Andrew J. Pierre, 'Introduction', in *Cascade of Arms: Managing Conventional Weapons Proliferation*, ed. by Andrew J. Pierre (Washington and Cambridge: Brookings Institution Press and The World Peace Foundation, 1997), pp. 4–5. See also Buzan and Herring, *The Arms Dynamic in World Politics*, p. 75.

39 Wilson, 'European Warfare 1815–2000', p. 206.

40 Thayer, *The War Business*, p. 39.

41 Coll, *Directorate S*, p. 667.

42 David Miller, *The Illustrated Dictionary of Tanks of the World From World War I to the Present Day* (London: Salamander Books, 2000), p. 47.

43 See Hook and Rothstein, 'New Rationales and Old Concerns About U.S. Arms-Export Policy', p. 153.

44 Robert Forsyth, *Luftwaffe Emergency Fighters* (Oxford: Osprey Publishing, 2017), pp. 76–77.

45 Ian Anthony, 'The Conventional Arms Trade', in *Cascade of Arms: Managing Conventional Weapons Proliferation*, ed. by Andrew J. Pierre (Washington and Cambridge: Brookings Institution Press and The World Peace Foundation, 1997), pp. 15–41 (p. 16).

46 Dorschner, 'Conflict Zone', p. 21.

47 Benoît Gomis, 'Criminal Opportunities', *Jane's Defence Weekly*, 60 (29 March 2023), pp. 26–29 (p. 28).

48 Jackson, *Mirage*, *passim*.

49 Boutin, 'Feeding the Lion', p. 234.

50 Rahul Bedi, 'Growing Pains', *Jane's Defence Weekly*, 55 (21 February 2018), pp. 22–30 (p. 30).

51 Rahul Bedi, 'India Signs Accord with Moscow to Lease Another SSN', *Jane's Defence Weekly*, 56 (13 March 2019), p. 8; Rahul Bedi, 'India Signs USD950m Deal for Two Russian-built Frigates', *Jane's Defence Weekly*, 55 (7 November 2018), p. 19.

## 7 Managing the Conventional Arms Trade

1 See Micah Zenko and Sarah Kreps, *Limiting Armed Drone Proliferation* (Council Special Report No.69) (New York: Council on Foreign Relations, Center for Preventative Action, 2014), pp. 8–13.

2 Lorell et al., *Going Global?*, pp. 104–08; United States Government Accountability Office, *DOD's Critical Technologies Lists Rarely Inform Export Control and Other Policy Decisions* (Washington: US Government Printing Office, 2006), p. 4.

3 Caitlin Harrington, 'US Seeks to Lift Export Sales Ban on F-22A', *Jane's Defence Weekly*, 43 (28 June 2006), p. 11.

4 United States, 'Arms Export Control Act of 1976' (22 U.S.C. Sec.2751 *et seq*), Chapter 2, Section 25.

5 United States, Government Accountability Office, *Export Controls: Challenges Exist in Enforcement of an Inherently Complex System* (Washington: Government Printing Office, 2006), pp. 7–13. See also Peter M. Leitner, *Decontrolling Strategic Technology, 1990–1992: Creating the Military Threats of the 21st Century* (Lanham: University Press of America, 1995), pp. 32–33.

6 Engelbrecht and Hanighen, *Merchants of Death*, p. 264.

7 David A. Cooper, *Competing Western Strategies Against the Proliferation of Weapons of Mass Destruction: Comparing the United States to a Close Ally* (Westport: Praeger Publishers, 2002), pp. 16–17.

8 William J. Long, 'Defining Strategic Exports in the 1990s: From Export Control to the Management of Technology Exchange', in *Export Controls in Transition: Perspectives, Problems, and Prospects*, ed. by Gary K. Bertsch and Steven Elliott-Gower (Durham: Duke University Press, 1992), pp. 105–27 (p. 105).

9 Malcolm Chalmers and Owen Greene, 'The Register in its First Four Years', in *Developing Arms Transparency: The Future of the UN Register*, ed. by Malcolm Chalmers, Mitsuro Donowaki and Owen Greene (Bradford: University of Bradford and Centre for the Promotion of Disarmament and Non-Proliferation, Japan Institute for International Affairs, 1997), pp. 9–23 (pp. 9–10).

10 See Thomas Jackson, 'From Under Their Noses: Rebel Groups' Arms Acquisition and the Importance of Leakages from State Stockpiles', *International Studies Perspectives*, 11 (May 2010), pp. 131–47 (pp. 135–37).

11 Jozef Goldblat, *Arms Control: The New Guide to Negotiations and Agreements* (London: SAGE Publications, 2002), p. 244.

12 See Mark Bromley, Neil Cooper and Paul Holtom, 'The UN Arms Trade Treaty: Arms Export Controls, the Human Security Agenda and Lessons of History', *International Affairs*, 88 (2012), pp. 1029–48 (pp. 1038–39); and Anna Stavrianakis, 'Controlling Weapons Circulation in a Postcolonial Militarised World', *Review of International Studies*, 45 (2019), pp. 57–76 (p. 57).

13 See Jennifer L. Erickson, *Dangerous Trade: Arms Exports, Human Rights, and International Reputation* (New York: Columbia University Press, 2015), pp. 101–03.

14 Howson, *Arms for Spain*, pp. 81–82. See also R.T. Naylor, 'The Rise of the Modern Black Market and the Fall of Supply-Side Controls', in *Combating Transnational Crime: Concepts, Activities and Responses*, ed. by Phil Williams and Dimitri Vlassis (London: Frank Cass, 2001), pp. 209–36 (p. 213).

15 See Lina Grip, 'History Never Repeats? Imports, Impact and Control of Small Arms in Africa', *Contemporary Security Policy*, 36 (2015), pp. 79–103 (pp. 85–86); and Moravcsik, 'Arms and Autarky in Modern European History', p. 25.

16 Jon Grevatt, 'Japan Looks to New Defence Policy to Boost Defence Industry', *Jane's Defence Weekly*, 49 (31 October 2012), p. 23.

17 Beth Stevenson and Guy Anderson, 'German Government Halts Defence Sales to Saudi Arabia', *Jane's Defence Weekly*, 55 (31 October 2018), p. 16.

18 Hugo Meijer, *Trading with the Enemy: The Making of US Export Control Policy toward the People's Republic of China* (Oxford: Oxford University Press, 2016), pp. 33–54.

19 Voice of America, 'US Treasury Promises to Tighten Sanctions on Russia' (29 May 2024) <www.voanews.com/a/us-treasury-promises-to-tighten-sanctions-on-russia/7634156.html> [accessed 30 May 2024]; Masood Farivar, 'US Warns About Increasing Use of Intermediaries to Evade Russia Sanctions' (6 March 2023), <www.voanews.com/a/us-warns-about-increasing-use-of-intermediaries-to-evade-russia-sanctions/6992824.html> [accessed 7 March 2023].

20 Chase, '"Strong Indignation", but Limited Retribution', p. 2; Associated Press, 'China Sanctions Lockheed Martin, Raytheon for Taiwan Sales'.

21 Jon Grevatt, 'Japanese MoD Says "No Collaboration" with Israel on UAV Development', *Jane's Defence Weekly*, 53 (21 September 2016), p. 24.

22 Charles Forrester, 'DSCA Tightens End-Use Monitoring Process', *Jane's Defence Weekly*, 56 (12 June 2019), p. 21.

23 Rahul Bedi, 'US Eyes Indian Military Counterweight to China', *Jane's Defence Weekly*, 47 (15 September 2010), p. 25.

24 Pat Host, 'Brazil, USA Sign Space TSA', *Jane's Defence Weekly*, 56 (27 March 2019), p. 11.

25 Zachary Fryer-Biggs, 'US Builds Database of Arms Given to Syrian Kurds', *Jane's Defence Weekly*, 54 (7 June 2017), p. 5.

26 Agence France-Presse, 'US Personnel Tracking American-Supplied Gear in Ukraine' (3 November 2022), <www.voanews.com/a/us-personnel-tracking-american-supplied-gear-in-ukraine-/6819038.html> [accessed 4 November 2022].

27 See Gareth Jennings, 'France Could Replace US Parts in SCALP to Bypass ITAR Restrictions for Egypt', *Jane's Defence Weekly*, 55 (8 August 2018), p. 10.
28 Wall, 'Export Issues Bedevil JSF', pp. 36–37.
29 See Hull and Markov, 'Trends in the Arms Market', pp. 236–37.
30 Reuters, 'US Imposes Sanctions on Military Procurement Network Aiding Russia' (14 November 2022), <www.voanews.com/a/us-imposes-sanctions-on-military-procurement-network-aiding-russia-/6833861.html> [accessed 14 November 2022]; Reuters, 'US Curbs Exports to Iranian Firms for Producing Drones for Russia' (31 January 2023), <www.voa.com/a/us-curbs-exports-to-Iranian-firms-for-producing-drones-for-Russia/6942647.html> [accessed 1 February 2023].
31 Bryen, *Technology Security and National Power*, pp. 60–61.
32 See Charles Forrester, 'Raytheon Penalised $8m following ITAR Violations', *Jane's Defence Weekly*, 50 (8 May 2013), p. 20; and Guy Anderson, 'ITT Pays the Penalty for ITAR Violation', *Jane's Defence Weekly*, 44 (4 April 2007), p. 18.
33 See Jon Grevatt, 'US Imposes Sanctions On Chinese Firms', *Jane's Defence Weekly*, 50 (20 February 2013), p. 18.
34 Sanders, *Arms Industries*, p. 4.
35 Joe McDonald, 'China Ukraine Envoy Urges Allies to "Stop Sending Weapons" to Kyiv', *Defense News* (3 June 2023), <www.defensenews.com/news/your-military/2023/06/02/china-ukraine-envoy-urges-allies-to-stop-dending-weapons-to-kyiv> [accessed 3 June 2023].
36 Katz and Bohbot, *The Weapon Wizards*, pp. 230 and 237.
37 Yaakov Katz, 'Block Remains in Israeli Sales to China', *Jane's Defence Weekly*, 48 (23 November 2011), p. 18.
38 James Bingham and Oscar Widlund, 'High-Level Protection', *Jane's Defence Weekly*, 56 (24 April 2019), pp. 26–31 (p. 30); Jon Grevatt, 'Russia and its Asian Clients Seek to Exploit CAATSA Loopholes', *Jane's Defence Weekly*, 56 (24 July 2019), p. 21.
39 Ch'i, *Warlord Politics in China 1916–1928*, p. 121; Howson, *Arms for Spain*, p. 81.
40 Sampson, *The Arms Bazaar*, p. 172. See also Anthony, 'The "Third Tier" Countries', p. 364.
41 Daniel R. Headrick, *The Tools of Empire: Technology and European Imperialism in the Nineteenth Century* (New York: Oxford University Press, 1981), p. 110. See also Bromley, Cooper and Holtom, 'The UN Arms Trade Treaty', p. 1031.
42 See Brian J. Given, *A Most Pernicious Thing: Gun Trading and Native Warfare in the Early Contact Period* (Ottawa: Carleton University Press, 1994), p. 58.
43 Stockholm International Peace Research Institute, Arms Embargo Archive, <www.sipri.org/databases/embargoes> [accessed 1 November 2023]
44 Erickson, *Dangerous Trade*, pp. 102–03.
45 See Zachary Fryer-Biggs, 'US Gathers 44 Countries in Push for Armed UAV Export Standards', *Jane's Defence Weekly*, 53 (12 October 2016), p. 13.
46 Brogan and Zarca, *Deadly Business*, pp. 175–76.
47 Lucie Béraud-Sudreau, 'Building Franco-German Consensus on Arms Exports', *Survival*, 61 (August–September 2019), pp. 79–98 (p. 79).
48 *Jane's Defence Weekly*, 'EU Builds a Bigger Fence', *Jane's Defence Weekly*, 24 (15 July 1995), p. 4.

49 Guy Anderson, 'EU Defence Export Frictions Emerge as a Growing Issue', *Jane's Defence Weekly*, 56 (6 March 2019), p. 23; Charles Forrester, 'Cracks Emerge in Franco-German Export Control Plans', *Jane's Defence Weekly*, 56 (13 February 2019), p. 23.

50 See Dinshaw Mistry, 'Technological Containment: The MTCR and Missile Proliferation', *Security Studies*, 11 (Spring 2002), pp. 91–122 (pp. 96–104).

51 Bromley, Cooper and Holtom, 'The UN Arms Trade Treaty', pp. 1032–34.

52 Goldblat, *Arms Control*, pp. 241–42.

53 Bromley, Cooper and Holtom, 'The UN Arms Trade Treaty', p. 1036.

54 Buzan and Herring, *The Arms Dynamic in World Politics*, p. 218.

55 Stavrianakis, 'Controlling Weapons Circulation in a Postcolonial Militarised World', p. 59; Daniel Wasserbly, 'US Signs Arms Trade Treaty', *Jane's Defence Weekly*, 50 (2 October 2013), p. 10.

56 Boutin, *American Technology Policy*, p. 102; Heigo Sato, 'Economic Security and Arms Transfer Policy of the United States: DTSI and Defense Cooperation with Allies', *NIDS Security Reports* No.4 (March 2003), pp. 90–108 (pp. 90–92).

57 See Bonsignore and Kogan, 'Fatal Attraction', p. 13.

58 Matthew Bell, 'Trade Treaties with US Remain in Limbo', *Jane's Defence Weekly*, 48 (1 June 2011), p. 19.

59 See Richard D. Fisher, Jr., 'China Assists North Korea with New 300 mm Rocket Artillery System', *Jane's Defence Weekly*, 53 (16 March 2016), p. 14; James Hardy, 'Documents Confirm China Shipped TELs to North Korea', *Jane's Defence Weekly*, 49 (20 June 2012), p. 17.

60 Bryen, *Technology Security and National Power*, pp. 60–61.

61 Robert C. Sellers, 'Appendix III', in *Armed Forces of the World: A Reference Handbook* (Third Edition), ed. by Robert C. Sellers (New York: Praeger Publishing, 1971), pp. 287–89.

62 Cragin and Hoffman, *Arms Trafficking and Colombia*, p. 52.

63 See Anthony Davis, 'United Wa State Army Parade Showcases Modernisation', *Jane's Defence Weekly*, 56 (1 May 2019), p. 15; and Wahyudi Soeriaatmadja, 'Indonesian-Filipino Terror Links Exposed', *The Straits Times* (3 February 2018), p. A2.

64 Mitsuro Donowaki, 'Addressing Light Weapons and Small Arms Proliferation', in *Developing Arms Transparency: The Future of the UN Register*, ed. by Malcolm Chalmers, Mitsuro Donowaki and Owen Greene (Bradford: University of Bradford and Centre for the Promotion of Disarmament and Non-Proliferation, Japan Institute for International Affairs, 1997), pp. 203–11 (p. 203).

65 Coll, *Directorate S*, pp. 138–39.

66 Jeremy Binnie, 'UAE Distances Itself from Munitions Found in Libya', *Jane's Defence Weekly*, 56 (10 July 2019), p. 18.

67 See Max Smeets, 'Cyber Arms Transfer: Meaning, Limits, and Implications', *Security Studies*, 31 (2022), pp. 65–91.

68 AIR International, 'Iraq', *AIR International*, 25 (August 1983), p. 54.

69 Garcia, 'Arms Transfers Beyond the State-to-State Realm', p. 156.

70 Shirley A. Kan, *Chinese Missile and Nuclear Proliferation: Issues for Congress* (Washington: Congressional Research Service, 1993), p. i.

71 Zhang, 'Harmonising the Management of Foreign and Domestic Affairs in Chinese Foreign Policy', pp. 155–57.

72 Taylor, *China's New Role in Africa*, p. 123.

73 John Boatman, 'USA and Taiwan in "Sub-COCOM" Talks', *Jane's Defence Weekly*, 12 (23 December 1989), p. 1392; Meijer, *Trading with the Enemy*, p. 7.

74 Noah Robertson, 'AUKUS Countries Update Rules on Sharing Defense Kit', *Defense News* (16 August 2024), <www.defensenews.com/pentagon/2024/08/15/aukus-countries-update-rules-on-sharing-defense-kit> [accessed 16 August 2024].

75 Boutin, *Economic Security and Sino-American Relations*, p. 86.

76 Matthew Smith, 'Canada Reforms Export Rules', *Jane's Defence Weekly*, 51 (11 June 2014), p. 36; Nick Cook, 'UK Hinders European Stealth Demonstrator Plan', *Jane's Defence Weekly*, 34 (4 October 2000), p. 3.

77 Lorell et al., *Going Global?*, pp. 121–23.

78 Matthew Bell, 'US-UK Defence Trade Treaty Takes Effect', *Jane's Defence Weekly*, 49 (18 April 2012), p. 5; Jon Grevatt, 'Canberra Finally Ratifies Trade Treaty with US', *Jane's Defence Weekly*, 49 (7 November 2012), p. 5.

79 Brogan and Zarca, *Deadly Business*, p. 224; Thayer, *The War Business*, p. 137.

80 Steve Coll, *Ghost Wars: The Secret History of the CIA, Afghanistan, and Bin Laden, from the Soviet Invasion to September 10, 2001* (New York: Penguin Books, 2005), p. 133.

81 Reuters, 'Israeli Attacks Squeeze Iranian Aerial Supplies to Syria, Sources Say' (2 September 2022), <www.voanews.com/a/israeli-attacks-squeeze-iranian-aerial-supplies-to-syria-sources-say/6728735.html> [accessed 3 September 2022].

82 Mary Beth Nikitin, *Proliferation Security Initiative (PSI)* (Washington: Congressional Research Service, 2011), p. 5.

83 Bradley Bowman, Ryan Brobst and Mark Montgomery, 'New Mideast Task Force Can Counter Iranian Arms Smuggling, But More Capabilities Are Needed', *Defense News* (10 May 2022), <www.defensenews.com/opinion/commentary/2022/05/09/new-mideast-task-force-can-counter-iranian-arms-smuggling-but-more-capabilities-are-needed> [accessed 10 May 2022].

84 Dinshaw Mistry, 'Beyond the MTCR: Building a Comprehensive Regime to Contain Ballistic Missile Proliferation', *International Security*, 27 (2003), pp. 119–49 (p. 119).

85 The International Institute for Strategic Studies, 'Iran Sanctions Halt Long-Range Ballistic-Missile Development', *Strategic Comments*, 18 (2012), pp. 1–3 (p. 3).

86 See Bermudez, *Shield of the Great Leader*, pp. 184–88; Reuben F. Johnson, 'But Further Strategic Weapon Tests Likely to Continue', *Jane's Defence Weekly*, 53 (8 June 2016), p. 8; Naylor, *Patriots and Profiteers*, p. 156; Signe Landgren, *Embargo Disimplemented: South Africa's Military Industry* (Oxford: Oxford University Press, 1989).

87 Hull and Markov, 'A Changing Market in the Arms Bazaar', p. 141.

88 Charles McC. Mathias, Jr., 'A New US Export Control Policy', in *National Security and Technology Transfer: The Strategic Dimensions of East-West Trade*, ed. by Gary K. Bertsch and John R. McIntyre (Boulder: Westview Press, 1983), pp. 159–69 (p. 166).

89 Quoted in Andrew Koch, 'USA Rethinks MTCR Options', *Jane's Defence Weekly*, 33 (10 May 2000), p. 22.

90 George Crown, 'Success of the Arms Embargo', in *South Africa: The Sanctions Report: Documents and Statistics*, ed. by Joseph Hanlon (London: The Commonwealth Secretariat, 1990), pp. 168–74 (p. 168).

91 See Daniel Salisbury, 'Exploring the Use of "Third Countries" in Proliferation Networks: The Case of Malaysia', *European Journal of International Security*, 4 (2019), pp. 101–22); and Reuters, 'The Supply Chain That Keeps Tech Flowing to Russia' (13 December 2022), <www.reuters.com/investigates/special-report/ukraine-crisis-tech-middlemen> [accessed 14 December 2022].

92 Charles Forrester and Matthew Smith, 'Up in Arms: The Impact of Europe's Sanctions on Russia', *Jane's Defence Weekly*, 51 (6 August 2014), pp. 20–21.

93 See Jeremy Binnie, 'Iran Unveils F-5F as "New" Fighter Type', *Jane's Defence Weekly*, 55 (29 August 2018), p. 16.

## 8 The Prospects for the International Arms Transfer System

1 Pat Host, 'Promise & Limitation', *Jane's Defence Weekly*, 55 (4 April 2018), pp. 24–30 (pp. 24–25); Tristan A. Volpe, 'Dual-Use Distinguishability: How 3D-Printing Shapes the Security Dilemma for Nuclear Programs', *Journal of Strategic Studies*, 42 (2019), pp. 814–40 (pp. 814–15).

2 Anthony Davis, 'Power Struggles', *Jane's Defence Weekly*, 59 (9 November 2022), pp. 18–25 (p. 21).

3 Stephen Losey, 'Future Fighter Program Poses Key Test for US Air Force's Design Methods', *Defense News* (30 August 2023), <www.defensenews.com/air/2023/08/30/future-fighter-program-poses-key-test-for-us-air-forces-design-method> [accessed 31 August 2023].

4 Stephen Losey, 'T-7 Tred Hawk Trainer Makes its Debut', *Defense News* (30 April 2022), <www.defensenews.com/air/2022/04/29/t-7-red-hawk-trainer-makes-its-debut> [accessed 30 April 2022].

5 See Marc Selinger, 'Lockheed Martin and Raytheon Back US Effort to Expand Use of 3D Printing', *Jane's Defence Weekly*, 59 (18 May 2022), p. 9.

6 Volpe, 'Dual-Use Distinguishability', p. 815.

# Bibliography


Acharya, A., *An Arms Race in Post-Cold War Southeast Asia: Prospects for Control* (Singapore: Institute of Southeast Asian Studies, 1994).

Agence France-Presse, 'US Personnel Tracking American-Supplied Gear in Ukraine' (3 November 2022), <www.voanews.com/a/us-personnel-tracking-american-supplied-gear-in-ukraine-/6819038.html> [accessed 4 November 2022].

AIR International, 'The Ayatollahs' Air Force', *AIR International*, 26 (June 1984), pp. 277–80.

———, 'Singapore', *AIR International*, 26 (March 1984), p. 110.

———, 'Iraq', *AIR International*, 25 (August 1983), p. 54.

———, 'Egypt', *AIR International*, 10 (May 1976), p. 210.

Alagappa, M., 'Asian Practice of Security: Key Features and Explanations', in *Asian Security Practice: Material and Ideational Influences*, ed. by M. Alagappa (Stanford: Stanford University Press, 1998), pp. 611–76. https://doi.org/10.1515/9780804765121-022

Alderman, D. et al., 'The Rise of Chinese Civil-Military Integration', in *Forging China's Military Might: A New Framework for Assessing Innovation*, ed. by T.M. Cheung (Baltimore: Johns Hopkins University Press, 2014), pp. 109–35.

Alley, R., 'Small Arms and Light Weapons: The Disjunction Problem', *Conflict, Security & Development*, 19 (2019), pp. 143–72. https://doi.org/10.1080/14678802.2019.1570722

Anderson, B., *Imagined Communities: Reflections on the Origins and Spread of Nationalism* (Revised Edition) (London: Verso, 1991).

Anderson, G., 'US Aerospace and Defence Exports Facing "Headwinds"', *Jane's Defence Weekly*, 56 (15 May 2019), p. 20.

———, 'EU Defence Export Frictions Emerge as a Growing Issue', *Jane's Defence Weekly*, 56 (6 March 2019), p. 23.

———, 'GAO Reports on Counterfeit Parts Probe', *Jane's Defence Weekly*, 49 (4 April 2012), p. 15.

———, 'Partnerships of Equality', *Jane's Defence Weekly*, 47 (20 January 2010), pp. 28–31.

———, 'QinetiQ Reveals Push for Fourth "Home" Market', *Jane's Defence Weekly*, 45 (23 July 2008), p. 22.

———, 'ITT Pays the Penalty for ITAR Violation', *Jane's Defence Weekly*, 44 (4 April 2007), p. 18.

Anderson, G. et al., 'Exports and Global Influence', *Jane's Industry Quarterly*, 1 (July 2008), pp. 3–9.

Anthony, I., 'The Conventional Arms Trade', in *Cascade of Arms: Managing Conventional Weapons Proliferation*, ed. by A.J. Pierre (Washington and Cambridge: Brookings Institution Press and The World Peace Foundation, 1997), pp. 15–41.

———, 'The "Third Tier" Countries: Production of Major Weapons', in *Arms Industry Limited*, ed. by H. Wulf (Oxford: Oxford University Press, 1993), pp. 362–83.

Arlinghaus, B.E., 'Social Versus Military Development: Positive and Normative Dimensions', in *Arms Production in Developing Countries: An Analysis of Decision Making*, ed. by J.E. Katz (Lexington: D.C. Heath and Co., 1984), pp. 39–50.

Arthur, G., 'Fincantieri Inks $1.3B Deal with Indonesia for Two Patrol Ships', *Defense News* (30 March 2024), <www.defensenews.com/naval/2024/03/29/fincantieri-inks-13b-deal-with-indonesia-for-two-patrol-ships> [accessed 30 March 2024].

Ashdown, P., *Nein: Standing Up to Hitler 1935–1944* (London: William Collins, 2018).

Associated Press, 'China Sanctions Lockheed Martin, Raytheon for Taiwan Sales' (17 February 2023), <www.voanews.com/a/china-sanctions-lockheed-martin-raytheon-for-taiwan-sales/6967494.html> [accessed 18 February 2023].

———, 'US: Russia to Buy Rockets, Artillery Shells from North Korea' (6 September 2022), <www.voanews.com/a/us-russia-to-buy-rockets-artillery-shells-from-north-korea/6733042.html> [accessed 7 September 2022].

———, 'China Makes Semi-Secret Delivery of Missiles to Serbia' (10 April 2022), <www.voanews.com/a/china-makes-semi-secret-delivery-of-missiles-to-serbia/6523269.html> [accessed 11 April 2022].

Australian Broadcasting Corporation, 'Russia Seeks Arms-for-Food Deal With North Korea, US Says' (31 March 2023), <www.abc.net.au/news/2023-03-31/us-russia-seeks-arms-for-food-deal-with-north-korea/102169302> [accessed 31 March 2023].

Axworthy, M., *Revolutionary Iran: A History of the Islamic Republic* (Second Edition) (London: Penguin Books, 2019).

Babb, C., 'Austin Hosts First In-Person Ukraine Defense Contact Group of 2024' (18 March 2024), <https://voanews.com/a/austin-hosts-first-in-person-ukraine-defense-contact-group-of-2024/7533349.html> [accessed 19 March 2024].

Ball, N., *Security and Economy in the Third World* (Princeton: Princeton University Press, 1988).

Bassett, R., Interview with Dan Burnham, Raytheon Chief Executive, *Jane's Defence Weekly*, 31 (31 March 1999), p. 32.

Bechtol, B.E., Jr., *North Korean Military Proliferation in the Middle East and Africa: Enabling Violence and Instability* (Lexington: The University Press of Kentucky, 2018).

Bedi, R., 'India Reverts to Russia for Defence Equipment Needs', *Jane's Defence Weekly*, 56 (3 July 2019), p. 23.

———, 'India Signs Accord with Moscow to Lease Another SSN', *Jane's Defence Weekly*, 56 (13 March 2019), p. 8.

———, 'India, Pakistan Look to Ease Tensions after Dogfights Over Kashmir's LoC', *Jane's Defence Weekly*, 56 (6 March 2019), pp. 4–5.

———, 'India Signs USD950m Deal for Two Russian-built Frigates', *Jane's Defence Weekly*, 55 (7 November 2018), p. 19.

———, 'Growing Pains', *Jane's Defence Weekly*, 55 (21 February 2018), pp. 22–30.
———, 'India Asks Japan to Offer Soryu Subs for Project 75I', *Jane's Defence Weekly*, 52 (4 February 2015), p. 25.
———, 'US Overtakes Russia as India's Main Materiel Supplier', *Jane's Defence Weekly*, 51 (20 August 2014), p. 6.
———, 'US Eyes Indian Military Counterweight to China', *Jane's Defence Weekly*, 47 (15 September 2010), p. 25.
Bedi, R., and Grevatt, J., 'Panetta to Talk Defence Sales on Trip to India', *Jane's Defence Weekly*, 49 (30 May 2012), p. 21.
Bekdil, B.E., 'Turkey Seeks to Repair Ties with Western Procurement Club', *Defense News* (6 June 2022), <www.defensenews.com/global/europe/2022/06/06/turkey-seeks-to-repair-ties-with-western-procurement-club> [accessed 7 June 2022].
Bell, M., 'US-UK Defence Trade Treaty Takes Effect', *Jane's Defence Weekly*, 49 (18 April 2012), p. 5.
———, 'Trade Treaties with US Remain in Limbo', *Jane's Defence Weekly*, 48 (1 June 2011), p. 19.
Bell, M., Bobbi, M., and Wagstaff-Smith, K., 'JSF: Weighing Up the Partner Nation Benefits', *Jane's Defence Weekly*, 47 (3 February 2010), p. 23.
Ben-David, A., 'Israel Cannot Fit Local EW Systems to its F-35s, Says US', *Jane's Defence Weekly*, 46 (2 December 2009), p. 16.
———, 'China Issue Undermines US-Israeli Defence Ties', *Jane's Defence Weekly*, 42 (27 April 2005), p. 6.
Béraud-Sudreau, L., 'Building Franco-German Consensus on Arms Exports', *Survival*, 61 (August–September 2019), pp. 79–98.
Berger, A., 'Disrupting North Korea's Military Markets', *Survival*, 58 (June–July 2016), pp. 101–30.
Bergman, R., *Rise and Kill First: The Secret History of Israel's Targeted Assassinations* (trans. Ronnie Hope) (London: John Murray, 2018).
Bermudez, J.S., Jr., *Shield of the Great Leader: The Armed Forces of North Korea* (St. Leonards: Allen & Unwin, 2001).
Bermudez, J.S., Jr., Cha, V., and Jun, J., 'Major Munitions Transfers from North Korea to Russia' (28 February 2024), <https://beyondparallel.csis.org/major-munitions-transfers-from-north-korea-to-russia> [accessed 4 March 2024].
Bingham, J., 'UN Report Reveals Extent of North Korean Arms Sales', *Jane's Defence Weekly*, 55 (11 April 2018), p. 8.
Bingham, J., and Widlund, O., 'High-Level Protection', *Jane's Defence Weekly*, 56 (24 April 2019), pp. 26–31.
Binnie, J., 'US Aircraft "On the Table" for UAE After Normalising Relations with Israel', *Jane's Defence Weekly*, 57 (2 September 2020), p. 16.
———, 'UAE Distances Itself from Munitions Found in Libya', *Jane's Defence Weekly*, 56 (10 July 2019), p. 18.
———, 'Iran Unveils F-5F as "New" Fighter Type', *Jane's Defence Weekly*, 55 (29 August 2018), p. 16.
———, 'Riyadh and Moscow Sign S-400 MOU', *Jane's Defence Weekly*, 54 (11 October 2017), p. 4.
———, 'Analysis: Iraq's Shia Militias Roll Out Heavy Rockets for IS Offensive', *Jane's Defence Weekly*, 52 (1 April 2015), p. 18.

———, 'Saudis Unveil DF-3 Ballistic Missiles', *Jane's Defence Weekly*, 51 (7 May 2014), p. 19.

Bitzinger, R.A., *Arming Asia: Technonationalism and Its Impact on Local Defense Industries* (London: Routledge, 2017).

———, *Towards a Brave New Arms Industry?* (Adelphi Paper No. 356) (London: International Institute for Strategic Studies, 2003).

Blank, S., 'Russia's Clearance Sale', *Jane's Intelligence Review*, 9 (November 1997), pp. 517–22.

Boatman, J., 'USA and Taiwan in "Sub-COCOM" Talks', *Jane's Defence Weekly*, 12 (23 December 1989), p. 1392.

———, 'USA's Growing Concern Over Co-operation', *Jane's Defence Weekly*, 12 (29 July 1989), p. 165.

Bokhari, F., 'Pakistan Takes Delivery of Home Produced JF-17', *Jane's Defence Weekly*, 46 (2 December 2009), p. 8.

Bokhari, F., and Novichkov, N., 'Pakistan, Russia Sign Defence Co-operation Accord', *Jane's Defence Weekly*, 51 (3 December 2014), p. 6.

Bonsignore, E., and Kogan, E., 'Fatal Attraction: The EU Defence Industry and China', *Military Technology*, 29 (June 2005), pp. 8–15.

Boutin, K., *Economic Security and Sino-American Relations: Progress Under Pressure* (Cheltenham: Edward Elgar, 2019).

———, 'Feeding the Lion: China and Defence Development in African States', *Defense & Security Analysis*, 34 (2018), pp. 232–48.

———, *American Technology Policy: Evolving Strategic Interests after the Cold War* (Dulles: Potomac Books, 2013).

———, 'Arms and Autonomy: The Limits of China's Defense-Industrial Transformation', in *The Modern Defense Industry: Political, Economic, and Technological Issues*, ed. by R.A. Bitzinger (Santa Barbara: Praeger Security International, 2009), pp. 212–26.

———, 'Emerging Defense Industries: Prospects and Implications', in *The Modern Defense Industry: Political, Economic, and Technological Issues*, ed. by R.A. Bitzinger (Santa Barbara: Praeger Security International, 2009), pp. 227–40.

Bowen, W.Q., *The Politics of Ballistic Missile Nonproliferation* (Houndmills: Macmillan Press, 2000).

Bowman, B., Brobst, R., and Montgomery, M., 'New Mideast Task Force Can Counter Iranian Arms Smuggling, But More Capabilities Are Needed', *Defense News* (10 May 2022), <www.defensenews.com/opinion/commentary/2022/05/09/new-mideast-task-force-can-counter-iranian-arms-smuggling-but-more-capabilities-are-needed> [accessed 10 May 2022].

Braybrook, R., 'The Shape of Things to Come', *AIR International*, 27 (September 1984), pp. 143–49.

Brobst, R., Hardie, J., and Bowman, B., 'World Leaders Should Press Switzerland On Arms Deliveries to Ukraine', *Defense News* (18 January 2023), <www.defensenews.com/opinion/commentary/2023/01/17/world-leaders-should-press-switzerland-on-arms-deliveries-to-ukraine> [accessed 18 January 2023].

Brogan, P., and Zarca, A., *Deadly Business: Sam Cummings, Interarms, and the Arms Trade* (New York: W.W. Norton & Co., 1983).

Bromley, M., Cooper, N., and Holtom, P., 'The UN Arms Trade Treaty: Arms Export Controls, the Human Security Agenda and the Lessons of History', *International Affairs*, 88 (2012), pp. 1029–48.

Bryen, S.D., *Technology Security and National Power: Winners and Losers* (New Brunswick: Transaction Publishers, 2016).

Buzan, B., and Herring, E., *The Arms Dynamic in World Politics* (Boulder: Lynne Rienner Publishers, 1998).

Carnoy, M., 'Multinationals in a Changing World Economy: Whither the Nation-State?' in *The New Global Economy in the Information Age: Reflections on Our Changing World*, ed. by M. Carnoy, M. Castells, S.S. Cohen and F.H. Cardoso (University Park: Pennsylvania State University Press, 1993), pp. 45–96.

Carr, E.H., *German–Soviet Relations Between the Two World Wars, 1919–1939* (New York: Harper & Row, 1966).

Chalmers, M., and Greene, O., 'The Register in its First Four Years', in *Developing Arms Transparency: The Future of the UN Register*, ed. by M. Chalmers, M. Donowaki and O. Greene (Bradford: University of Bradford and Centre for the Promotion of Disarmament and Non-Proliferation, Japan Institute for International Affairs, 1997), pp. 9–23.

Chang, I., *Thread of the Silkworm* (New York: Basic Books, 1995).

Chase, M.S., '"Strong Indignation," but Limited Retribution: China's Response to U.S. Arms Sales to Taiwan', *China Brief*, 11 (14 October 2011), pp. 1–4.

———, *Taiwan's Security Policy: External Threats and Domestic Policies* (Boulder: Lynne Rienner Publishers, 2008).

Cheung, T.M., *Fortifying China: The Struggle to Build a Modern Defense Economy* (Ithaca: Cornell University Press, 2009).

Ch'i, H.S., *Warlord Politics in China 1916–1928* (Stanford: Stanford University Press, 1976).

Clarke, D.L., O'Connor, D.B., and Ellis, J.D., *Send Guns and Money: Security Assistance and U.S. Foreign Policy* (Westport: Praeger Publishers, 1997).

Cole, J.M., 'Taiwan's Surveillance Radar "Will Not Track Satellites"', *Jane's Defence Weekly*, 49 (29 February 2012), p. 10.

Coll, S., *Directorate S: The C.I.A. and America's Secret Wars in Afghanistan and Pakistan, 2001–2016* (London: Allen Lane, 2018).

———, *Ghost Wars: The Secret History of the CIA, Afghanistan, and Bin Laden, from the Soviet Invasion to September 10, 2001* (New York: Penguin Books, 2005).

Conca, K., 'Third World Military Industrialization and the Evolving Security System', in *The Highest Stakes: The Economic Foundations of the Next Security System*, ed. by W. Sandholtz et al. (New York: Oxford University Press, 1992), pp. 141–64.

Connors, S., Interview with Shane O'Neill, CEO of Timoney Technology Limited. *Jane's Defence Weekly*, 53 (9 November 2016), p. 34.

Cook, C., 'Friends Over Factories', *Foreign Affairs* (27 March 2023), <www.foreignaffairs.com/united-states/friends-over-factories> [accessed 28 March 2023].

Cook, N., 'UK Hinders European Stealth Demonstrator Plan', *Jane's Defence Weekly*, 34 (4 October 2000), p. 3.

Cooper, D.A., *Competing Western Strategies Against the Proliferation of Weapons of Mass Destruction: Comparing the United States to a Close Ally* (Westport: Praeger Publishers, 2002).

Cragin, K., and Hoffman, B., *Arms Trafficking and Colombia* (Santa Monica: RAND Corporation, 2003).

Cranny-Evans, S., 'Big Spenders', *Jane's Defence Weekly*, 57 (27 May 2020), pp. 25–29.

Crown, G., 'Success of the Arms Embargo', in *South Africa: The Sanctions Report: Documents and Statistics*, ed. by J. Hanlon (London: The Commonwealth Secretariat, 1990), pp. 168–74.

Cupp, O.S., 'Defence Consolidation in the US', in *Handbook of Defence Politics: International and Comparative Perspectives*, ed. by I. Wilson III and J.J.F. Forest (London: Routledge, 2008), pp. 361–69.

Dasgupta, S., 'China Boosts Military Spending Amid Ukraine Uncertainties' (5 March 2022), <www.voanews.com/china-boosts-military-spending-amid-ukraine-uncertainties/6471773.html> [accessed 6 March 2022].

Davis, A., 'Myanmar Air Force Inducts New FTC-2000Gs to Replace K-8s', *Jane's Defence Weekly*, 59 (21 December 2022), p. 16.

———, 'Power Struggles', *Jane's Defence Weekly*, 59 (9 November 2022), pp. 18–25.

———, 'United Wa State Army Parade Showcases Modernisation', *Jane's Defence Weekly*, 56 (1 May 2019), p. 15.

Demarais, A., 'Why China Hasn't Come to Russia's Rescue', *Foreign Affairs* (28 April 2023), <www.foreignaffairs/com/china/why-china-hasnt-come-russias-rescue> [accessed 2 May 2023].

Deutch, J.M., and Moniz, E.J., 'How America Can Make Industrial Policy Work', *Foreign Affairs* (7 September 2022), <www.foreignaffairs.com/united-states/how-america-can-make-industrial-policy-work> [accessed 17 August 2023].

Dominguez, G., 'Type 15 Light Tank Enters Service in Xinjiang', *Jane's Defence Weekly*, 58 (10 February 2021), p. 15.

———, 'UN Report Highlights Role of Foreign Players in North Korean Arms Sales', *Jane's Defence Weekly*, 56 (20 March 2019), p. 4.

———, 'Russia to Deliver First Four Su-35s to China in 2016', *Jane's Defence Weekly*, 53 (28 September 2016), p. 6.

———, 'N Korean "Scuds" Can Hit USN in Japan', *Jane's Defence Weekly*, 53 (6 July 2016), p. 8.

Dong, J.H., 'Industry: Into a New Era', *Jane's Defence Weekly*, 16 (16 November 1991), pp. 965–67.

Donowaki, M., 'Addressing Light Weapons and Small Arms Proliferation', in *Developing Arms Transparency: The Future of the UN Register*, ed. by M. Chalmers, M. Donowaki and O. Greene (Bradford: University of Bradford and Centre for the Promotion of Disarmament and Non-Proliferation, Japan Institute for International Affairs, 1997), pp. 203–11.

Dorschner, J., 'Conflict Zone', *Jane's Defence Weekly*, 56 (27 March 2019), pp. 20–25.

Dougherty, M.J., *Chinese Tanks & AFVs: 1950–Present* (London: Amber Books, 2019).

Elliot, J., 'The "Other" Military Aircraft Programmes', *Military Technology*, 22 (July 1998), pp. 54–61.

Elliot, J., and Bonsignore, E., 'Asia's "New" Aerospace Industry: At the Turning Point?' *Military Technology*, 22 (February 1998), pp. 24–32.

Engelbrecht, H.C., and Hanighen, F.C., *Merchants of Death: A Study of the International Armament Industry* (New York: Dodd, Mead & Co., 1934).

Erickson, J.L., *Dangerous Trade: Arms Exports, Human Rights, and International Reputation* (New York: Columbia University Press, 2015).

Farah, D., and Braun, S., *Merchant of Death: Money, Guns, Planes, and the Man Who Makes War Possible* (Hoboken: John Wiley & Sons, 2007).

Farivar, M., 'US Warns About Increasing Use of Intermediaries to Evade Russia Sanctions' (6 March 2023), <www.voanews.com/a/us-warns-about-increasing-use-of-intermediaries-to-evade-russia-sanctions/6992824.html> [accessed 7 March 2023].

Fiorenza, N., 'Belgium Procures SPHs and Mortar Carriers from France', *Jane's Defence Weekly*, 60 (20 December 2023), p. 15.

———, 'Zelensky's European Tour Yields More Weapons for Kyiv', *Jane's Defence Weekly*, 60 (24 May 2023), p. 15.

———, 'Belgium Chooses F-35, Invests in Armoured Vehicles and MALE UAVs', *Jane's Defence Weekly*, 55 (31 October 2018), p. 4.

Fish, T., 'LTTE Navy is "Defunct", Says Sri Lankan MoD', *Jane's Defence Weekly*, 44 (26 September 2007), p. 14.

Fisher, R.D., Jr., 'China Assists North Korea with New 300 mm Rocket Artillery System', *Jane's Defence Weekly*, 53 (16 March 2016), p. 14.

Fitzpatrick, M., 'Iran and North Korea: The Proliferation Nexus', *Survival*, 48 (Spring 2006), pp. 61–80.

Forczyk, R., *Case Red: The Collapse of France, 1940* (Oxford: Osprey Publishing, 2017).

Forrester, C., 'DSCA Tightens End-Use Monitoring Process', *Jane's Defence Weekly*, 56 (12 June 2019), p. 21.

———, 'Cracks Emerge in Franco-German Export Control Plans', *Jane's Defence Weekly*, 56 (13 February 2019), p. 23.

———, 'Paris, Riyadh Agree New Procurement Deal', *Jane's Defence Weekly*, 55 (18 April 2018), p. 21.

———, 'Algeria Aims to Expand its Defence Industrial Output', *Jane's Defence Weekly*, 51 (17 September 2014), p. 22.

———, 'Raytheon Penalised $8m Following ITAR Violations', *Jane's Defence Weekly*, 50 (8 May 2013), p. 20.

Forrester, C., and Smith, M., 'Up in Arms: The Impact of Europe's Sanctions on Russia', *Jane's Defence Weekly*, 51 (6 August 2014), pp. 20–21.

Forsyth, R., *Luftwaffe Emergency Fighters* (Oxford: Osprey Publishing, 2017).

Fryer-Biggs, Z., 'US Builds Database of Arms Given to Syrian Kurds', *Jane's Defence Weekly*, 54 (7 June 2017), p. 5.

———, 'US Gathers 44 Countries in Push for Armed UAV Export Standards', *Jane's Defence Weekly*, 53 (12 October 2016), p. 13.

Gallo, W., 'Ukraine's Call for Weapons Remains Tough Sell in South Korea' (1 March 2023), <www.voanews.com/a/ukraine-call-for-weapons-remains-tough-sell-in-south-korea/6985407.html> [accessed 3 March 2023].

Gansler, J.S., *The Defense Industry* (Cambridge: The MIT Press, 1980).

Garcia, D., 'Arms Transfers beyond the State-to-State Realm', *International Studies Perspectives*, 10 (May 2009), pp. 151–68.

Gelfand, L., 'South Sudan Set to Buy Mi-17 Transport Helos', *Jane's Defence Weekly*, 47 (15 September 2010), p. 18.

———, 'Delivery of Su-30MKAs to Algeria Revives Arms Deal', *Jane's Defence Weekly*, 45 (11 June 2008), p. 21.

Giovanzanti, A., 'Supercharged in the Sky', *Jane's Defence Weekly*, 59 (2 March 2022), pp. 22–29.

Given, B.J., *A Most Pernicious Thing: Gun Trading and Native Warfare in the Early Contact Period* (Ottawa: Carleton University Press, 1994).

Goldblat, J., *Arms Control: The New Guide to Negotiations and Agreements* (London: SAGE Publications, 2002).

Golich, V., 'Aviation's Technology Imperative and the Transformation of the Global Political Economy', in *Technology, Culture and Competitiveness: Change and the World Political Economy*, ed. by M. Talalay, C. Farrands and R. Tooze (London: Routledge, 1997), pp. 180–95.

———, 'From Competition to Collaboration: The Challenge of Commercial-Class Aircraft Manufacturing', *International Organization*, 46 (Autumn 1992), pp. 899–934.

Gomis, B., 'Criminal Opportunities', *Jane's Defence Weekly*, 60 (29 March 2023), pp. 26–29.

Gordon, Y., and Komissarov, D., *Soviet and Russian Military Aircraft in Asia* (Manchester: Hikoki Publications, 2014).

Gosselin-Malo, E., 'Rafales on the Upswing? French Fighter Eyes Additional Mideast Sales', *Defense News* (7 September 2023), <www.defensenews.com/air/2023/09/07/rafales-on-the-upswing-french-fighter-eyes-additional-mideast-sales> [accessed 8 September 2023].

Gould, J., 'Here's What Global Weapons Chiefs Will Discuss this Month in Brussels', *Defense News* (10 September 2022), <www.defensenews.com/pentagon/2022/09/09/heres-what-global-weapons-chiefs-will-discuss-this-month-in-brussels> [accessed 10 September 2022].

———, 'US Pledges $391 Million for Euro Allies to Buy American to Backfill Weapons Donations to Ukraine', *Defense News* (26 April 2022), <www.defensenews.com/global/europe/2022/04/25/us-pledges-391-million-for-euro-allies-to-buy-american-to-backfill-weapons-donations-to-ukraine> [accessed 26 April 2022].

Gould, J., and Sprenger, S., 'Ukraine Weapon Switcheroos Are Flushing Soviet Arms Out of Europe', *Defense News* (29 April 2022), <www.defensenews.com/global/europe/2022/04/28/ukraine-weapon-switcheroos-are-flushing-soviet-arms-out-of-europe> [accessed 29 April 2022].

Goulden, J.C., with Raffio, A.W., *The Death Merchant: The Rise and Fall of Edwin P. Wilson* (London: Sidgwick & Jackson, 1984).

Grant, C., 'Global Defence Industry', *The Economist*, 343 (14 June 1997), pp. 3–18.

Grant, N., *Mauser Military Rifles* (Oxford: Osprey Publishing, 2015).

Grevatt, J., 'US Senate Committee Approves Proposed Taiwan Policy Law', *Jane's Defence Weekly*, 59 (28 September 2022), p. 4.

———, 'Powering Up', *Jane's Defence Weekly*, 58 (26 May 2021), pp. 18–23.

———, 'Good Enough', *Jane's Defence Weekly*, 56 (20 November 2019), pp. 22–27.

———, 'Slow and Steady', *Jane's Defence Weekly*, 56 (31 July 2019), pp. 24–30.

———, 'Russia and its Asian Clients Seek to Exploit CAATSA Loopholes', *Jane's Defence Weekly*, 56 (24 July 2019), p. 21.

———, 'US "Normalises" Defence Trade with Taiwan', *Jane's Defence Weekly*, 56 (10 July 2019), p. 5.

———, 'US Voices Concerns About Indian S-400 Buy', *Jane's Defence Weekly*, 56 (26 June 2019), p. 17.

———, 'China's AVIC Begins Sale of Shipbuilding Arm', *Jane's Defence Weekly*, 56 (8 May 2019), p. 20.

———, 'Toughening Up', *Jane's Defence Weekly*, 56 (24 April 2019), pp. 20–25.

———, 'Seoul Expands Import Substitution Drive', *Jane's Defence Weekly*, 56 (20 March 2019), p. 18.

———, 'United States, India Advance Trade and Technology Initiative', *Jane's Defence Weekly*, 56 (27 March 2019), p. 18.

———, 'DAPA Unveils Plan to Develop Industrial Base', *Jane's Defence Weekly*, 55 (26 September 2018), p. 24.

———, 'Japan Paves Way for Defence Sales in Southeast Asia', *Jane's Defence Weekly*, 54 (15 November 2017), p. 18.

———, 'South Korea, US to Sign Industry Sharing Accord', *Jane's Defence Weekly*, 53 (30 November 2016), p. 19.

———, 'Japanese MoD Says "No Collaboration" with Israel on UAV Development', *Jane's Defence Weekly*, 53 (21 September 2016), p. 24.

———, 'Thailand Makes Defence Development a Priority', *Jane's Defence Weekly*, 53 (22 June 2016), p. 21.

———, 'Indonesia Announces Offset Programme', *Jane's Defence Weekly*, 51 (16 April 2014), p. 20.

———, 'US Imposes Sanctions On Chinese Firms', *Jane's Defence Weekly*, 50 (20 February 2013), p. 18.

———, 'Thai Offset Plans Could be Derailed by Moves to Reinstate Countertrade', *Jane's Defence Weekly*, 49 (5 December 2012), p. 17.

———, 'Canberra Finally Ratifies Trade Treaty with US', *Jane's Defence Weekly*, 49 (7 November 2012), p. 5.

———, 'Japan Looks to New Defence Policy to Boost Defence Industry', *Jane's Defence Weekly*, 49 (31 October 2012), p. 23.

———, 'Taiwan Starts Offset Negotiations Over F-16', *Jane's Defence Weekly*, 48 (12 October 2011), p. 20.

———, 'Indonesia Bails Out Defence Groups with $1bn of Funding', *Jane's Defence Weekly*, 48 (13 July 2011), p. 19.

———, 'S Korea Considers Offset Changes in Bid for Investment', *Jane's Defence Weekly*, 47 (17 March 2010), p. 18.

———, 'Japan Export Ban Leaves Industry "at a Standstill"', *Jane's Defence Weekly*, 46 (4 March 2009), p. 23.

Grevatt, J., and Anderson, G., 'Seoul Outlines Policy Shift Towards Industrial Collaboration', *Jane's Defence Weekly*, 56 (15 May 2019), p. 21.

Grip, L., 'History Never Repeats? Imports, Impact and Control of Small Arms in Africa', *Contemporary Security Policy*, 36 (2015), pp. 79–103.

Gunn, S., 'War and the Emergence of the State: Western Europe, 1350–1600', in *European Warfare 1350–1750*, ed. by F. Tallett and D.J.B. Trim (Cambridge: Cambridge University Press, 2010), pp. 50–73.

Ha, Y.S., 'South Korea', in *Arms Production in Developing Countries: An Analysis of Decision Making*, ed. by J.E. Katz (Lexington: D.C. Heath and Co., 1984), pp. 225–33.

Hamburg Institute for Economic Research, Kiel Institute for World Economics, and National Research Council, *Conflict and Cooperation for High-Technology Industry* (Washington: National Academy Press, 1996).

Hardy, J., 'South Korea Signs Up for 40 F-35As', *Jane's Defence Weekly*, 51 (1 October 2014), p. 9.

———, 'Documents Confirm China Shipped TELs to North Korea', *Jane's Defence Weekly*, 49 (20 June 2012), p. 17.

———, 'UNSC Investigates Chinese Link to North Korean TEL', *Jane's Defence Weekly*, 49 (25 April 2012), p. 6.

Harrington, C., 'US Seeks to Lift Export Sales Ban on F-22A', *Jane's Defence Weekly*, 43 (28 June 2006), p. 11.

Harris, B., 'Biden Arms Deal Policy Seeks to Balance Human Rights and Competition', *Defense News* (24 February 2023), <www.defensenews.com/pentagon/2023/02/23/biden-arms-deal-policy-seeks-to-balance-human-rights-and-competition> [accessed 24 February 2023].

———, 'Congress Passes Bill to Loan U.S. Military Equipment to Ukraine and Allies', *Defense News* (29 April 2022), <www.defensenews.com/congress/2022/04/28/congress-passes-bill-to-loan-us-military-equipment-to-ukraine-and-allies> [accessed 29 April 2022].

Hastings M., and Jenkins, S., *The Battle for the Falklands* (London: Pan Books, 2022).

Hayward, K., 'The Globalisation of Defence Industries', *Survival*, 43 (Summer 2001), pp. 115–32.

Headrick, D.R., *The Tools of Empire: Technology and European Imperialism in the Nineteenth Century* (New York: Oxford University Press, 1981).

Heitman, H.R., 'South Africa "Seeks Defence Self-Reliance"', *Jane's Defence Weekly*, 48 (30 March 2011), p. 16.

Herschelman, K., 'Independence Through Industry', *Jane's Defence Weekly*, 56 (3 April 2019), pp. 20–30.

Hess, M., *Economic War: Ukraine and the Global Conflict between Russia and the West* (London: Hurst & Co., 2023).

Hewish, M., 'Re-directing the Defense R&D Pipeline', *International Defense Review*, 26 (July 1993), p. 555.

Hewson, R., 'Cruise Missile Technology Proliferation Takes Off', *Jane's Intelligence Review*, 17 (October 2005), pp. 41–45.

———, 'Chinese Su-27 Upgrade Funds Russian Project', *Jane's Defence Weekly*, 40 (8 October 2003), p. 5.

Hobson, S., 'Picking Your Partner', *Jane's Defence Weekly*, 18 (4 July 1992), pp. 43–46.

Hook, S.H., and Rothstein, D.B., 'New Rationales and Old Concerns About U.S. Arms Export Policy', in *Guns and Butter: The Political Economy of International Security*, ed. by P. Dombrowski (Boulder: Lynne Rienner Publishers, 2005), pp. 153–78.

Host, P., 'Brazil, USA Sign Space TSA', *Jane's Defence Weekly*, 56 (27 March 2019), p. 11.

———, 'Promise & Limitation', *Jane's Defence Weekly*, 55 (4 April 2018), pp. 24–30.

Howarth, H.M.F., 'The Malaysian Armed Forces', *International Defense Review*, 16 (September 1983), pp. 1225–31.

Howson, G., *Arms for Spain: The Untold Story of the Spanish Civil War* (New York: St. Martin's Press, 1998).

Hu, H., 'Building Up the Island Nation', *Jane's Defence Weekly*, 21 (22 January 1994), pp. 24–25.
Hughes, C., 'Japan's Emerging Arms Transfer Strategy: Diversifying to Re-centre on the US-Japan Alliance', *The Pacific Review*, 31 (2018), pp. 424–40.
Hull, A., and Markov, D., 'Trends in the Arms Market: Part Two', *Jane's Intelligence Review*, 9 (May 1997), pp. 232–38.
———, 'A Changing Market in the Arms Bazaar', *Jane's Intelligence Review*, 9 (March 1997), pp. 140–42.
International Defense Review, 'Matra's International Strategy', *International Defense Review*, 22 (July 1989), p. 887.
The International Institute for Strategic Studies, 'Iran Sanctions Halt Long-Range Ballistic-Missile Development', *Strategic Comments*, 18 (July 2012), pp. 1–3.
———, 'Consolidating Europe's Defence Industries: Big Rewards, Big Obstacles', *Strategic Comments*, 11 (June 2005), pp. 1–2.
———, *The Military Balance 1987–1988* (London: International Institute for Strategic Studies, 1987).
Jackson, J.H., 'Reshaping of the Defence Industry', *Jane's Defence Weekly*, 12 (25 November 1989), pp. 1153–55.
Jackson, P., *Mirage* (Shepperton: Ian Allan, 1985).
Jackson, T., 'From Under Their Noses: Rebel Groups' Arms Acquisition and the Importance of Leakages from State Stockpiles', *International Studies Perspectives*, 11 (May 2010), pp. 131–47.
*Jane's Defence Weekly*, 'Industry', *Jane's Defence Weekly*, 57 (9 December 2020), 42–46.
———, 'Nigeria Unveils Indigenous Ship', *Jane's Defence Weekly*, 49 (13 June 2012), p. 16.
———, 'New Interests Spur Force Development', *Jane's Defence Weekly*, 25 (22 May 1996), pp. 23–26.
———, 'EU Builds a Bigger Fence', *Jane's Defence Weekly*, 24 (15 July 1995), p. 4.
———, 'Climbing the Industrial Ladder', *Jane's Defence Weekly*, 20 (31 July 1993), pp. 20–25.
Jennings, G., 'Rotary Recap', *Jane's Defence Weekly*, 59 (14 September 2022), pp. 16–23.
———, 'France Could Replace US Parts in SCALP to Bypass ITAR Restrictions for Egypt', *Jane's Defence Weekly*, 55 (8 August 2018), p. 10.
———, 'UAE Set to Upgrade Mirage 2000 Fighters', *Jane's Defence Weekly*, 54 (22 November 2017), p. 7.
———, 'Afghan Air Force to Field Black Hawk Helicopters in Place of Mi-17s', *Jane's Defence Weekly*, 53 (30 November 2016), p. 6.
———, 'US Looks to Contain Iran with Arms Sales to Allies', *Jane's Defence Weekly*, 50 (1 May 2013), p. 4.
———, 'UK Throws Weight Behind Saab's Gripen F-X2 Bid', *Jane's Defence Weekly*, 46 (18 November 2009), p. 13.
Johnson, R.F., 'Russian Industry Makes Push into the Iranian Market', *Jane's Defence Weekly*, 53 (23 November 2016), p. 9.
———, 'Users of Russian Hardware Facing Spare Parts Dilemma', *Jane's Defence Weekly*, 53 (15 June 2016), p. 22.
———, 'But Further Strategic Weapon Tests Likely to Continue', *Jane's Defence Weekly*, 53 (8 June 2016), p. 8.

———, 'PLA May Finally Receive S-400 SAMs', *Jane's Defence Weekly*, 51 (16 April 2014), p. 8.

———, 'Losses, Gains Emerge as Talent Pool Heads Home', *Jane's Defence Weekly*, 46 (4 March 2009), p. 24.

Jones, B., 'Putin Backs Ankara-Moscow S-400 Sales Negotiations', *Jane's Defence Weekly*, 54 (14 June 2017), p. 17.

Jowett, P.S., *Modern African Wars (5): The Nigerian-Biafran War 1967–70* (Oxford: Osprey Publishing, 2016).

Judson, J., 'Rafael Pitches Latest Spike Variant for US Army's Long-Range Weapon for Helos', *Defense News* (17 June 2022), <www.defensenews.com/digital-show-dailies/eurosatory/2022/06/17/rafael-pitches-latest-spike-variant-for-us-armys-long-range-weapon-for-helos> [accessed 20 June 2022].

Kahwaji, R., 'Making Headway', *Defense News* (26 May 2003), pp. 19–20.

Kan, S.A., *Chinese Missile and Nuclear Proliferation: Issues for Congress* (Washington: Congressional Research Service, 1993).

Karniol, R., 'Linking Defence with Economic Progress', *Jane's Defence Weekly*, 24 (25 November 1995), p. 40.

———, 'Taiwan to Slash its IDF Fighter Production', *Jane's Defence Weekly*, 19 (3 April 1993), p. 5.

Katz, Y., 'Block Remains on Israeli Sales to China', *Jane's Defence Weekly*, 48 (23 November 2011), p. 18.

———, 'Israel Seeks Rapport with China Over Iran', *Jane's Defence Weekly*, 48 (22 June 2011), p. 19.

———, 'Israel Offered F-35s in Return for West Bank Deal', *Jane's Defence Weekly*, 47 (24 November 2010), p. 6.

Katz, Y., and Bohbot, A., *The Weapon Wizards: How Israel Became a High-Tech Military Superpower* (New York: St. Martin's Press, 2017).

Kazimiroff, P., 'Russian Industry Wary of Su-35 Sale to China', *Jane's Defence Weekly*, 49 (21 March 2012), p. 5.

Keatinge, T., *Developing Bad Habits: What Russia Might Learn from Iran's Sanctions Evasion* (London: Royal United Services Institute, 2023).

Kehoe, J.W., and Brower, K.S., 'US and Soviet Weapon System Design Practices', *International Defense Review*, 15 (June 1982), pp. 705–12.

Kemp, D., 'Spotlight Falls on UK, US Export Controls', *Jane's Defence Weekly*, 41 (3 March 2004), p. 8.

Kemp, I., 'The Execution of "Project Babylon"', *Jane's Defence Weekly*, 14 (24 November 1990), p. 1010.

Kennedy, G., *The Military in the Third World* (New York: Charles Scribner's Sons, 1974).

Kington, T., 'German-Italian Tank Kerfuffle Dings Vision of Europeanized Arms', *Defense News* (14 June 2024), <www.defensenews.com/global/2024/06/14/german-italian-tank-kerfuffle-dings-vision-of-europeanized-arms> [accessed 15 June 2024].

———, 'Italy Readies Quick Sale of Patrol Ships to Indonesia Amid China Fears', *Defense News* (27 October 2023), <www.defensenews.com/global/europe/2023/10/27/italy-readies-quick-sale-of-patrol-ships-to-indonesia-amid-china-fears> [accessed 28 October 2023].

Koch, A., 'USA Rethinks MTCR Options', *Jane's Defence Weekly*, 33 (10 May 2000), p. 22.

Koistinen, P.A.C., *State of War: The Political Economy of American Warfare, 1945–2011* (Lawrence: University Press of Kansas, 2012).

———, *Beating Plowshares into Swords: The Political Economy of American Warfare, 1606–1865* (Lawrence: University Press of Kansas, 1996).

Konstam, A., *British Motor Gun Boats 1939–45* (Oxford: Osprey Publishing, 2010).

Kramer, M., 'The Global Arms Trade After the Persian Gulf War', *Security Studies*, 2 (Winter 1992), pp. 260–309.

Krause, K., *Arms and the State: Patterns of Military Production and Trade* (Cambridge: Cambridge University Press, 1992).

Kua, K.S., *Questioning Arms Spending in Malaysia: From Altantuya to Zikorsky* (Petaling Jaya: Suara Rakyat Malaysia, 2010).

Lai, B., *The Chinese People's Liberation Army Since 1949: Ground Forces* (Oxford: Osprey Publishing, 2012).

Landgren, S., *Embargo Disimplemented: South Africa's Military Industry* (Oxford: Oxford University Press, 1989).

Lee, Y.C., 'Implications of China's Aircraft Carrier Development' (Carlisle: US Army War College, 2012).

Leitner, P.M., *Decontrolling Strategic Technology, 1990–1992: Creating the Military Threats of the 21st Century* (Lanham: University Press of America, 1995).

Le Mière, C., Li, G., and Inkster, N., 'China', in *Afghanistan: To 2015 and Beyond*, ed. by T. Dodge and N. Redman (London: The International Institute for Strategic Studies, 2011), pp. 219–30.

Lert, F., and Novichkov, N., 'Egypt to Buy the Two Ex-Russian Mistral-Class Helicopter Carriers', *Jane's Defence Weekly*, 52 (30 September 2015), p. 5.

Lewis, J., 'North Korea's Juche Rocket' (23 January 2013), <https://lewis.armscontrolwonk.com/archive/6177/north-koreas-juche-rocket> [accessed 25 January 2013].

Li, X., *A History of the Modern Chinese Army* (Lexington: University Press of Kentucky, 2007).

Lohnstein, M., *Royal Netherlands East Indies Army 1936–42* (Oxford: Osprey Publishing, 2018).

Long, W.J., 'Defining Strategic Exports in the 1990s: From Export Controls to the Management of Technology Exchange', in *Export Controls in Transition: Perspectives, Problems, and Prospects*, ed. by G.K. Bertsch and S. Elliott-Gower (Durham: Duke University Press, 1992), pp. 105–27.

Looney, R.E., *Third-World Military Expenditure and Arms Production* (Houndmills: Macmillan Press, 1988).

Lorell, M.A. et al., *Going Global? U.S. Government Policy and the Defense Aerospace Industry* (Santa Monica: RAND Corp., 2002).

Losey, S., 'US Air Force, Boeing Reach Deal on Prototype E-7', *Defense News* (22 July 2024), <www.defensenews.com/air/2024/07/22/us-air-force-boeing-reach-deal-on-prototype-e-7> [accessed 13 August 2024].

———, 'Future Fighter Program Poses Key Test for US Air Force's Design Method', *Defense News* (30 August 2023), <www.defensenews.com/air/2023/08/30/future-fighter-program-poses-key-test-for-us-air-forces-design-method> [accessed 31 August 2023].

———, 'F-16s Key Step for Ukraine, But Won't Be "Game-Changer", SECAF Says', *Defense News* (23 May 2023), <www.defensenews.com/air/2023/05/22/f-16s-key-step-for-uktraine-but-wont-be-game-changer-secaf-says> [accessed 23 May 2023].

———, 'Russia Burning Through Ammunition in Ukraine at "Extraordinary" Rate', *Defense News* (5 December 2022), <www.defensenews.com/smr/reagan-defense-forum/2022/12/04/russia-burning-through-ammunition-in-ukraine-at-extraordinary-rate> [accessed 5 December 2022].

———, 'T-7 Red Hawk Trainer Makes its Debut', *Defense News* (30 April 2022), <www.defensenews.com/air/2022/04/29/t-7-red-hawk-trainer-makes-its-debut> [accessed 30 April 2022].

Louscher, D.J., and Salomone, M.D., *Technology Transfer and U.S. Security Assistance: The Impact of Licensed Production* (Boulder: Westview Press, 1987).

Louscher, D.J., and Schwarz, A.N., 'Patterns of Third World Military Technology Acquisition', in *The Dilemma of Third World Defense Industries: Supplier Control or Recipient Autonomy?* ed. by K.I. Baek, R.D. McLaurin and C.I. Moon (Boulder: Westview Press, 1989), pp. 33–56.

Mabee, B., *The Globalization of Security: State Power, Security Provision and Legitimacy* (Basingstoke: Palgrave Macmillan, 2009).

McDonald, J., 'China Ukraine Envoy Urges Allies to "Stop Sending Weapons" to Kyiv', *Defense News* (3 June 2023), <www.defensenews.com/news/your-military/2023/06/02/china-ukraine-envoy-urges-allies-to-stop-sending-weapons-to-kyiv> [accessed 3 June 2023].

Machi, V., 'Lockheed, Rheinmetall Pair Up to Build Europe-made Rocket Launcher', *Defense News* (24 June 2023), <www.defensenews.com/global/europe/2023/06/23/lockheed-rheinmetall-pair-up-to-build-europe-made-rocket-launcher> [accessed 24 June 2023].

———, 'Czech Army to Get Leopard Tanks Under Berlin-Prague Arms Swap', *Defense News* (12 October 2022), <www.defensenews.com/global/europe/2022/10/11/czech-army-to-get-leopard-tanks-under-berlin-prague-arms-swap> [accessed 12 October 2022].

———, 'How the F-35 Swept Europe, and the Competition it Could Soon Face', *Defense News* (4 September 2022), <www.defensenews.com/global/europe/2022/09/04/how-the-f-35-swept-europe-and-the-competition-it-could-soon-face> [accessed 5 September 2022].

McNab, C., *Armies of the Iran-Iraq War 1980–88* (Oxford: Osprey Publishing, 2022).

Mader, G., 'Austrian Typhoon Delay Possible', *Jane's Defence Weekly*, 44 (16 May 2007), p. 11.

Mahnken, T.G., *Uncovering Ways of War: U.S. Intelligence and Foreign Military Innovation, 1918–1941* (Ithaca: Cornell University Press, 2002).

Maiolo, J., *Cry Havoc: The Arms Race and the Second World War, 1931–41* (London: John Murray, 2010).

Majumdar, O., 'Bangladesh to Procure Bayraktar TB2 But Remains Silent On Numbers', *Jane's Defence Weekly*, 59 (10 August 2022), p. 16.

Malenic, M., 'US Targets Exportability as Part of Acquisition Overhaul', *Jane's Defence Weekly*, 49 (21 November 2012), p. 10.

Martin, T., and Schmidt, R., *A Case Study of the F-20 Tigershark* (Report P-7495-RGS) (Santa Monica: RAND Corporation, 1987).

Mathias, C.M., Jr., 'A New US Export Control Policy', in *National Security and Technology Transfer: The Strategic Dimensions of East-West Trade*, ed. by G.K. Bertsch and J.R. McIntyre (Boulder: Westview Press, 1983), pp. 159–69.

Matthews, R., 'Indonesian Strategy is Put to the Test', *Jane's Defence Weekly*, 19 (20 March 1993), pp. 29–30.

Meagher, T.R., 'The Future of the Global Defense-Industrial Base: A Case Study of the LTV Sale', *International Defense Review*, 26 (January 1993), pp. 71–73.

Meijer, H., *Trading with the Enemy: The Making of US Export Control Policy toward the People's Republic of China* (Oxford: Oxford University Press, 2016).

Mihalka, M., *The Measurement and Modelling of Arms Accumulation: The Middle East as a Case Study* (Cambridge: Massachusetts Institute of Technology, 1975).

Miller, D., *The Illustrated Dictionary of Tanks of the World from World War I to the Present Day* (London: Salamander Books, 2000).

Mistry, D., 'Beyond the MTCR: Building a Comprehensive Regime to Contain Ballistic Missile Proliferation', *International Security*, 27 (2003), pp. 119–49.

———, 'Technological Containment: The MTCR and Missile Proliferation', *Security Studies*, 11 (Spring 2002), pp. 91–122.

Monaghan, S., 'Challengers and Challenges: The Promise and Perils of UK Leadership', *Defense News* (20 January 2023), <www.defensenews.com/opinion/commentary/2023/01/19/challengers-and-challenges-the-promise-and-perils-of-uk-leadership> [accessed 20 January 2023].

Moran, T.H., and Mowery, D.C., 'Aerospace and National Security in an Era of Globalization', in *Techno-Security in an Age of Globalization: Perspectives from the Pacific Rim*, ed. by D.F. Simon (Armonk: M.E. Sharpe, 1997), pp. 226–50.

———, 'Aerospace', *Daedalus*, 120 (1991), pp. 135–54.

Moravcsik, A., 'Arms and Autarky in Modern European History', *Daedalus*, 120 (1991), pp. 23–45.

Mulholland, D., Interview with Richard Moon, Chief Executive of Thales Defence, *Jane's Defence Weekly*, 35 (18 April 2001), p. 40.

Murphy, J., 'DIS "Incompatible" with US Policy, Says UK Official', *Jane's Defence Weekly*, 43 (12 April 2006), p. 21.

Naylor, R.T., *Patriots and Profiteers: Economic Warfare, Embargo Busting, and State-Sponsored Crime* (Second Edition) (Montreal and Kingston: McGill-Queen's University Press, 2008).

———, 'The Rise of the Modern Arms Black Market and the Fall of Supply-Side Control', in *Combating Transnational Crime: Concepts, Activities and Responses*, ed. by P. Williams and D. Vlassis (London: Frank Cass, 2001), pp. 209–36.

Neuman, S.G., 'Defense Industries and Global Dependency', *Orbis*, 50 (Summer 2006), pp. 429–51.

———, 'Third World Arms Production and the Global Arms Transfer System', in *Arms Production in Developing Countries: An Analysis of Decision Making*, ed. by J.E. Katz (Lexington: D.C. Heath and Co., 1984), pp. 15–37.

Nikitin, M.B., *Proliferation Security Initiative (PSI)* (Washington: Congressional Research Service, 2011).

Nolan, J.E., *Military Industry in Taiwan and South Korea* (Houndmills: Macmillan Press, 1986).

Noppen, R.K., *Ottoman Navy Warships 1914–18* (Oxford: Osprey Publishing, 2015).

Novichkov, N., 'Tor-M1s Help Pay Debt to Beijing', *Jane's Defence Weekly*, 33 (15 March 2000), p. 13.

Oden, M., 'Cashing In, Cashing Out, and Converting: Restructuring of the Defense Industrial Base in the 1990s', in *Arming the Future: A Defense Industry for the 21st Century*, ed. by A.R. Markusen and S.S. Costigan (New York: Council on Foreign Relations Press, 1999), pp. 74–105.

Pabriks, A., 'Latvia's Defense Minister: The Security of Supply Can Solve Crises', *Defense News* (8 December 2022), <www.defensenews.com/outlook/2022/12/05/latvias-defense-minister-the-security-of-supply-can-solve-crises> [accessed 9 December 2022].

Parker, G., *The Military Revolution: Military Innovation and the Rise of the West, 1500–1600* (Second Edition) (Cambridge: Cambridge University Press, 1996).

Pepper, S., 'Aspects of Operational Art: Communications, Cannon, and Small Wars', in *European Warfare 1350–1750*, ed. by F. Tallett and D.J.B. Trim (Cambridge: Cambridge University Press, 2010), pp. 181–202.

Phipps, G., and Hardy, J., 'But Taipei Will Still Push for F-16C/D Purchase', *Jane's Defence Weekly*, 48 (28 September 2011), p. 6.

Pierre, A.J., 'Introduction', in *Cascade of Arms: Managing Conventional Weapons Proliferation*, ed. by A.J. Pierre (Washington and Cambridge: Brookings Institution Press and The World Peace Foundation, 1997), pp. 1–12.

———, 'Toward an International Regime for Conventional Arms Sales', in *Cascade of Arms: Managing Conventional Weapons Proliferation*, ed. by A.J. Pierre (Washington: Brookings Institution Press; and Cambridge: The World Peace Foundation, 1997), pp. 369–436.

———, *The Global Politics of Arms Sales* (Princeton: Princeton University Press, 1982).

Pollack, J., 'Ballistic Trajectory: The Evolution of North Korea's Ballistic Missile Market', *The Nonproliferation Review*, 18 (July 2011), pp. 411–29.

Potter, M., *Outlaws Inc.: Flying with the World's Most Dangerous Smugglers* (London: Sidgwick & Jackson, 2011).

Rahmat, R., 'Japan to Boost Defence Sales in Asia as Part of Diplomatic Strategy', *Jane's Defence Weekly*, 54 (25 January 2017), p. 7.

Ralston, D.B., *Importing the European Army: The Introduction of European Military Techniques and Institutions into the Extra-European World, 1600–1914* (Chicago: University of Chicago Press, 1996).

Rangsimaporn, P., 'Russia's Debate on Military-Technological Cooperation with China', *Asian Survey*, 46 (2006), pp. 477–95.

Reed, C., and Starr, B., 'Defending the Industrial Realm', *Jane's Defence Weekly*, 17 (11 April 1992), pp. 629–30.

Reuters, 'US Tries to Woo India Away From Russia With Aircraft' (17 February 2023), <www.voanews.com/a/6967153.html> [accessed 18 February 2023].

———, 'US Curbs Exports to Iranian Firms for Producing Drones for Russia' (31 January 2023), <www.voanews.com/a/us-curbs-exports-to-iranian-firms-for-producing-drones-for-russia/6942647.html> [accessed 1 February 2023].

———, 'The Supply Chain that Keeps Tech Flowing to Russia' (13 December 2022), <www.reuters.com/investigates/special-report/ukraine-crisis-russia-tech-middlemen> [accessed 14 December 2022].

———, 'US Imposes Sanctions on Military Procurement Network Aiding Russia' (14 November 2022), <www.voanews.com/a/us-imposes-sanctions-on-military-procurement-network-aiding-russia-/6833861.html> [accessed 15 November 2022].

———, 'Israeli Attacks Squeeze Iranian Aerial Supplies to Syria, Sources Say' (2 September 2022), <www.voanews.com/a/israeli-attacks-squeeze-iranian-aerial-supplies-to-syria-sources-say/6728735.html> [accessed 3 September 2022].

Richardson, L.D., 'COTS Conundrum', *Jane's Defence Weekly*, 49 (25 January 2012), pp. 29–32.

Roaten, M., 'US to Send Second Patriot Air-Defence Battery to Ukraine', *Jane's Defence Weekly*, 61 (24 July 2024), p. 4.

Robertson, N., 'AUKUS Countries Update Rules on Sharing Defense Kit', *Defense News* (16 August 2024), <www.defensenews.com/pentagon/2024/08/15/aukus-countries-update-rules-on-sharing-defense-kit> [accessed 16 August 2024].

———, 'With Pause in US Aid, Ukraine's Allies Rally to Ponder What's Next', *Defense News* (19 March 2024), <www.defensenews.com/pentagon/2024/03/19/with-pause-in-us-aid-ukraines-allies-rally-to-ponder-whats-next> [accessed 20 March 2024].

Robinson, T., 'Getting a Slice of the Cake', *Military Technology*, 30 (November 2006), pp. 8–17.

Rodan, S., 'Israel, USA Claim Egyptian Missile Links with N Korea', *Jane's Defence Weekly*, 33 (23 February 2000), p. 18.

Roque, A., 'New Truck-Mounted Harpoon Launchers Headed to Ukraine', *Jane's Defence Weekly*, 59 (29 June 2022), p. 5

Roque, A., and Herschelmann, K., 'SACEUR Warns Against Selling F-35 to Turkey if Ankara's S-400 Buy Proceeds', *Jane's Defence Weekly*, 56 (13 March 2019), p. 4.

Rose, A., *The Lion and the Fox: Two Rival Spies and the Secret Plot to Build a Confederate Navy* (New York: Mariner Books, 2022).

Ross, A.L., 'World Order and Arms Production in the Third World', in *The Implications of Third World Military Industrialization: Sowing the Serpents' Teeth*, ed. by J.E. Katz (Lexington: D.C. Heath and Co., 1986), pp. 277–92.

———, *Arms Production in Developing Countries: The Continuing Proliferation of Conventional Weapons* (RAND Note N-1615-AF) (Santa Monica: RAND Corporation, 1981).

Ruitenberg, R., 'KNDS Will Set Up Shop in Ukraine to Repair Heavy Weapons, Make Ammo', *Defense News* (8 June 2024), <www.defensenews.com/global/europe/2024/06/07/knds-will-set-up-shop-in-ukraine-to-repair-heavy-weapons-make-ammo> [accessed 8 June 2024].

———, 'Norway's View On Long War in Ukraine Drives Easing of Arms Export Rule', *Defense News* (18 January 2024), <www.defensenews.com/global/europe/2024/01/17/norways-view-on-long-war-in-ukraine-drives-easing-of-arms-export-rule> [accessed 18 January 2024].

Sae-Liu, R., 'Second Song Submarine Vital to China's Huge Programme', *Jane's Defence Weekly*, 32 (18 August 1999), p. 17.

Salisbury, D., 'Exploring the Use of "Third Countries" in Proliferation Networks: The Case of Malaysia', *European Journal of International Security*, 4 (2019), pp. 101–22.

Sampson, A., *The Arms Bazaar: From Lebanon to Lockheed* (New York: The Viking Press, 1977).

Sanders, R., *Arms Industries: New Suppliers and Regional Security* (Washington: National Defense University, 1990).

Sariibrahimoglu, L., 'Strategic Operator', *Jane's Defence Weekly*, 48 (27 April 2011), pp. 24–31.

Sasidharan, A., 'Kaveri to be Revived with French Assistance', *Jane's Defence Weekly*, 54 (22 February 2017), p. 7.

Sato, H., 'Economic Security and Arms Transfer Policy of the United States: DTSI and Defense Cooperation with Allies', *NIDS Security Reports* No.4 (March 2003), pp. 90–108.

Saw, D., 'The Emergence of the Third World Aircraft Industry', *Military Technology* 12 (April 1988), pp. 42–52.

Scott, R., 'Steller Systems Trials Scaled Offshore Insertion Craft', *Jane's Defence Weekly*, 61 (10 April 2024), p. 13.

———, 'Coming Of Age', *Jane's Defence Weekly*, 60 (26 April 2023), pp. 20–25.

———, 'Refreshed or Rehashed?' *Jane's Defence Weekly*, 59 (6 April 2022), pp. 18–21.

———, 'Intrinsically Exportable', *Jane's Defence Weekly*, 56 (2 October 2019), pp. 22–27.

———, 'Global Matrix', *Jane's Defence Weekly*, 43 (19 April 2006), pp. 24–28.

Seldin, J., 'US Security Aid to Israel to Arrive in Coming Days' (8 October 2023), <https://voanews.com/a/us-to-send-carrier-strike-group-to-mediterranean-in-support-of-israel/7301975.html> [accessed 9 October 2023].

———, 'US Pushing Central, South American Countries to Give Ukraine Quick Military Boost' (20 January 2023), <www.voanews.com/a/us-pushing-central-south-american-countries-to-give-ukraine-quick-military-boost-/6927591.html> [accessed 21 January 2023].

Selinger, M., 'Lockheed Martin and Raytheon Back US Effort to Expand Use of 3D Printing', *Jane's Defence Weekly*, 59 (18 May 2022), p. 9.

Sellers, R.C., 'Appendix III', in *Armed Forces of the World: A Reference Handbook* (Third Edition), ed. by R.C. Sellers (New York: Praeger Publishers, 1971), pp. 287–89.

Shanson, L., 'Building on Offsets', *Jane's Defence Weekly*, 14 (15 December 1990), pp. 1248–49.

Sharma, A., 'India to Boost Output, Fearing Shortfall from Russia', *Defense News* (8 April 2022), <www.defensenews.com/global/asia-pacific/2022/04/07/india-to-boost-arms-output-fearing-shortfall-from-russia> [accessed 8 April 2022].

Shiffman, G.M., *Economic Instruments of Security Policy: Influencing Choices of Leaders* (London: Palgrave Macmillan, 2006).

Smeets, M., 'Cyber Arms Transfer: Meaning, Limits, and Implications', *Security Studies*, 31 (2022), pp. 65–91.

Smith, M., 'Canada Reforms Export Rules', *Jane's Defence Weekly*, 51 (11 June 2014), p. 36.

Smith, M., and Anderson, G., 'European A&D Giants Call for MALE UAS Programme', *Jane's Defence Weekly*, 50 (26 June 2013), p. 23.

Smith, M., *The Real Special Relationship: The True Story of How the British and US Secret Services Work Together* (London: Simon & Schuster, 2022).

Soeriaatmadja, W., 'Indonesian-Filipino Terror Links Exposed', *The Straits Times* (3 February 2018), p. A2.

Son, K.Y., 'N. Korea to Use Shanghai as Benchmark for SEZ', *The Korea Times* (26 January 2001), <www.koreatimes.co.kr/times/200101/t2001012617322840111184.htm> [accessed 28 August 2002].

Soper, K., 'Russia Completes Assembly of Iveco LMV 4x4s', *Jane's Defence Weekly*, 51 (19 November 2014), p. 14.

Sprenger, S., 'The Race to Arm Ukraine Highlights West's Worry of Losing Tech Secrets', *Defense News* (9 June 2022), <www.defensenews.com/global/europe/2022/06/08/the-race-to-arm-ukraine-highlights-wests-worry-of-losing-tech-secrets> [accessed 9 June 2022].

Sprenger, S., and Gould, J., 'US Officials Balance Arms Sales Push Against Securing Tech Secrets', *Defense News* (8 September 2022), <www.defensdenews.com/pentagon/2022/09/07/us-officials-balance-arms-sales-push-against-tech-protection-needs> [accessed 8 September 2022].

Stafrace, C., *Arab Air Forces* (Carrollton: Squadron/Signal Publications, 1994).

Starr, B., 'S Koreans Cool Hornet Deal', *Jane's Defence Weekly*, 14 (10 November 1990), p. 921.

Stavrianakis, A., 'Controlling Weapons Circulation in a Postcolonial Militarised World', *Review of International Studies*, 45 (2019), pp. 57–76.

Stevenson, B., and Anderson, G., 'German Government Halts Defence Sales to Saudi Arabia', *Jane's Defence Weekly*, 55 (31 October 2018), p. 16.

Stockholm International Peace Research Institute, Arms Embargo Archive, <www.sipri.org/databases/embargoes> [accessed 1 November 2023].

———, *The Arms Trade with the Third World* (Harmondsworth: Penguin Books, 1975).

Stone, M., 'Ukraine War Spurs European Demand for U.S. Arms, But Not Big-Ticket Items' (17 February 2023), <www.reuters.com/world/europe/ukraine-war-spurs-european-demand-us-arms-not-big-ticket-items-2023-02-17> [accessed 18 February 2023].

Strazzari, F., and Tholens, S., 'Another Nakba: Weapons Availability and the Transformation of the Palestinian National Struggle, 1987–2007', *International Studies Perspectives*, 11 (2010), pp. 112–30.

Sweetman, B., 'The Big Seven Vie for Survival', *Jane's Defence Weekly*, 16 (14 September 1991), pp. 476–79.

Taylor, I., *China's New Role in Africa* (Boulder: Lynne Rienner Publishers, 2009).

Thayer, G., *The War Business: The International Trade in Armaments* (London: Weidenfeld and Nicolson, 1969).

Tigner, B., 'More Nations Join Danish-led NATO Group to Bulk-buy PGMs', *Jane's Defence Weekly*, 54 (15 November 2017), p. 12.

———, 'EDA Warns Europe to Address Critical Defence Dependencies', *Jane's Defence Weekly*, 48 (27 April 2011), p. 15.

Todd, D., 'Naval Shipbuilding: Prerequisite for Rising Powers?' *International Defense Review*, 24 (March 1991), pp. 229–34.

Tödtling, F., 'The Uneven Landscape of Innovation Poles: Local Embeddedness and Global Networks', in *Globalization, Institutions, and Regional Development in Europe*, ed. by A. Amin and N. Thrift (Oxford: Oxford University Press, 1994), pp. 68–90.

Tooze, A., *The Wages of Destruction: The Making and Breaking of the Nazi Economy* (London: Allen Lane, 2006).

Trebilcock, C., 'The British Armaments Industry 1890–1914: False Legend and True Identity', in *War, Economy and the Military Mind*, ed. by G. Best and A. Wheatcroft (London: Croom Helm, 1976), pp. 89–107.

United States, 'Arms Export Control Act of 1976' (22 U.S.C. Sec. 2751 *et seq*).

United States, Congress, Office of Technology Assessment, 'Global Arms Trade: Commerce in Advanced Military Technology and Weapons' (Washington: Office of Technology Assessment, June 1991).

———, *Arming Our Allies: Cooperation and Competition in Defense Technology* (Washington: US Government Printing Office, 1990).

United States Government Accountability Office, *DOD's Critical Technologies Lists Rarely Inform Export Control and Other Policy Decisions* (Washington: US Government Printing Office, 2006).

———, *Export Controls: Challenges Exist in Enforcement of an Inherently Complex System* (Washington: US Government Printing Office, 2006).

United States, Office of the White House, 'National Security Presidential Memorandum Regarding U.S. Conventional Arms Transfer Policy' (Washington: Office of the White House, 19 April 2018).

Vernon, R., and Kapstein, E.B., 'National Needs, Global Resources', in *Defense and Dependence in a Global Economy*, ed. by R. Vernon and E.B. Kapstein (Washington: Congressional Quarterly, Inc., 1992), pp. 1–22.

Voice of America, 'US Treasury Promises to Tighten Sanctions on Russia' (29 May 2024), <www.voanews.com/a/us-treasury-promises-to-tighten-sanctions-on-russia/7634156.html> [accessed 30 May 2024].

———, 'Taliban Hand in Smuggling of US Arms Clear, Despite Denials' (17 July 2023), <www.voanews.com/a/fact-check-/7184125.html> [accessed 20 July 2023].

Volpe, T.A., 'Dual-Use Distinguishability: How 3D-Pringting Shapes the Security Dilemma for Nuclear Programs', *Journal of Strategic Studies*, 42 (2019), pp. 814–40.

Wagstaff-Smith, K., 'PFI: Unfairly Maligned?' *Jane's Defence Weekly*, 48 (2 March 2011), pp. 28–31.

Wall, R., 'Export Issues Bedevil JSF', *Aviation Week & Space Technology*, 158 (3 March 2003), pp. 36–37.

Wang, Z., 'China Confronts Globalization: Conceptualizing Economic Security and Governance', in *Globalisation and Economic Security in East Asia: Governance and Institutions*, ed. by H.E.S. Nesadurai (London: Routledge, 2006), pp. 62–84.

Wasserbly, D., 'US Signs Arms Trade Treaty', *Jane's Defence Weekly*, 50 (2 October 2013), p. 10.

———, 'Brazil to Make F-X2 Decision in "April or May"', *Jane's Defence Weekly*, 47 (21 April 2010), p. 10.

Wheeldon, H., 'JSF Technology Transfer Remains an Unproven Art', *Jane's Defence Weekly*, 44 (16 May 2007), p. 21.

Widakuswara, P., 'Russia Receiving Hundreds of Iranian Drones, Plans to Produce Them: White House' (9 June 2023), <www.voanews.com/a/7130137.html> [accessed 10 June 2023].

Wilson, M., 'European Avionics into the 1990s and Beyond', *Jane's Defence Weekly*, 2 (1 September 1984), pp. 335–43.

Wilson, P.A., and Parachini, J.V., 'Russia's Military Aircraft Exports Are Headed for a Nosedive', *Defense News* (21 October 2022), <www.defensenews.com/opinion/commentary/2022/10/20/russias-military-aircraft-exports-are-headed-for-a-nodedive> [accessed 21 October 2022].

Wilson, P.H., 'European Warfare 1815–2000', in *War in the Modern World Since 1815*, ed. by J. Black (London: Routledge, 2003), pp. 192–216.

Wong, P.K., 'The Proliferation of Technology-Based International Strategic Alliances: Contrasting Perspectives', in *Techno-Security in an Age of Globalization: Perspectives from the Pacific Rim*, ed. by D.F. Simon (Armonk: M.E. Sharpe, 1997), pp. 165–85.

Yarhi-Milo, K., Lanoszka, A., and Cooper, Z., 'To Arm or to Ally? The Patron's Dilemma and the Strategic Logic of Arms Transfers and Alliances', *International Security*, 41 (Fall 2016), pp. 90–139.

Yeng, B.S., 'Understanding the Chinese Defence Industry', *Military Technology*, 11 (March 1987), pp. 36–53.

Yeo, M., 'Taiwan Launches its First Homemade Submarine', *Defense News* (29 September 2023), <www.defensenews.com/global/asia-pacific/2023/09/29/taiwan-launches-its-first-homemade-submarine> [accessed 30 September 2023].

Young, P.L., 'Clandestine Trade in Arms: A Matter of Ways and Means', *Jane's Intelligence Review*, 12 (May 2000), pp. 48–51.

Zaloga, S.J., *Superguns 1854–1991: Extreme Artillery from the Paris Gun and the V-3 to Iraq's Project Babylon* (Oxford: Osprey Publishing, 2018).

———, *The M47 and M48 Patton Tanks* (Oxford: Osprey Publishing, 1999).

Zenko, M., and Kreps, S., *Limiting Armed Drone Proliferation* (Council Special Report No. 69) (New York: Council on Foreign Relations, Center for Preventative Action, June 2014).

Zarate, J.C., *Treasury's War: The Unleashing of a New Era of Financial Warfare* (New York: Public Affairs, 2013).

Zhang, Q.M., 'Harmonising the Management of Foreign and Domestic Affairs in Chinese Foreign Policy', in *China Under Xi Jinping: Its Economic Challenges and Foreign Policy Initiatives*, ed. by B.S. Shao (Leiden: Brill Publishing, 2015), pp. 143–66.

# Index

www.ingramcontent.com/pod-product-compliance
Ingram Content Group UK Ltd.
Pitfield, Milton Keynes, MK11 3LW, UK
UKHW041133071026
15587UKWH00009B/468

9 781804 131268